THE ART OF
SINGING

Da Capo Press Music Reprint Series

MUSIC EDITOR
BEA FRIEDLAND
Ph.D., City University of New York

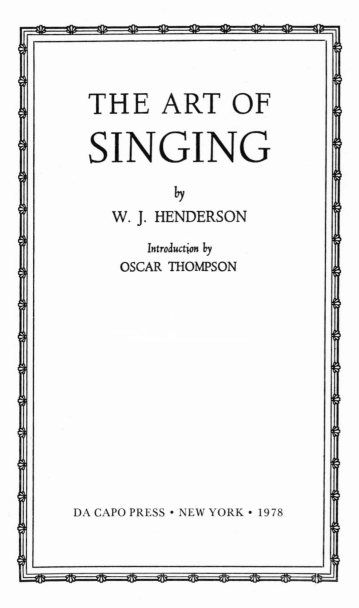

THE ART OF
SINGING

by
W. J. HENDERSON

Introduction by
OSCAR THOMPSON

DA CAPO PRESS • NEW YORK • 1978

Library of Congress Cataloging in Publication Data

Henderson, William James, 1855-1937
  The art of singing.

  (Da Capo Press music reprint series)
  Reprint of the ed. published by Dial Press, New York.
  Contains The art of the singer, first published in
1906, and a collection of articles principally from *The
New York Sun* compiled by Oscar Thompson and Irving
Kolodin.
  1. Singing. I. Title.
[ML820.H496A8 1978]   784.9   78-4953
ISBN 0-306-77593-X

Published by Da Capo Press, Inc.
A Subsidiary of Plenum Publishing Corporation
227 West 17th Street, New York, N.Y. 10011

THE ART OF SINGING

THE ART OF SINGING

by

W. J. HENDERSON

Introduction by
OSCAR THOMPSON

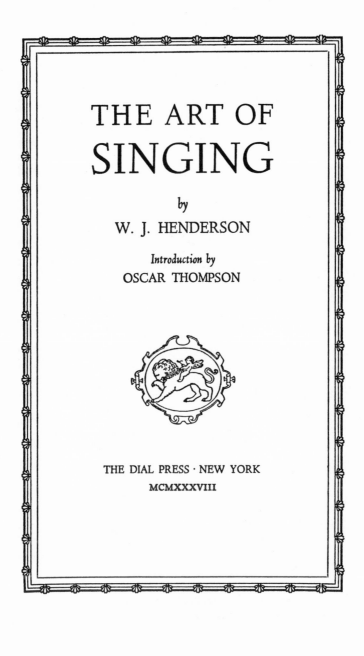

THE DIAL PRESS · NEW YORK
MCMXXXVIII

Contents

PART II

A Lifetime of Reviewing

CONTENTS

Acknowledgments

THE PUBLISHERS WISH TO STATE THAT ALL THE material in Part II is from the *New York Sun*, except "The Nineteenth Century's Greatest Singers," which is from *Munsey's Magazine*, and "The Need of a Standard of Voice Production," which is from *The Laryngoscope*. The publishers also wish to express their thanks to Mr. Irving Kolodin for his collaboration with Mr. Thompson in choosing and collating the critical articles which compose Part II.

Introduction

INTO THE MAKING OF THIS BOOK HAS GONE MUCH
that can honestly pass as a labor of love. For W. J.
Henderson dearly loved singing, his long life
through, and those who have collected his writings for this volume dearly loved W. J. Henderson.
In part, but only in part, *The Art of Singing* paral-
lels and duplicates his earlier volume, *The Art of
the Singer*. In his preface to that book, Henderson
expressed the hope that the teacher, the student
and the lover of singing would find set forth clearly
and comprehensively what he had been able to
learn in twenty-five years of careful study and
original research pertaining to the singer's art. But
that quarter of a century was only about half of
the long period which Henderson, as a professional
critic and investigator, devoted to music and to
his great love of song. He did not stop with *The
Art of the Singer*, which was first published in
1906, almost half a lifetime (as lifetimes ordinarily
are calculated) before he was to lay down his pen.

He wrote on, as a critic and as an enthusiast on singing, up to almost the hour of his death in the summer of 1937. As was honestly said of him in his sixties and seventies, and still later, when he had turned eighty, his was the freshest style among the music critics in New York. *The Art of the Singer* became but a fraction of what he had written about singing.

Much that represented his most mature and most mellow views on the vocal art appeared else-where, occasionally in magazines and musical or other special periodicals, but chiefly in his remark-able discussional articles for the New York *Sun*, and before 1902, the New York *Times*. Considered in detail or in their entirety, no more thoughtful and influential articles on music have appeared in the American press; though Henderson, with char-acteristic modesty and generosity, would have pointed to the writings of Henry E. Krehbiel and Philip Hale as having done more for music than his own. Each played his part, as did others of the critical "Old Guard"—James G. Huneker, Henry T. Finck, and Richard Aldrich, not to overlook William Foster Apthorp in Boston—but it is with

Henderson that we have here to do. With his passing, there was manifest a need for the preservation
in some permanent form of much that he had
written about singing outside of the covers of *The
Art of the Singer.*

Perhaps the best of Henderson is found in his
famous "Saturday articles" for the *Sun.* In these
he often summed up and amplified his day-to-day
reviews. Good reading as were his first thoughts,
his second ones were still better. With the most
scrupulous impartiality, the most impersonal application of his long-considered criteria, the clearest
discernment and the most unflagging curiosity he
analyzed the singing of the multitude of vocal
artists who came before him. In the course of more
than a half century of critical writing for New
York newspapers, he was called upon to pass judgment on virtually every singer of any importance
who entered upon the American scene. No other
first critic was so relentless with himself in this
matter of hearing and writing about the singers
who came and went, though of course the competi-
tion of other musical events often required his
presence elsewhere when singers appeared. It was

his policy never to send an assistant to review a concert, recital or opera performance of consequence if he could be there himself. And if there was only one event of an evening, even though that one was not very important, usually it was the assistant, not Henderson, who had the night off. In consequence, Henderson in his later years was in a position to say—though he did not bother to say it—that the Henderson hallmark, his stamp of critical approval or the contrary, was on every singer really worth considering who had come to New York between the middle eighteen-eighties and 1937. Although he was writing at the time the Metropolitan opened its doors in 1883, and had already acquired a rich background through his attendance on performances at the old Academy of Music and the associations of his father's theater, his first newspaper work was in secondary positions; hence it was to others that the plums of the reviewing fell. But from 1887, when he became critic for the *Times*, there were criticisms by Henderson to be read almost daily through nearly fifty years. A staggering number of these were concerned with singing, either as heard at the opera or in the concert halls.

From the time he took up his duties of critic on the *Times* and until he rounded out his career on the *Sun*, Henderson kept scrap-books of his writings, one for every season, in which were carefully pasted, dated and indexed every criticism he wrote. In later years he also filed in this manner the reviews of his assistants. Even before 1887, when music became his chief concern, he had kept such a scrap-book, in which are to be found reviews of performances at the Academy of Music and of the earliest years of the Metropolitan, side by side with articles on yachting, of which he was a devotee and an expert; news stories written as a reporter, fiction, poetry, book reviews, correspondence for the *Saturday Review* of London and an astonishing variety of other writings, still good reading for anyone with the inclination to cast himself back into the currents of the early eighties.

It was W. J. Henderson's desire that *The Art of the Singer* be reissued and he had gone over it from cover to cover at the time of his death, satisfying himself that what he had written in 1906 was phrased as he would want it to appear in 1936. When he died without having completed this pur-

pose, there devolved upon the undersigned, with
the whole-hearted collaboration of his associate, Mr.
Irving Kolodin, a new labor of love, that of col-
lecting and editing their chief's other writings on
singing and singers, so that a new volume could be
issued, one that would be no less representative
but more comprehensive—as W. J. Henderson's
parting contribution to the art he loved. Here,
therefore, have been collated articles and excerpts
of articles, the most vital and significant of many
hundreds that could have been used, as Part II of a
volume in which *The Art of the Singer* is Part I.

Fascinating in their immediacy, their sense of the
living present rather than the dead past, are Henderson's summations of the Metropolitan careers
of singers like the de Reszkes, Lilli Lehmann,
Sembrich, Nordica, Melba, Caruso and others, up
to and including the days of Farrar, Ponselle,
Jeritza, Tibbett and favorites of our own time.
These articles constitute a virtual history of opera
for a half century in New York. Beyond that, they
may be considered the most notable exposition of
music criticism ever brought together in America.
They are examples of the clarity of thought and

the corresponding clarity of writing that set Henderson apart as a writer on music. They are models of literary style as well as of critical evaluation. In reflecting the man as well as delineating the critic, they show him big enough to modify and even to reverse his judgment, but he seems never to have been radically mistaken in his first estimates of singers.

Several valuable supplementary volumes might be devoted to Henderson's daily criticisms. But these have had to be foregone in the selection of the material for this book because of the number and scope of his more extended writings on singing. It is in order, however, to make some further reference to them in this introduction. A study of the day-to-day reviews shows that about Nordica, Dippel, Calvé, Schumann-Heink and Gadski, to mention a few particularly interesting cases, Henderson wrote much more favorably as time passed than he did when they first appeared. Nordica, indeed, he came to regard as one of the greatest artists of her time and she, with Sembrich and Jean de Reszke, he singled out for thanks in his preface to *The Art of the Singer*, because of assistance given him in the way of information and practical demonstrations. There is much eulogy of the art of Sembrich, but Henderson did not hesitate to point out on one occasion the presence of the glottis stroke in her singing. That vocal blemish, with the tremolo and the exaggerated portamento, he repeatedly brands as "vicious."

Most latter-day criticism appears of the "pussy-foot" variety, beside the bluntness of many of his early reviews, as when he says of one singer: "She ought to leave the stage at once and study under a competent teacher. This may seem like harshness but if a soprano will wear her glottis on her sleeve for critics to peck at, she is likely to hear things severe but nevertheless to her advantage." Over and over, however, he is found making allowances for the nervousness of newcomers and for vocal indispositions; and it is not to the fledglings, but to artists of some standing or pretensions, that he points in citing "interesting object lessons in how not to sing." For a review like that of Tetrazzini's first appearance at the Manhattan Opera House there is no other word but "masterpiece." Yet it can be duplicated, at least in part, many times along the

way from those days when the incomparable Lilli
Lehmann stood where Flagstad now stands, and
when the Metropolitan's Wagner was sung reg-
ularly in Italian. "Cigno gentil" sang Lohengrin in
his "addio" to the swan. Hans Sachs, Pogner,
Kothner, Beckmesser flourished as "I Maestri di
Cantori." Of Lehmann it is rather startling to read
that she took the florid phrases of the part of
Norma so deliberately that her singing of these passages would scarcely have been tolerated from one
of the older Italian prime donne. And still more
startling to read that the celebrated Herr Niemann,
New York's first Tristan, fairly "murdered" some
of his music, particularly the Spring Greeting in
"Die Walkure." But with even the great artists,
there were good nights and bad nights, as Henderson reviewed them, and he did not hesitate to write
in high praise of Calvé at one performance and
take her to task for cheapening her art at another.
He had mildly derogatory things to say about
Jean de Reszke's voice, which—at first, perhaps
more than later—he did not regard as either an
exceptionally beautiful or important organ—though
he extolled his art. "There is always a but" he wrote

in one review. Patti had her limitations, as Caruso had his faults. But they were great vocalists, and like Ternina, like Lehmann, like Nordica, like Flagstad, they left with Henderson memories of beautiful singing that could never fade. He was no automaton. He listened with his heart as well as his intellect and his ears. One feels in his reviews how he was set resonating by what he heard and his words have the vibrations of a chiming bell. Dispassionate as he made it his business to be, and humorous as often was his approach to the routine that presented for him little of emotional appeal, there courses through his writings the strong pulsations of the man who feels as well as thinks. He was a critic whose response to beauty was emotional as well as intellectual. If he became (in Lawrence Gilman's happy phrase) a "mellow ironist," that was because he had reason to know that beauty is by no means inseparable from music or its performance—and W. J. Henderson had to hear music and write about it almost every day!

OSCAR THOMPSON

PART I
The Art of the Singer

What Is Singing?

SINGING IS THE INTERPRETATION OF TEXT BY MEANS of musical tones produced by the human voice.

This is a definition. It ought also to be a self-evident proposition. But it is not. Go where you will among singers and listen to their talk and you will hear an endless reiteration of one thought—how best to produce beautiful tones. It is not at all astonishing that this should be the case because the method of tone-formation presents problems of immediate import to the singer. If he cannot fathom the secrets of his own throat he must stop at the very threshold of his art. When he essays to sing he discovers that certain tones refuse to flow, that they are veiled, or that his throat is unduly strained in their delivery. Something is wrong with the method.

Again he sets out on the weary search for a voice-teacher. Again he finds one who has rediscovered the secret of Porpora. Again he trudges through weary pages of solfeggi.

At length he tries once more to sing songs, and lo! now he has troubles with tones which before flowed spontaneously.

This is a very sad and common experience among singers. No wonder that they think and talk altogether of the art of tone-production.

Yet from this custom a grave misfortune comes upon the art of song. The edifice stops too often with its foundation. We get tone, tone, and tone. Singing becomes *vox et præterea nihil*. All the world is a music-box and all the men and women merely tinklers. The human voice is treated purely as a musical instrument, and it performs melodies inarticulately, as a violin does. Nine tenths of the songs we hear are songs without words. And when we do hear the words they are either mangled in the formation or neglected in the matter of significance. We are furnished with little books containing the texts of the songs to be sung. These little books are useful to those who do not understand the language in which the texts of the songs are written. They ought not to have any other use. When they are employed to tell us what is the meaning of the song which the singer is singing, they are a confession of great weakness.

The listener who does not understand the text of a song to which he is listening is as much at sea as an audience at a college commencement listening to the Greek salutatory. Give the audience a printed translation of the salutatory, and you put them in the position of the listeners with the texts of the songs. A part of the cause of this trouble lies in the lack of general acquaintance with German, Italian, and French. But an audience listening to songs with English texts is as much at sea most of the time as it is when the other languages are employed. That is the singer's fault.

It is a fault which begins with the singer's award of the first place in his consideration to beauty of tone. It is both right and wrong that he should do this. This was sometime a paradox, but now it is a truism.

The public, the unthinking public, is perfectly content to accept what the majority of singers give it—beautiful tone, the intoning of melodic sequences by the voice. But that is not singing any more than striking all the keys correctly is piano playing.

Singing is the interpretation of text by means of musical tones produced by the human voice.

Hence the force of the paradox. If the tones are not beautiful they cannot be musical. Therefore it is right that the singer should first learn to make musical tones. But if he stop there, he is wrong. He must use the tones to interpret the text. It is no concern whatever of the real artist that his hearers are willing to accept half a loaf. He must insist upon the dignity of his art. He must refuse to allow the burial of its intellectuality.

To sing mere sounds is a senseless performance no matter how much those sounds tickle the ears of the dear public, no matter how large the price paid the singer for their utterance.

And it is the artist who must educate the public. Critics may write till doomsday, but their efforts must continually prove futile in the presence of the deeds of the exponents of the art. Of what avail is it that the critics cease not to preach that the singing of a Melba is not to be compared with that of a Sembrich, as long as Melba continues to sing as she does and to enchant the unthinking with the mere tones of her ravishing voice? A few singers of the Melba type can do in a year evil

which two or three Sembrichs and Lehmanns cannot undo in six.

The opera, indeed, is a wholesale destroyer of
high ideals of song. Two-thirds of the people who
attend it do not make the slightest attempt to find
out what the singers are saying, and content themselves with drinking in the merely sensuous elements of vocal music. It is no wonder that many
opera-singers become slothful. Others, whose enunciation is most admirable, substitute mere articulation for interpretation.

There is a vast difference between the two.

The evils of mere sound singing come from a
misconception of the nature of song. If every singer
would write on the tablets of his mind the definition of singing given herewith it would be a happy
thing for vocal art. Let it be a daily maxim: Singing
is the interpretation of text by means of musical
tones produced by the human voice. Let it be
understood that in song, as in the Wagnerian
drama, the music is not the end, but a means. The
radical error of the entire Italian school of singing,
despite its proclamation of other belief, lay in the

fact that in actual practice it held that the ultimate purpose of vocal technic was the production of beautiful tone. The fundamental truth is that the object of vocal technic is the vitalization of text by musical tone, and that the creation of the tone must be for that purpose and that alone.

I have already shown that the pure beauty of song cannot be diminished by a practice based upon this theory. Unmusical tone is wholly excluded by the primary definition of singing. There is no dispute that a pure musical tone formed by the human throat has beauty. The secrets of the Italian method, if it had any secrets, are applicable to the highest forms of interpretative singing. Indeed, no singer can accomplish all that is within the scope of his voice in the matter of interpretation unless that voice is perfectly disciplined. Even the mastery of colorature is absolutely essential to perfection. For example, who can sing "Glockenthürmer's Töchterlein" or "Aufträge" without the training of the colorature school?

In short, we have arrived at that period in the development of vocal art when we may look upon the splendid technical achievements of the eighteenth century and the early part of the nineteenth as the necessary foundations of a vocal art. But they were not the whole of it. They possessed the potentialities, and enabled certain gifted individuals— the Farinellis, the Senesinos, the Pastas, and the Malibrans—to produce moving effects. But the Italian opera schools of these times lacked a perception of the elementary truth which forced its way to recognition with the spread of the songs of Schubert and Schumann and with the gradual ascent to supremacy of the dramas of Wagner.

That elementary truth is contained in the definition of singing offered herewith.

2

The Artist and the Public

TO HEAR THE SINGING TEACHERS TALK, ONE WOULD think that everyone and no one possessed the true Italian school. Each teacher claims it, and vehemently denies that anyone else knows anything about it. Of course the explanation of this state of affairs is that some one is deficient in regard for the truth. But there is another cause for the apparently contradictory statements, and that is pure ignorance. There are many teachers of singing in these days who know as much about the right schooling of the voice as they do about the establishment of secondary meridians or about suggestive therapeutics.

Teachers or no teachers, it is plain to every careful observer that the race of beautiful singers is diminishing with every year, and that in its place there is growing up a generation of harsh, unrefined, tuneless shouters, whom we are asked to accept as dramatic impersonators on the lyric stage, because of a particularly vigorous style of declamation or a significant facial expression. Meanwhile our own ears are becoming vitiated and many of us are complacently listening to the worst sort of singing out of tune and applauding it as if infidelity to the pitch were an evidence of independent conception. We sit calmly while a leading tenor produces as many different qualities of voice as registers, bleats in his lower tones, swallows half of his upper ones, and gurgles in all. We are perfectly content that a contralto shall hold a leading place while she never sustains any tone or attacks one directly, but is always sliding through infinitesimal degrees of pitch as if her voice were on skates. And when we do hear a soprano who not only gives us the dramatic meaning of the music which she sings, but sings every measure with a beautiful tone, we applaud her no more than we do another who rarely sings in tune and always with a sour quality.

Whose fault is it that the public is so woefully deficient in discrimination? The public is not an expert, never was, and never will be. It does not go beneath the surface in the world of what it is pleased to call amusements. It is idle, careless, and indifferent to the critical questions of art. If it is amused for the moment it is satisfied. The performer is paid and applauded, and so, "on with the dance." If the artist be frivolous, flippant, unskilled, the education of the facile public down to his level is his work, and he is to be blamed for it. The maintenance of a high standard of art is the duty of the artist. If he waits for the public to undertake this work he will see his art go to the dogs.

The public has always had to be led and always will have to be led by the men and women of genius. Did the public in ante-Calvé times ever demand that "Carmen" should be interpreted as Calvé used to interpret it? Did the public ever demand that "Tristan" should be sung as Jean de Reszke sang it until he showed that that was the way it ought to be sung? No, the leader in artistic matters must always be the artist. And so bad singers lead the public to endure and even to applaud bad singing.

There is a good deal of loose argument against method in these days. It begins with some such utterance as that which Fétis made half a century ago when he wrote: "The mechanical part of sing-

ing, even the most perfect, is an indispensable part
of the merit of a good singer, but it is not all. The
most successful delivery of the voice, the best regu-
lated respiration, the purest execution of the ornaments, and what is very rare, the most perfect intonation, are the means by which a great singer
expresses the sentiment which animates him, but
they are nothing more than means, and he who
should persuade himself that the whole art of the
singer is comprised in them might sometimes give
his audience a degree of tranquil pleasure, but
would never cause them to experience vivid emotion."

This is perfectly true, but it is not true that
because the purity of the vocal method is only a
means it can be sacrificed for the sake of a warmth
of temperament, a knowledge of styles, a fine diction, or a complete understanding of the significance of a song. The first business of a singer is to
sing. That means to deliver to the hearer the notes
set down by the composer, not some other note or
notes an eighth of a tone above or below those set
down. The singer is bound to deliver the notes just
as firmly as he is bound to deliver the words of the

text and not those of some other text. In the second place, he is under obligations to deliver them purely, in a good round tone, free from harshness, breathiness, or any other bad quality, which should distract the attention of the sensitive listener from the poetry of the words and music. This is a plain and unadorned statement of the primary obligations of the singer, yet how many fulfill them? Are we to believe that there was once an age of vocal fable, or is it really true that there were once singers of a far different sort from the vast majority of those we hear now?

It is said that Farinelli cured Philip of Spain of an attack of melancholia which threatened his reason. He did it by singing beautifully. Raff is said to have brought the relief of tears to the Princess Belmont when her sanity was in danger because of immense grief. Senesino, a great singer, once forgot his own part, and on the stage threw his arms around the neck of Farinelli after that singer had sung an air with surpassing beauty. Gabrielli broke down with emotion on the stage after hearing Marchesi sing a cantabile. Crescentini, when he sang in "Romeo and Juliet," caused the grim Napoleon and all his court to shed tears.

Is it true that these singers knew something which is now a lost art? I for one do not believe it. It is my firm conviction that the acquisition of a beautiful vocal style is in the power of anyone who will take the trouble to go through the necessary study.

There is the rub. The necessary study is the one thing that so few are willing to undertake. The ignorant, when they hear a woman like Madame Sembrich sing, say: "Oh, what a voice!" The voice, the voice, the gift of God, is praised, and the art, which is the result of long and hard and sometimes bitterly painful struggle, is not discerned. Thousands of persons imagine that singing such as Madame Sembrich's is a pure gift. To a certain extent the bounty of nature is to be thanked for such music as this woman gives us, for it is not possible by any process of teaching to manufacture such a voice. But if Madame Sembrich's art were not perfect, she would not always sing beautifully, no matter how lovely the natural voice, and, furthermore, the natural beauty of her voice would long ago have been destroyed. Ten years of reckless, unmethodical use of such a voice would take all the velvet off it and leave us only the rags of what once was.

It is hard, it is almost impossible, to make the young singers of to-day believe this. They all laugh when the old story of Caffarelli and Porora is told, but that tale, exaggerated though it be, carries with it a sound text. Patience, devotion, sincerity. These must be the watchwords of the student of singing. The planting is slow and laborious; the harvest long and rich. Let the student approach the portals of the divine art with all humility, prepared to linger on the threshold till the first step can be firmly taken. Jacob served seven years for Rachel and then served seven more. Jean de Reszke served twenty years' apprenticeship for his Siegfried and his Tristan, and his memory will live as long as the art of song.

3

Fundamental Breathing

THE FIRST THING A SINGER MUST LEARN IS HOW TO control his breath. Everyone breathes and most of us find it no effort to do so. But try to sing and you discover that you must first acquire a system of managing the breath. If you have no system your tones are unsteady or they refuse to cling to the pitch. Your phrases are broken. Your singing is labored and spasmodic. You are an organ pipe fed by defective bellows.

In this, the fundamental feature of vocal technics, there are as many differences among professors as in the later details of the art. All the teachers agree that good tone production, which is the basis of all good singing, rests upon the management of the breath, and that it is therefore essential that every pupil should acquire a correct method of breathing. The teacher, when asked what he means by a correct method of breathing, will tell you that he means one which is in accord with nature, which is not artificial or strained. After that comes the deluge. You would not suppose that there could be more than one such method, but you will find by inquiry that there are several.

One set of masters will tell you that in order to draw in your breath according to the laws of nature you must begin by causing your abdomen to protrude in order that your diaphragm may have room to operate. The next set will tell you that this is radically wrong, and that in beginning an inspiration you should contract the muscles of the abdomen, causing it to flatten. Another set will tell you to pay no attention at all to your breathing, but just get as much air as you can into your lungs and then go ahead and sing.

After you have drawn in the breath, you have to expel it, because it is with the expulsion of the air from the lungs through the vocal cords that tone comes. Here again the different schools of teachers will tell you different ways of doing it. One set will say that when you begin the expulsion of the breath you must push out the abdomen and forcibly contract the muscles of your sides around the lower ribs.

Another set will tell you that this is rank heresy and that you will never be able to support your tones if you try to breathe in such a crazy manner. This set will tell you that in beginning the expulsion of the breath you must forcibly flatten the abdomen and give a good hard push with the diaphragm.

Again you will be told that in sustaining the tone thus begun you must permit your chest to sink gradually, keeping up a steady pressure upon the lungs with the intercostal muscles. Another party will urge you not to let your chest sink at all, but resolutely to raise it higher and higher as the air flows out of the lungs, thus keeping the tone pure and even. You pay your money, but you have great difficulty in taking your choice.

Among these different schools the student is like to be ground as wheat between millstones. He studies, let us say for a year with one master and is dissatisfied with his progress. He goes to another and is told that everything he does is wrong from the foundation up. He has to learn a wholly new method of breathing, of tone support, of voice placement, etc. He begins to think that singing is an abnormal art that is not founded on nature at all; that it is all a matter of theory and artificiality, and from that moment he is as much adrift as a rudderless and dismasted ship in a gale of wind.

Nevertheless, if one takes the trouble to read about the teaching of the older masters, whose pupils certainly knew how to sing, he finds little disagreement in regard to the matter of breathing. Most of the old teachers had not a great deal to say about it. They seemed to believe that if one systematically practiced drawing in deep breaths and letting them out slowly, turning every bit into tone, the power to breathe in just that necessary way would eventually be acquired. Curiously enough we find some rational and careful observers, who are not tied to any pet master's theory, thinking just the same thing in our own day. Most of them have come down the Garcia line.

It would be interesting to know how many teachers of the present time have ever made attempts to proceed empirically and at the same time systematically. Take this matter of breathing. The right way to find out how best to breathe in producing tone is not to decide first how you should breathe and then make tones accordingly, but to make tones till you find out how they can be made best.

Suppose a teacher of singing should take a sound, healthy, well-developed, athletic young man of some seventeen or eighteen years with a good natural voice, strip him and stand him up and say to him, "Sing this note as clearly and as gently and as long as you can, but without straining." Then when the young man sang, suppose the teacher should carefully observe the play of his form, the movements of his abdomen and chest, and find out how that youth, having no theories and no intentions about breathing, inspired and expelled air in the formation of tone.

Suppose the teacher were to continue that process with fifty or a hundred young people, would he not be likely to have a far sounder basis for the foundation of a belief as to the right way to breathe in singing than by reading the arguments of theorists backed by diagrams (not always correct) of the skeleton and lungs?

It is safe to say that the teacher who tries this sort of empiricism will learn that the abdomen is not forcibly pushed forward in inspiration. He will also learn that in expiration the abdomen does not protrude, as it is made to appear to do in a misleading diagram in Lamperti's recently published and generally excellent book, "The Technics of Bel Canto."

To make the abdomen protrude in expiration requires a special effort of the will, a concentration on the act of breathing and a deliberate perversion of nature. Let nature alone and she will in the end flatten the walls of the abdomen in breathing. The reasons are easily set forth.

The principal muscle used in respiration is the diaphragm, a dome-shaped partition extending across the trunk between the chest and the abdominal cavity. When you draw in breath the diaphragm contracts and at the same time presses downward upon the abdominal cavity. This causes the abdomen naturally to expand, but it is not forcibly pushed out. In fact, it pushes itself forward, but only at the beginning of the inspiration. As the lower ribs by muscular action expand, the lower parts of the lungs are filled and this expansion of the lower portion of the chest draws up the abdomen a little till the first protrusion almost disappears.

When you exhale the breath the muscles of the abdominal walls contract and press against the viscera, which in turn press against the diaphragm, pushing it upward and thus causing the cavity of the chest to diminish. Of course in this process the abdominal wall flattens.

In the practice of deep breathing, after the lungs have been filled the air should be retained for two or three seconds before exhalation. This retention is not to be accomplished by closing the vent in the larynx.

That method is correct for a diver, but it is incorrect for a singer, because it is contrary to the fundamental rule that there should never be any tightness or gripping anywhere. It calls for a conscious muscular strain in the throat and there should never be any strain there. The breath must be retained simply by the action of the diaphragm and rib muscles. The throat must be kept lax and open. All the breathing muscles must be held firmly in the position which they naturally take when the inspiration is completed, and by that power and that alone must the breath be retained. In exhalation the distended lungs must begin their contraction wholly by the release of the inhalation pose of the muscles. No push need be applied till the point is reached at which natural contraction ceases. Then the student may will to expel still more breath by the operation of the diaphragm and other muscles.

The fundamental secret of breathing in singing is to breathe deeply and easily and to keep the breath under perfect control. The singer need not concern himself with the operation of the muscles. Let him fix his mind on learning to draw in breath steadily without effort till his lungs are filled and then to let the breath flow out again easily, steadily and softly. As David Frangçon-Davies has very wisely said in his "The Singing of the Future," one should learn to emit just enough breath to make a whisper, and then convert it into a tone. This is what the old Italian masters meant when they continually told their pupils to learn how to "filar il tuono," or "spin the tone." The air should flow out in a gossamer filament.

Now, if a student concentrates his mind on this

and practises breathing it is a thousand to one that the muscles of the body will take care of themselves. Unless they have been deliberately taught to do the thing incorrectly they will go about it in the right way. It is necessary to know what is the right way in order that we may ascertain whether we have acquired the wrong way.

But the teacher who causes his pupil to draw a few deep breaths and let them out slowly, and finds that Nature has been permitted to take her own course, makes a grievous error if he launches into a demonstration of breathing method. Salvatore Marchesi has wisely said: "When explaining the physico-mechanical process of breathing to beginners it is essential to make them understand that natural laws have provided for its independence of our will, as is observed in sleeping. Therefore every intentional preparation or effort made in order to draw more air into the lungs will produce the contrary result, hindering the freedom of the natural process."

You will read many hundreds of pages of type on the subject of singing without finding anything more pregnant with good sense than this. The great point on which the student should focus his thought is not the direction of the muscles in breathing, but the acquisition of a deep, steady respiration and the ability to keep the outgoing column of air under perfect control. That is the beginning of singing. It is the foundation on which all else rests.

If you cannot manage your breath you can never acquire a pure, steady, even flow of tone, the basis of what is called *cantilena*. If you have no cantilena you are no singer. You may succeed in becoming a declaimer of the vicious Bayreuth type, but you will never breathe out the love song of Siegmund or the farewell of Wotan, the narrative of Waltraute or the liebestod of Isolde.

Much less will you ever sing the "Voi che sapete" or "batti batti" of Mozart or the "Roi de Thule" of Gounod or the "O mai piu" of Verdi. You can never be a singer unless you have a good legato style, for that is the bedrock of bel canto, and there is no legato without perfect breath control.

4

Breathing and Attack

IT IS NOT ENOUGH THAT THE SINGER SHALL MERELY breathe. He must breathe the breath of life into his singing. Before he can do that, he must learn to breathe with perfect freedom. The right way for singers to breathe is the way one employs when he stretches himself upon his bed for sleep and begins the steady deep breathing which invites to calm repose. This sort of breathing is diametrically opposed to violent or determined effort. It is not the sort of breathing which some athletes practise and which they call "deep breathing."

That consists in straining every muscle of the torso in a prolonged and violent effort to stretch the lungs to the cracking point. Chest labor of this kind has no relationship whatever to singing. No one can control his breath and turn it all into tone if he crams his lungs in that fashion. The strain of retention would be too great and he would have to relieve the muscles of the body by blowing off some of the bottled-up breath. When the athlete takes in his deep breath in that fashion he lets it out much faster and in a much bigger column than the singer.

The singer again cannot breathe as the athlete does after a race. This manner of breathing is entirely involuntary. It is an effect, not a cause. It is produced by violent physical effort, and it is characterized by a lively heaving of the chest and rising and falling of the shoulders, which will not answer at all for singing. Clavicular breathing has no place in artistic singing. Whenever you see a singer heaving up his shoulders before the beginning of each phrase, make up your mind that there is something radically wrong with his tone formation. Listen to his attack and you will find that it invariably begins with a strangulated tone, which at the conclusion of the phrase dwindles to a wheeze. "No cantilena here" should be the sign hung over the head of every singer who employs the hoisted shoulder process in singing.

The lungs are much like a pair of bellows, and the throat is related to them as the nozzle is to the real bellows. The part of the bellows which expands

and contracts most in drawing in and pushing out
air is the part furthest from the nozzle, and you
will find that the same thing is true of the human
apparatus. The diaphragm and the muscles of the
lower ribs are the chief agents in breathing deeply
and quietly.

Any heaving of the upper chest or shoulders
must disturb the poise of the larynx, which contains
the sounding reeds of the voice. Any disturbance
of the poise of the larynx calls for some effort in
the throat to offset it, and the singer should never
make efforts with his throat.

It is quite true that certain throat muscles are
employed in singing. But if the breathing, the
attack and the tone formation are correctly conceived, these muscles will operate normally and
without interference from other muscles which
should not be employed. The result is a feeling of
perfect freedom or relaxation. The word "relaxation" is used in this book to express a condition,
not of looseness, but of absence of tightness, which
is a very different thing.

All the muscles of the throat should be easy and
reposeful in good tone formation. They should not

be subjected to any pulls or shocks. Singers should never be conscious of effort in the throat; they should feel it all below the throat in the muscles of the body. The whole neighborhood of the throat should be kept quiet.

Now comes the inevitable question: What is the singer to do when called upon to sing long phrases rapidly succeeding one another? How is he to draw in a good big breath without making a sudden and violent effort? Well, the answer to this is that he is not to attempt to draw in such a breath.

Madame Sembrich, who is a past mistress of sustained and smooth delivery, is a firm advocate of the use of the half breath in singing. In other words, instead of attempting to let the whole body of air exude from the lungs and then completely replenish it, one should take half breaths before the storehouse is empty, and thus keep it occupied.

By this method a series of sustained phrases may be sung without any apparent break in the continuous flow of tone. The interruption of the stream of sound required for half a breath is very brief and will not convey any noticeable stoppage to an audience. The muscular effort needed to take half a breath is comparatively small, much less than half that needed for a quick, deep inspiration, and hence the strain on the physical organization of the singer is less and the possibility of disturbing the poise of the tone forming organ much smaller.

It must be distinctly understood that the half breath is not to be used except when it is absolutely necessary. When the singer can advantageously get the full breath, he should take it. The object of the half breath is to prevent depletion in passages where there is not time to get a full inspiration.

We are now approaching the point at which this matter of breathing connects itself with the attack of tone, the beginning of actual singing. And here must come the final caution about breathing. The singer must never try to take in too much breath, for that will result in the trouble which Lilli Lehmann says affected her in her early days.

"I always felt," she says, "as if I must let out some of the breath before beginning to sing." Poor Nature was uttering her protest and misguided human will was trying to stifle it. Breathe easily, opulently, but not willfully. Let the demands of the voice, not the operation of your will govern breath-

ing. On this vital point a quotation may be profit-
ably made from the excellent "Philosophy of
Singing," by Clara Kathleen Rogers, who was
aforetime the Clara Doria of operative note. She
declaims vigorously against consciously working
the diaphragm.

"What is required in breathing," she says, "is
expansion without unnecessary tension. The lungs
must fill themselves in proportion as the breath is
exhausted under the regulation of their own law—
that of action and reaction—and not by any conscious regulating of the diaphragm on the part of
the singer, as this leads inevitably to a mechanical
and unspontaneous production of tone.

"Singers will understand me better if I say that
there must be no holding, no tightness anywhere,
but the frame of the body must remain plastic or
passive to the natural acts of inhaling and exhaling,
as in this way only can perfect freedom of vocal
expression be obtained."

This is sound talk and should be carefully tucked
away in the memory closet of every student of
singing. Lilli Lehmann, in her treatise on her own
way of singing, advocates a wholly different

method, but her book discloses the secret that this
method was devised to meet certain physical dis-
qualifications with which Lehmann had to contend
in girlhood. In other words, she acquired her manner of breathing when she was making earnest
efforts to overcome a natural shortness of breath.
She therefore fell into the habit of willfully operat-
ing her breathing muscles instead of permitting
them to operate in response to the demands of tone.

She tells us that she breathed that way for
twenty-five years, and then learned from a horn
player with remarkably long wind that although he
set up his diaphragm very firmly in inspiration, he
relaxed it when he began to play. Madame Lehmann
tried that way in singing, and says she obtained
"the best results." So in the end the principle of
"no holding, no tightness anywhere," came home
to her.

This seems to be a suitable point at which to
insert a letter from a physician who has made a
special study of the physical operations of singing.
He says:

I believe the essential of proper breathing is to stand
erect, with the shoulders in absolutely normal (but erect)

position. This results in the elevation of the upper part of
the thoracic wall, lifting the ribs so that the action of the
chest is for the time being suspended, giving free action
to the diaphragm—which is the sole breath regulator in the
act of singing. At the close of a series of phrases—at the
end of a paragraph, if I may use such a word for descrip-
tive purposes—in the music, where a pause of sufficient
length is available, the bony walls of the chest are col-
lapsed for the purpose of removing a modicum of car-
bonic-acid gas, which must of necessity accumulate and
which is immediately replaced with fresh air by the
restoration of the erect position before the commencement of the next act singing.

To go beyond this in instructing a pupil is to introduce
error, to substitute the conscious for what must be uncon-
scious action to be effective and, finally and worst of all,
to wallow in the sea of error which will simply be a
measure of the anatomical attainments of the teacher and
the teacher's judgment in a field for which no adequate
training is possible.

Shakespeare (the English teacher of music) has shown
that considerable air pressure is necessary to the attainment of good quality of tone in singing. The essence of
his work is the reserve quantity of breath required at the
end of a phrase. It is a good feature.

I have carefully observed the method of the greatest
singers, and I believe that the above statements, simple as
they are, cover the entire field, so far as it relates to breath
control. Beyond this we go into questions of natural
attributes and temperament of the pupil.

Three words must ever be kept in mind when
thinking of breathing in the art of song: These

words are "slow," "gentle," "deep." All the old masters insisted that breathing in song should be of the character described by these three terms. If the reader desires the names of some of these masters, here they are: Nicolo Porpora, Antonio Bernacchi, Antonio Pistocchi, Leonardo Leo, Domenico Gizzi, Francesco Durante, Giuseppe Amadori and Francesco Brivio. The fundamentals of the method taught by these masters were the pure legato and sonorous, beautiful tone. To this they added training in vocal agility, but it must be ever borne in mind that this training was superimposed on a course of instruction in breathing and tone formation.

If the student has learned to breathe slowly, deeply and gently, so that he can emit from his windpipe a steady column of air which is under perfect control, he must next solve the question of the attack of tone. It is unnecessary here to enter upon a long description of the operations of the vocal cords. It will be enough to say that they are two membranous bands stretching across the upper opening of the larynx. Air expelled from the lungs and passing through these cords sets them in vibration, when they are brought close together and set taut by their muscular fibers acting under the operation of the will to make a vocal sound.

The action of the vocal cords is entirely automatic. When one breathes without desiring to speak they relax and leave a wide passage between them for the air. Sometimes they lie snugly at rest behind the two ventricular bands which stretch across the larynx just in front of them. When the person is about to make a vocal sound the cords rush out of their hiding places and, bringing their edges close together, form a narrow slit, through which the air rushes, setting the membranes in vibration and producing sound. And that is the act of phonation.

It is the same in both speech and song. The singer, however, has a purpose different from the speaker's. The singer aims to produce a tone which shall be musical, that is, absolutely the same in pitch from beginning to end. The voice of a person speaking ranges through infinitesimal gradations of pitch. If it does not, he acquires what is graphically described as a "sing song" delivery. Furthermore, a speaker cares little whether his tone is beautiful or not. It would add much to the joys of living if we all did think a little about our speaking voices, but we do not. Public speakers might improve vastly in this matter, but they are usually satisfied if they can make their tones big enough to reach all their hearers.

Now the singer in the search after smooth, round, musical tone, speedily finds out that the first secret is the attack, the beginning of the tone. This attack begins with what is called the stroke of the glottis, which in plain English means the flying together of the two vocal cords. If the singer thinks of the tone apart from its motor, the air column, he will fall into one or two vices: either his vocal cords will come together before the air strikes them from below, or afterward. If they do the former, the air will forcibly open them and a little clucking sound will be caused.

This is not quite accurately described by some of the authorities on singing as the audible stroke of the glottis. It is most unbeautiful and is the most vicious form of bad attack. It occurs almost entirely on words beginning with vowels. Consonantal beginnings make it nearly impossible, or at any rate cover it up. But a passage beginning with "Ah" is likely to bring out this vice in all its ugliness. The long English E is the next sound after "Ah" to encourage it.

When once a singer has fallen into this pernicious habit of attack, it seems as if he could never rid himself of it. Women seem fonder of it than men, for some reason not clear to this writer. But it is exceedingly wearisome to hear a soprano go clucking through an opera like a hen calling her brood. The other form of bad attack is the H form. In this bad attack the singer wills to exhale the breath before willing to make tone, and the result is that his tone begins with an aspirate. If he wishes to sing "I am lonely to-night" he perforce sings "Hi am lonely." These are the two opposites to a good attack, which consists in willing the cords to set themselves for a tone at precisely the moment when the column of air strikes them. Sir Morel Mackenzie says:

"The regulation of the force of the blast which strikes against the vocal cords, the placing of these in the most favorable position for the effect which it is desired to produce, and the direction of the vibrating column of air are the three elements of artistic production. These èlements must be thoroughly coördinated—that is to say, made virtually one act, which the pupil must strive by constant practice to make as far as possible automatic."

A perfect attack is rare. Yet in our own time we have had the privilege of hearing not a few singers who possessed it. The present writer always found that one of the greatest beauties of Melba's delivery in the best days of her exquisite voice was the perfection of her attack. The technical term seems altogether unsuitable to a description of the manner in which she began a tone.

It was not an attack at all. She just opened her lips, and the tones dropped out like the pearls from the mouth of the princess in the fairy tale. Or one might liken an attack of this kind to the beginning of the flow of water when a faucet is turned. The clucking attack sounds like the lighting of gas; the aspirated attack like the turning on of electric light in which the click of the switch always precedes the appearance of illumination.

Lehmann's attack was imperfect throughout her career. Doubtless her artificial method of breathing was at fault. At any rate, she aspirated a large percentage of those tones which had to be taken on open vowels. Caruso has a perfect attack, and he breathes with consummate ease. Therefore his tone is rich, round and sustained.

But students who observe Caruso must not forget that some of his gifts are exceptional. He possesses lung capacity far beyond the normal. He sings amazingly long phrases with apparently careless ease. No art will enable a singer to imitate him in this, for he is equipped with a most extraordinary pair of bellows.

When he does not drive great blasts out of them in the endeavor to supply the vulgar demand for huge sounds, the quality of his voice, floated on a deep and perfectly controlled stream of air, is something beautiful beyond description. As long as we have such singing we need not altogether despair of vocal technic.

5

Practice in Beginning Tones

AN ENDEAVOR HAS BEEN MADE TO SHOW CLEARLY
that the question of attack is not one admitting of
many words. The vocal cords should set for the
tone at the very instant that the column of breath
moving up the windpipe strikes them. That is the
secret of pure bell-like attack. The student will
naturally ask how he is to know when he is getting
this kind of attack. There are two ways of ascertaining. One is by one's own sensations and the
other is by the report of a competent hearer. It is in
the later capacity that the trained teacher is essential. One's sensations are pretty good guides in this
particular matter, but they are deceptive in other
details of singing. One cannot hear his own voice
as others hear it, and the teacher is the guide whose
experienced ear detects vocal error and who knows
the cause of it.

However, some readers may wish to know what
the sensations are. Purposely shut your throat, as

if you were trying to avoid swallowing something distasteful to you, and then give a quick, smart push with your breath. Do this in a whisper. You will get a little explosive sound like the beginning of a feeble cough. This will provide you with the sensation made by bringing the vocal cords together before expelling the air.

Try the same thing again, uttering the sound "ah" when you expel the breath, and you will get the effect and sensation together. Now utter the word "halt," but make the initial "h" long, thus "h-h-h-halt." You will find that in order to do this you must blow out breath and suddenly choke it off by bringing the vocal cords together to make the "ah" sound. This will bring clearly to your notice the sensation of the aspirated attack.

In singing a word beginning with an open vowel you should not feel either of these sensations. You should feel that your lungs contain sufficient air for the formation of the tone which you are about to produce, and that the tone begins by the passing of the breath through the throat.

Attack should be practiced with the minimum amount of effort. A good attack can never be acquired by practicing with a big tone. The employment of a big tone presupposes the inhalation of much breath, and no neophyte in singing is competent to manage a large body of breath. Bad attack is sure to result from any attempt to do so. The attack and much more must be acquired before singing in full volume should be attempted.

Taking in a large quantity of breath is at all times hazardous. The singer should inhale just as much breath as he needs for the tone he is about to produce, and there is no standard of mental judgment for this. The natural demand of the lungs is the best guide. You will find that they will protest equally against being starved and against being crammed. If they are stretched too much the muscular strain of retention will affect not only them, but also the throat, and you will without question get a tone sadly afflicted with vibrato.

Anything which tends to tie up the vocal cords, to rob them of perfect ease (that is, in so far as sensation goes) will bring on vibrato. On the other hand, if they are actually relaxed, that is not properly set taut for the formation of a tone, the voice will surely wabble, and every tone will be unsteady and uncertain in pitch.

The breathing behind the attack, then, must be well within the power of the lungs. Practice deep, gentle and slow breathing, but in singing never attempt to fill the lungs to their utmost capacity. The athlete who can do a hundred yards in ten seconds flat and who is jogging along at a fourteen-second gait has the same feeling of ease and elasticity in his limbs as the singer should have in his chest when he is breathing properly.

Feeling this way he will not ruin his attack by tightening up the throat in the effort to help the lungs hold in, nor by opening it up too much in the effort to help the air out. David Frangçon-Davies in his admirable work, "The Singing of the Future," says that we should draw just enough breath for a whisper and then convert it into tone.

A sigh of contentment is his standard of breathing. He advises the singer to draw a sigh of contentment, then to repeat that sigh and exhale it in tone. It is by no means bad advice. In practicing attack, however, it would be well to think rather of the whisper than the sigh. A sigh is sometimes pretty deep. Think of a whisper, then, and inhale breath as if about to utter one. Then make your attack with that amount of breath.

Now follows the natural question, "What am I to attack?" Attack a vowel sound. That is the answer. In general let consonants alone in the early stages of your practice, with one exception. The letter L is kind to the student of attack. It is recommended by most of the old masters as aiding in setting the mouth, lips, tongue, etc., in the natural position or the production of a good tone.

These same masters also advocate the use of the vowel sound best represented by the syllable "Ah" as the safest for the early stages of tone formation. They believed that in the utterance of this sound the throat was well opened and the tongue and palate brought into good positions.

This is true as far as it goes, but it is not the whole secret. The "ah" sound is the best open vowel sound, provided there be no artificiality in its utterance. Now if one puts much thought on the position of the tongue or the palate, there will be artificiality, and the most probable result will be the placing too far back of the tone, which results in what is called throatiness.

In studying attack one should not fix his mind on the position of the tongue at all. What he should keep before him is the imperative necessity of having everything about his throat and mouth in a position creating a sensation of comfortable freedom, of elastic ease.

The runner runs with his legs and lets his arms swing relaxed. The singer sings with his breath and should let his throat and mouth feel relaxed. Of course the vocal cords are not relaxed, but there is no unnatural pull or haul on any of the muscles attached to the larynx. If one undertakes to force his tongue into some cramped position advocated by teachers as the best for tone production, he will speedily learn that when he tries to sound certain vowels the tongue will fight for liberation to assume its function in the formation of that sound.

We make tone with our larynx, but vowels with that and the mouth combined. The lips and tongue have to do their share. Now when you sing "ah," it is perfectly easy to permit the tongue to lie flat in the mouth with its edge touching the teeth all around. That is what the old masters taught. But note this: You must simply let the tongue lie there. You must not force it. Sing "ah" once with your tongue perfectly relaxed. Just don't think about it at all. You will find that the tone comes out easily and without causing any sensation or discomfort in your throat.

Now sing it again, but this time gently push the tongue forward so as to make it press very lightly against the teeth. In other words, feel for the teeth and make sure that the tongue is touching them. You will now discover a sensation of discomfort in your throat, a feeling as if the passage was partly stopped, and if you can hear your voice clearly you will note that your "ah" sound has altered perceptibly toward the short "a," as in "fan."

Continue to sing your "ah" sounds that way and you will end by having a flat, wooden and un-vibrant tone, utterly unfavorable to artistic song. All your "ah" sounds will come out precisely as those of Ernst van Dyck did after his voice had lost all semblance of a musical organ, and for ex-actly the same reason.

Singing this sort of an "ah" is called singing "too

open." The truth is precisely the opposite. It is singing too closed. The tongue being forcibly pushed forward pulls up its own posterior part and crowds the throat passage so that the free emission of air is blocked. A strangulated, bleating quality of tone is the result. Therefore in practicing attack with "ah" concentrate your mind entirely on the quality of the tone, and let your poor throat and tongue alone. Let them fall into a state of security and repose.

You may perhaps deceive yourself about this matter. Hence the need of an unprejudiced ear, that of the teacher. He must tell you when your tone sounds strained or muffled, and you must try to think it more free and open. Then draw in your breath as if for a whisper and sigh out the "ah" in placid contentment. The older masters, as we have noted, or at any rate many of them, believed in prefixing an "l" to the "ah" sound. There is much to be said in favor of this practice. No other consonant so little impedes the flow of tone. No other gives so little interruption to it when sounded in the middle of a word.

On the other hand, the simple stroke of the

tongue against the teeth made in forming this consonant brings the tongue down into a very good position for the proper emission of a round and sonorous "ah." The one thing to be borne in mind is that the student must in the end learn to sing his "ah" without the help of the "l," because it is on words beginning with open vowels that bad attack is most likely to occur.

If what has thus far been printed here in regard to the art of singing means anything at all, it means that it is not such a complicated and recondite process as it is generally represented to be. "Sing as you speak," says Jean de Reszke. This is not a scientific statement of the case. The kind of tones employed in speaking are different from those used in singing, as has already been noted.

In speaking breath is taken without any thought just as often as it is necessary to replenish the store in the lungs. In singing it is essential to look ahead and perceive where breath can be conveniently taken without disturbing the outline of the melody which is sung. Again, in speaking we do not particularly concern ourselves about the quality of our tones, but permit them to issue from the throat in their spontaneous timbre.

In singing we aim to produce the most beautiful tones of which our throats are capable. But, on the other hand, the normal operations of the lungs and throat are the foundations of good singing. The dust thrown in the eyes of students consists of a cloud of mystery constructed out of queer theories of artificial breathing and unnatural tone formation. Back to nature as closely as we can go should ever be the singer's ideal.

One of the writer's acquaintances has declared it to be his belief that there is no such thing as a natural method of singing, because singing is an artificial achievement. It is art. We were never intended by nature to sing, but simply to speak. In a measure this is true. Singing is art, while speaking is nature. But singing can be done by methods entirely opposed to nature, and also by other methods amicably related to her. These latter methods are all simple, the others are all complex.

The truth is that while speaking is nature, singing is nothing more than nature under high cultivation. The culture of wild flowers has in some instances given us beautiful additions to the garden.

Speaking is like the wild rose; singing like the American Beauty. The student of singing should always keep this thought in mind, and when he finds himself confronted with some theory which makes the act of drawing and exhaling the breath or beginning the emission of a tone appear to be a complex process, depending on the voluntary guidance of a number of muscles and ligaments, he should examine it very closely and with suspicion.

The art of singing is an æsthetic art, not an anatomical study. It begins with an ideal dwelling in the realm of the conception of tonal beauty, not in the domain of correct movement of muscles. The problem of the great masters of the early period was to ascertain the best way of singing beautiful tones on every vowel sound throughout the entire range of a voice, not to find how to operate certain parts of the body and decide that such operation ought to give the tone.

They reasoned from the tone to the operation, not from the operation to the tone. Too many modern theorists seem to proceed in the latter way, and that is why they build up complicated and unnatural processes which confuse students and do incalculable harm.

6

About Tone Formation

ATTACK SHOULD BE PRACTICED BY ALL BEGINNERS in the medium range of their voices only. Indeed, no exercises in the extreme upper or lower parts of the singer's scale should ever be undertaken except by students sufficiently far advanced to be able to do so without strain.

By strain here is meant forcible pulls on the muscles of the throat. Perfect emission of tone presupposes complete freedom of these muscles. They should operate entirely normally, and if they do the singer will not feel their operation. If they do not operate normally there will be a perceptible pull somewhere. The only way to avoid contracting muscular habits of this sort is for the student to take everything easily at first. Sing always a trifle below mezzo forte, but not altogether piano, for singing down to a complete piano is likely to result in flabbiness of the vocal cords.

The attack, then, should be practiced at first on the syllables "la" and "ah" in the tones which come most easily to the singer in the middle of the voice and at a little less than half power. The next step forward is practice of attack on other simple vowel sounds. The student should use at first only long O, long E (English) and Oo. These are perfectly pure vowel sounds and can be utilized safely.

In the beginning it is wiser to let the others alone. Some of them are compound, and others are conducive to bad tone if sung by a person who has not yet acquired any command of attack and tone formation. In the end, of course, every singer must learn to sing all vowel sounds on all notes of his scale.

It is true that some never acquire ability to do this. Sometimes this inability is caused by peculiar conformation of the mouth, and again it is the product of pure laziness in practice. The celebrated tenor Brignoli was so indolent in this matter that he found it most comfortable to sing all his upper middle tones on the vowel sound "ah," and all his high notes on the long Italian I. Hence he was wont at times to alter his text so that he sang simply "Ah, si," over and over. Such a performance would not be tolerated in these days of realistic opera.

While practicing attack the young singer must

acquire a knowledge of correct tone placing. He cannot go on singing without any knowledge of this. Now, tone placing is a much-vexed question. Anyone who observes carefully the art of the eminent singers of the Metropolitan Opera House will find many differences in their methods of placing. Those who do so observe will furthermore find some rather pointed warnings against the acquirement of bad habits.

Tone placing is a term which shares with more than two-thirds of the nomenclature of singing technics a sad lack of scientific accuracy. The terminology of the art is more than half figurative. Such expressions as "chest register," "head register," or examples, are figures of speech, not scientific appellations. So, too, tone placing is a figurative expression. Tone formation is a more accurate phrase, but it does not, considered simply as a piece of English, mean precisely the same thing as tone placing.

When singing teachers talk about tone placing they have in their minds a clear idea, but it is one hard to put before a student. The whole matter rests largely upon the intellectual conception of tone, but it has also a distinct physical aspect. The question first to be considered is, how best to make use of the natural resonating parts of the body which are set in vibration by the sung tone and which reënforce and enrich it.

What makes your voice have a different quality from that of your friend? Both are originally made by those two little thin bands in the larynx called vocal cords. Let that fact never slip out of mind. Voice is made by vocal cords, but it is modified by other agents acting in union with those cords.

Helmholtz demonstrated that every musical sound was complex. There is a fundamental tone and certain other sounds called upper partials or harmonics or overtones. These overtones are not perceived by the untrained ear, but they exist nevertheless. In the ringing of a large bell they become perfectly audible to the most casual observer, but in tones more closely knit they melt into the whole and pass unobserved.

Now let us imagine some abstract tone producer capable of emitting elementary pitch without quality. Let us suppose that we caused this tone producer to sound its note first through a cylindrical tube, next through a hollow ovoid, next through a conical tube and finally through an oblong box, like a thirty-two-foot organ pipe. We should in each case get a different quality of tone, and for want of a better term we should say that these tones had different timbres.

Some theoreticians are of the opinion that timbre is affected by the nature of the substance through which the tones are sounded, and that a human voice acquires part of its difference from a clarinet (for example) because it is formed in different material. This theory has of late been warmly opposed, and Mahillon Brothers, a firm of Belgian cornet makers, conducted a series of experiments to show that cornets, scientifically made of wood, brass, copper, iron or other materials, all sounded alike, provided only that the bores were identical in every particular.

The point to be made here, however, is that whether it is owing wholly to the shape of the cavity or partly to the substance of which it is made, the difference in timbres is caused by the prominence of some upper partials and the retirement of others. The upper partials are all present in the resonating cavities above mentioned, but the cylinder will emphasize certain ones, while the conical tube will bring forward others, and thus we get a difference in timbres, whether the substance of which the tube is made be the same or not.

Now in the human being difference of tone is caused by differences in the shape of the parts of the person which vibrate in sympathy with vocal tone. Study of throats with the laryngoscope shows that the epiglottis (termination of the air passage above the glottis) differs in different individuals. That in itself would be enough to cause some variety in voices. The shape of the throat is not precisely the same in every human being, and that is another cause. Here we have a case in which it is surely not the substance, but the shape in which it is molded that causes the prominence of some upper partials and the obscurity of others in such a way as to make difference in voices.

This is not all. The vibrations of the vocal cords in producing sounds are carried down the larynx to the chest, and so the shape of the chest plays a part in coloring the voice. Again, because the air blast is propelled through the cords into the cavity of the throat, the throat is set in vibration, and these vibrations are carried up into the cavities of the nose.

Furthermore, there are cavities in the bones of the skull, in the forehead and just over the rear of the roof of the mouth. Anatomists have shown that these vary somewhat in shape and size in different persons. Now the vibratory waves caused by sound in the throat are carried up and communicated to these cavities, and their formation thus influences the quality of one's tone.

It is owing not only to differences in the length and thickness of vocal cords but also to these other differences in shape and size, which affect the upper partials of a tone, that human voices have different timbres, that Melba sounds different from Sembrich or Caruso from Jean de Reszke. It is in the formation of the cords and the resonating cavities as they are called, that singers receive the gift of nature in the shape of a voice.

Timbre is also affected by the action of the palatal muscles called the tensores, which lower the soft part of the roof of the mouth and at the same time give it a certain amount of firmness. It is also affected by the levatores palati, which lift the soft palate. Acting alone this lifting of the soft palate produces throaty tone. When the tensores and levatores work against one another so as to produce a perfect balance of power, the singing tone is rich and noble.

The question of tone placing, then, resolves itself into this: Is it possible by taking thought about the various resonators to bring out the best qualities of a singing voice? The experience of nearly three centuries of study and experiment by singers and teachers of singing has resulted in a consensus of opinion that it is. In spite of this there are still some who do not believe in any consideration of the resonating cavities, while others are foolish enough to think they can utilize some one of them at the expense of all the others.

Perhaps the clearest illustration of what is meant by this is to be found in overemployment of the resonance of the nasal cavity. The person who has this habit purposely drives the greater part of the air which has come through his vocal cords upward into the passage leading from the rear of the mouth into the nostrils. The result is a nasal twang in every tone, or in common speech the singer sings through his nose.

Joseph Sheehan, the tenor of Mr. Savage's English opera company, went to Paris one summer and studied three months. About all that his teacher could manage to teach him in that time was that he should utilize the nasal resonators, which he had previously not used at all. The result was that when Mr. Sheehan came back to America and sang Rhadames in "Aïda" he was generally informed that he sang through his nose, whereupon he lamented bitterly that he had spent three months and much honest coin in learning to do something wrong.

The French masters, however, are generally prone to overestimate the part played by nasal cavities in tone formation. These cavities must be used, but not disproportionately. The French tongue makes their use imperative, because no one can sing such words as "rien" or "bien" without using them.

The proper way to employ the nasal cavities is to let them entirely alone. In speaking one does not think about them and they attend to their business. In singing one should think of them only as much as is necessary to avoid closing them. They should be left open so that they may freely communicate with the rear arch of the mouth, and thus the resonating cavities not only of the nose but also of the head will without any thought on the part of the singer perform their natural offices and bring out the natural timbre of the tones.

The French say we should sing "dans le masque," by which they mean to convey the idea of projecting tone through the mouth and nose, but not through one at the sacrifice of the other.

But this is not all. The singer must use some art in focusing the tones in the mouth. This is one of the most important details of singing, because upon its proper execution depends largely the beauty of the tone. Furthermore a proper conception of the point at which one should aim to focus tone leads to a correct position of the organs employed in the formation and thus prevents the taking of unnatural positions certain in the long run to injure the voice.

For the beginner, then, practicing entirely in the medium register, the point upon which the tone should be focused is the front of the hard palate, the roof of the mouth where it begins to curve downward toward the upper teeth. Remember that you cannot make a tone there. You make it with your vocal cords. Remember also that you cannot place it there. What you really do is to think it there. When you do that, you involuntarily put your mouth into the correct position.

In other words, each tone should sound as if it were made just behind the teeth. When tones are placed too far forward they sound as if they were between the teeth, because of the too great pull on the tensores palati, and this gives them a hard, metallic quality. When placed too far back there is undue strain on the levatores palati and the tones assume a throaty sound.

In the formation of tones the lips are not to be forgotten, as their position has not a little influence on vocal sounds. Only general rules can be laid down for this detail. The one fundamental law of good tone production, that there should be no holding or tightness, no forcing, but a feeling of comfortable relaxation, stands good here. The mouth must of course be opened. Some singers open it too much, others not enough. The old masters advocated opening it sufficiently to admit the forefinger.

Many singers, however, will find that their tones flow most freely when the mouth is opened just a little more widely than this.

Some teachers and some singers believe that the secret of good tone lies in pushing forward the lips. The mouth is resolutely opened in the form of the letter O, the lips being compelled to protrude somewhat. Sbriglia of Paris is the most ardent advocate of this style, and yet Jean de Reszke, who studied with him for a time, discarded it in the very beginning. Madame Nordica employs it and is a firm believer in it. Madame Sembrich, on the other hand, employs the horizontal oval, or letter O laid on its side. This lip formation, the old masters asserted, gives the tones a beautifully soft sonority, suitable for the expression of feeling.

If, however, this position be exaggerated, as in a forced smile, the inevitable result is "white voice." Now there are occasions when "white voice" may be employed for passing effects, but to fall into the habit of using it all the time is to make emotional expression absolutely impossible. A finished artist ought to be able to color tone at will, but for the student only the best and most beautiful sonority must be sought. Therefore let him avoid all forced positions of the lips. On this point may be advantageously quoted some sensible words of Albert Bach, the London master:

"The teacher must from the outset ascertain with the greatest care the position of the mouth that is easiest and most suitable for each pupil and attend to its being constantly maintained. Even very small variations in the dimensions of the mouth strikingly alter the formation of the tone.

"The Bernacchi school of Bologna says opening the lips more or less by a tenth of an inch is of marked influence on the tone. With some singers whose organization permits only a moderate separation of the jaws in the production of the vowel E (eigh) a scarcely perceptible elevation of the point of the tongue prevents the free passage of the tone on this vowel.

"Each face, mouth and tongue being formed differently, special trials have to be made with every beginner in order that it may be established in what way he can form the tone with the greatest ease and beauty."

The old masters were especially skillful in ascertaining the best way for each pupil to get the best results. This was largely owing to the fact that they were not mere theorists. They had a great store of experience and tradition to lean upon and they had ready solutions of most of the problems raised by individuality. They were not hidebound at all. Their method was flexible and adaptable in detail, but solid and immovable in fundamentals.

7

Registers of the Voice

Giovanni lamperti says: "there is no doubt that the greater part of the difficulties encountered at a change of register, as well as the uneven tones within one and the same register, may be traced to faulty breathing. At a change of register especially the breathing must be calm and easy. When it is so and the body is in a normal position, with the mouth and pharynx suitably opened, no one will experience difficulty at a change of register."

Here again speaks the voice of experience and culture in the fertile field of Italian tradition. Singing teachers who have feared that pupils might regard the science of singing as too simple to justify the exorbitant prices asked for instruction in it are among the chief inculcators of perplexing ideas about the registers of the voice. We have been asked to believe that there are three different methods of producing tones, namely, the chest, the medium and the head. The truth is that all the tones of the voice are produced by the vibration of the vocal cords, and these cords are caused to vibrate by the passage through them of air from the lungs.

It is equally true that there are changes in the position of the larynx at different places in the scale of each singer, and that the sensations caused by these changes sometimes produce feelings of discomfort and lack of freedom in the act of singing. In striving to get rid of these feelings singers often resort to some abnormal pull among the throat muscles and thus acquire a bad method of singing certain tones.

When they have acquired such a method there is a marked difference between the tones produced without the abnormal pull and those produced with it, and this difference is called inequality of registers. One of the problems, therefore, that confront the student of singing is how to equalize his registers, which is simply another way of saying how to sing throughout his scale without materially altering the character of his voice. The words of Giovanni Lamperti, quoted above, should suggest fruitful reflection to many who have been bamboozled by the pretentious nonsense put forward by so many professors of this art.

There is no question whatever that a mechanical change in the production of tone does take place in the upper range of any voice, or in what is now called the head register. Giulio Caccini in his "Nuove Musiche," written at the beginning of the seventeenth century, when the study of artistic singing was just stepping from the portals of the church to the doors of the theater, recognizes the two registers, which he designates as "voce piena" and "voce finta." Literally these terms mean "full voice" and "disguised voice." They correspond to what believers in two registers now call lower, or chest, and head registers.

The writers of the master songs of church counterpoint utilized the head tones of men in their works. We have the careful account of Cerone (1613) on this matter, and he recognized two registers—chest and head. Since, therefore, the head voice (so-called) has been known and systematically used since the earliest period of the art of singing, we may accept it as a demonstrated fact.

The name is not quite satisfactory; but few of the terms used in the practice of singing are. This expression, "head voice," simply means that the notes in its range seem to cause vibrations in the skull or some part of it, whereas the physical feeling of vibration in the medium register is in the pharynx and in the lowest tones in the upper part of the chest.

Here we are again confronted with an inexact terminology. Most masters of singing divide registers into three—chest, medium and head. Very few of them hold that there is any change of mechanical operation in the passage from the chest to the medium. They are speaking merely of division of the scale. For practical purposes, it is convenient to use the three terms, but their true meaning must never be forgotten.

Sir Morell Mackenzie made many careful experiments and laryngoscopic investigations into this subject, and exhaustively reviewed the work of leading scientists and teachers. His conclusion, while it may not be that accepted by all the best contemporaneous masters of singing, is nevertheless worthy of serious attention. He found just the same number of registers as Caccini found three centuries ago—namely, a chest and a head.

In the chest register the pitch of the tones is raised, according to Mackenzie, by an increase of the tension of the vocal cords, and also by an almost microscopic addition to their length. In the head register, the pitch is raised by a gradual shortening of the vibrating reed, which is not quite so tense as in the chest register.

In other words, when the pitch has been raised as far as possible by an increase of tension on the vocal cords, the mechanical process is altered, and additional notes can be obtained by a different method. In producing these additional notes the vocal cords relax a trifle and then substitute for vibrations involving their entire length vibrations of only a part of it.

The cords come together just as they do in the natural lower tones, and then a small aperture near one end opens and allows itself to be set in vibration by the air blast. This produces the head tones, and the problem of the singer is to learn how to pass from the lower register into this one without so great a change in the quality of the voice as to cause a shock to the sensitive ear.

Mackenzie calls attention to the fact that all the scientific investigators of the voice have found only two registers. He names Müller, Mandl, Battaile, Vacher, Koch, Meyer, Gougenheim. and Lermoyez. Teachers of singing, on the other hand, have almost always held that there are at least three registers, and some of them have discovered as many as five. These five cannot be anything more than arbitrary divisions of the scale. There are not four changes in the anatomical process of voice production. There is only one, and that is the one which takes place at the transition from the "voce piena" to the "voce finta."

The sensation of vibration in the chest caused by singing the lowest tones of the voice is easily explained. When the lowest tones are sung the vocal cords have placed upon them the smallest amount of tension. They make slow and heavy vibrations just as the big pipes of an organ do, and these vibrations, being near the chest, communicate themselves to it, and the singer feels them. When the tones are pitched high the vibrations are short and rapid and are felt less in the chest than in their own immediate neighborhood.

In sounding the lowest tones of the voice the

larynx sinks, and that brings the vocal cords nearer to the chest. This sinking of the larynx is caused by the natural relaxation of the muscles, so that the tension on the vocal cords may be reduced. When the singer emits a medium tone the increased tension draws the larynx up a little, but a very little.

The student of singing, however, need not concern himself at all with the physiological formation of chest and head tones. What he must do is to ascertain at what point his voice naturally passes from one to the other, and then learn how to make the passage easily, smoothly and imperceptibly. In the voices of women this passage appears to cause more trouble than it does in those of men. At least such is the testimony of some experienced and competent masters of the art.

Nothing better has been said on this subject than the words of Lamperti with which this article begins. Practice and keen listening are the two elements which must enter into this operation of equalizing the registers. The chief object to be kept in mind is making the transition without introducing any feeling of constriction in the throat. As

Meyer has well said, one sings with his body through his throat, but not with his throat. Of course he is referring entirely to the propulsion of power.

Careful and correct breathing will go a long way toward the solution of the troublesome problems of equalizing registers. Together with these must go that nice mental conception of tone without which the singer can never become an artist. The student must form a clear and settled idea of the quality of tone for which he is to seek throughout his voice. He must therefore formulate his ideal for his high tones on those of the medium register, which are the most easily and spontaneously formed.

It is for this reason that he must carry on all his early practice on his medium tones. They must be correctly produced before more difficult notes are undertaken. When the student can sing with some ease and freedom up to the point at which he becomes conscious of a change in the mechanism it will be time for him to consider seriously the solution of the question of crossing the Rubicon. The point at which the change from the chest to the head register takes place is not the same in all voices.

The passage from the low to the medium register in women's voices is usually from E on the lowest line of the treble clef to F, and that from the medium to the high from E flat in the top space to F. The chest register of a tenor will usually run no higher than the E at the top of the middle octave. That of a baritone will go as high as E flat and that of a genuine bass up to D.

It must be borne in mind, however, that these are generalizations. No hard and fast rules can be laid down in regard to a matter which presents considerable variety. One thing is quite certain, and that is the point of alteration can readily be decided by the ear of a teacher, if not by the sensations of the student.

The golden rule in the treatment of the registers is to keep them in a normal state. The lowest register below the clef is that in which the vocal cords are least tense, and therefore the tones can never be given great sonority in that region. Any attempt to do so will lead to squeezing with the muscles through the involuntary endeavor to steady the cords against the undue pressure of air. This will produce a harsh and disagreeable tone, and if the practice is continued it will work great injury to the voice.

It is still more dangerous to try to carry up the chest (here including the medium) register beyond its limits. This, again, brings an unnatural strain upon the mechanism of the voice, and because the effort required to produce the high tones in this way is very great the damage to the voice is correspondingly large.

Lamperti recommends for practice in equalizing the registers the use of the four notes of the chords of C major and D flat major. He advises his pupil to sing the chord ascending in one breath with careful attention to legato, and then, after taking a breath, to sing it down again. This exercise introduces the low E and F, on which the passage from the low to the medium is likely to occur. A similar exercise is recommended, going up as far as G above the clef, for crossing the bridge between the medium and head registers.

Paul Marcel, a prominent Parisian teacher, whose book on singing is filled with common sense, advises the pupil to practice the passage from E flat to E and afterward from E flat to F without any stroke and carrying the voice lightly from one note to the other. "By this practice," he says, "the voice will be rendered homogeneous and the pupil will become able to use it without a feeling of fatigue and without making those Tyrolean sounds so injurious to the voice and so disagreeable to the ear."

One of the most excellent adjuncts to the mastery of the transition from the medium to the head register is the fact that the mechanism of head tones can be carried down a little below the limits of the head register. In other words, the tones at the transition point can be sung in the head register as well as in the chest. The last one or two semi-tones of the chest register can be sung with the mechanism of the head register. This gives the singer the option of producing these tones in one of two ways, either to afford relief to the voice or to produce significant effects of tone color.

Albert Bach, the London teacher, advises his pupils to practice passing from one register to another by forming a short scale with the transition note in its middle. Then sing this scale up and down "gently and with little expense of breath." In going up the transition note is to be sung with the mechanism of the lower register and in coming down with that of the upper. The present writer has no direct knowledge of the value of this method of practice, but it is based on the principles underlying those recommended by other masters, and it sounds reasonable.

In dealing with this entire question of registers the singer must ever bear in mind that an important element in the solution of the problems is tone-placing. The singer is always afraid that the tones of his low register will not carry. That is why he so often resorts to pushing. If the tones are correctly formed they will carry. That is the sum of the whole matter.

Almost all the authors of treatises on singing, and, indeed, many singers with whom this writer has discussed the subject, lay down points of aim for the placing of head tones. These points are not the same as that used for the placing of chest tones. We are told that the place for chest tones is the front of the hard palate; that for head tones the soft palate.

The truth is that a deal of nonsense is talked and written on this subject. Clara Kathleen Rogers in "The Philosophy of Singing" comes very close to the truth when she says that one must recognize the point of vibration in each register, but must not make any deliberate attempt to place the tone there.

Knowing full well what is likely to meet with the derision of some good teachers, the present writer does not hesitate to say that many singers play havoc with their upper tones by trying to do too much to assist the natural process of their formation.

Some forcibly open their mouths laterally by drawing back the corners of the lips, a method which invariably whitens the tone. Others violently throw up their chins and thus bring to bear a sudden pull on the top of the larynx, a pull which disturbs the poise of the vocal mechanism.

What the singer ought to do is to keep the muscles of his throat in a condition of ease and elasticity. He should not, in any circumstances, make efforts with his throat. He should open his mouth freely and naturally, simply by dropping the lower jaw, not by pulling at the lips. He should let his tongue lie comfortably in the lower part of his mouth, so that the whole back of the throat will be free to resonate and to permit the passage of the air.

Then, with the lungs sufficiently filled, he should propel the air with the diaphragm and rib muscles steadily and with just the necessary power (and no more) through the vocal cords. Let him *think* the tone—think its pitch, its quality and its pose. In thinking the latter let him aim to get the whole cavity of the mouth in resonance and to permit the nasal resonance chambers to do their part. Sing the high tones firmly "dans le masque," as the French say.

That does not mean through the nose, but through the mouth and with a feeling of perfect freedom in the nasal passages. The student who follows all the hints given in this chapter will have no serious troubles with the break between registers.

8

Messa di Voce and Portamento

GIOVANNI LAMPERTI SAYS THAT THE MESSA DI VOCE should not be attempted till the pupil has attained a considerable degree of agility. This idea is in direct opposition to those held on the same subject by many other excellent teachers. The messa di voce is the sounding of a sustained tone with a swell, that is, by beginning it piano, increasing it to full voice and then diminishing it again to piano. Why agility, which means the ability to sing runs and florid passages, should be acquired before the messa di voce is begun is a question which I find myself quite unable to answer.

The ability to sing a good messa di voce depends entirely on the control of the breath and the consequent steadiness and gradation of tone. Now, the control of breath is the first thing the student has to learn, and from his command of it he derives confidence in his power to sustain a steady tone and to emit it with a degree of force such as he chooses.

Therefore the next step ought logically to be toward the messa di voce, in which are combined the elements of tone mastery. Furthermore, it is by proceeding from the emission of tone sustained at a dead level to the sounding of tones varied in dynamic force that we throw off the shackles of monotony of style. It is by the emission of tones swelling and diminishing that we impart to song that wavelike undulation which gives it vitality and tonal vivacity.

Messa di voce was practiced by the earliest singers. It is mentioned as far back as Caccini and is particularly described by Mazzochi, writing in 1638. These old masters, however, do not lay down rules as to whether it should be attempted before or after the acquirement of a certain amount of agility. It must not be forgotten that at the beginning of the seventeenth century, and indeed some time before that, singers were capable of executing ornamental music. Archilei, a soprano of the time, was much praised for her skill in adding ornaments to a melody.

Nevertheless an examination of the recitatives of the first operas and oratorios, the works of Peri,

Caccini and Cavaliere will convince one that the stilo rappresentativo, as it was called, must have depended for its expressiveness very largely on beauty of tone, pure legato style and the messa di voce, by which flexibility and eloquence are imparted to long passages of sustained tones.

Mancini said: "Un vero ed attimo artista se ne serve in qualunque nota di valore la messa di voce." A true artist avails himself of the messa di voce on every tone. This is going much too far, but it serves to show in what estimation this beautiful ornament of song was held at a time when the technics of singing were most thoroughly understood. Another later master, D'Aubigny, in commenting on the need of perfect breath control for the execution of this device says: "The beginning and the end of the note must resemble the wafting of the evening breeze: one perceives its beginning without being able to define it; one is still listening to its termination when the note has already died away."

Two or three points must be kept in mind in singing messa di voce: In the first place the mouth must not be twisted or tortured; yet something has to be done with it. It must be kept nearly equally

open throughout the tone. The tone must be carefully attacked and then gently brought forward, by
which it will gain not a little in carrying power. In
the beginning of the singer's study messa di voce
should be practiced entirely in the medium tones of
the scale. No attempts at using it in the higher or
lower notes should be made till the elementary
exercises in the formation of these tones have been
completed.

In singing messa di voce in the higher tones the
mouth naturally needs to be opened a little more
fully at the forte. Otherwise the tones will sound
compressed. On the contrary, as the tone is gradually diminished the mouth should be gradually
permitted to diminish its opening so that the current of air forming the piano tone shall not be too
much scattered and the tone thus lose its carrying
power.

In spite of the dictum of Mancini, previously
quoted, the old Italians seem to have had moderate
notions about the employment of the messa di voce.
Tosi says: "Una bella messa di voce in bocca di un
professore che non sia avaro, e non se ne serva, che
su le vocali aperti, no manca mai di fare un ottimo

effetto." Which means: A beautiful messa di voce in the mouth of a professor who uses it with discretion and only on clear vowels will never fail to produce a fine effect.

Clara Kathleen Rogers says in regard to the method of making a messa di voce: "Singers often think they are making a crescendo when, in fact, they are doing nothing of the kind. This is when they press on some of the throat muscles in their ignorance of how a crescendo is made, and associate the physical pressure with an increase of volume of sound.

"They do not really hear an increase of sound, but they take it for granted that there must be one in response to the pressure, which pressure, in point of fact, simply hardens the tone, or renders it tremulous—sometimes both. If we would acquire the skill to swell or decrease the volume of tone at will, we must understand and bear in mind that it is the breath, and the breath alone, that is physically responsible for the increase and decrease of tone, and not muscular pressure or procuring a larger space in the throat for the tone to expand in by depressing the larynx."

In practicing the messa di voce let the student begin precisely as in the first exercises of tone production. Let him sing the syllable "la" (the *a* sounded as in "father") on tones in the middle of his voice. Let the attack be piano, delicate, but perfectly bell-like in its clearness. Let the inhalation of breath previous to the attack be moderate, so that the respiratory apparatus may be under complete control without any sense of tightness.

Then breathe out the tone gently and steadily, increasing the force of the air blast gradually so that in the middle of the tone a moderate forte is reached, or a natural full tone. Then diminish the power of the air blast gradually till the tone dies away imperceptibly. Great care will be necessary in the diminuendo to avoid allowing some of the air to escape without turning into tone. This will produce a faint hissing sound and impurity of tone.

It is also very likely to render the final part of the tone unsteady. This part of the tone, then, must be watched. Listen to a fine trumpeter play the opening notes of Wagner's "Rienzi" overture, and you will get a good conception of the messa di voce, except that the trumpeter will produce a forte of much greater power than a singer should desire to get.

The early Italian singers were in the habit of using very often, in company with the messa di voce, the portamento. Later singers used the portamento by itself, and it came to be one of the most admired features of artistic singing. It is used not a little in our time, but it is greatly abused.

Portamento means the sliding of the voice through the infinitesimal gradations of tone lying between a note and the ensuing one. This languorous progress of the voice is capable of much expression when judiciously employed, but when it becomes a habit it is deplorable, because then it leads to scooping.

It ruins correct attack and is actively hostile to accurate intonation. Once let a singer fall into the scooping habit and he will never more attack the tone which he intends to sing. He will strike into the scale somewhere below the tone and then slide up to it like a bad 'cello player feeling along the fingerboard for the position.

The secret of a pure and elegant execution of the portamento lies in the preservation of the pose of the first tone. The singer must aim to avoid a mental conception which will lead him to anticipate the second tone. He must pose his voice for the initial note, and think that pose all the time while his voice is gliding through the intervals between it and the second note. The emphasis in the mind must lie on the first note. Otherwise a scoop and not a portamento will be the result.

No special form of exercise is required for the acquirement of a good portamento. It will develop naturally if the student keep his mind upon it when he finds it advantageous for the production of a good effect. The main thing to be borne in mind is that it is a device to be used sparingly. It cannot be introduced artistically very often. When it is really needed it makes for beauty, but it should never be introduced merely for its own sake.

Those who heard the famous singers of the eighteenth century were unanimous in their praise of the manner in which these artists used the messa di voce and the portamento. We read that such great singers as Farinelli, Caffarelli, Faustina and Cuzzoni produced the most beautiful effects by means of these two devices of song. But it is indisputable that

their messa di voce was employed much more liberally than their portamento.

They knew well how to contrast with the portamento the clean glide from one tone to another,
without touching the intervening tones, called by
the Italians "di slancio." The student in practicing
portamento should frequently introduce this contrast in order that he may not lose hold of the perfect purity of his legato. An over-use of portamento
is ruinous to a clean legato.

On the other hand the liberal employment of the
messa di voce will impart to the voice a beautiful
flexibility. Let it be understood that flexibility refers
solely to the dynamics of tone, while agility is the
term signifying the power to produce tones in rapid
succession. A singer who is entirely without agility
can possess a perfect command of the messa di voce
and by means of it and other devices of expression
give eloquence to every air.

The acquirement of the technics of the messa di
voce and the portamento is one thing, while judgment in the use of these graces of song is quite
another. It is unfortunate, but it is true, that few of
the famous singers of the operatic stage are good

models in this respect. There is a vast amount of positive vulgarity of style in the singing designed to captivate the ostentatious part of humanity called Society, or the equally unrefined part which stands behind the orchestra rail and shouts "bravo" at every high tone.

The student should not be deceived by these things. He should aim always to be an artist, and the true artist combines continence in the use of his powers with refinement, taste and elegance.

9

The Acquirement of Agility

IT IS QUITE TRUE THAT THIS IS NOT THE DAY OF THE colorature singer. The modern lyric drama makes little use of the feats of agility with which the singers of a century ago astonished their auditors. The German lied, the reigning element in the song recital, narrows the sphere of vocal agility still more. Only in the oratorio does the singer of the present seem to be in imperative need of ability to execute cleverly what the earliest masters called "diminutions." Handel is inexorable in his demands, and Handel is apparently immortal, as he well deserves to be.

Nevertheless agility is essential to every singer. The singer who has a command of florid style possesses a reserve store of technic which will always be of incalculable value to him. The vocal music of to-day is not embroidered with runs, trills, groups and other ornaments, as the operas of the late seventeenth century were, but it does contain thousands

90

of progressions which can be executed with perfect smoothness and fluency by the agile voice, but by the singer untrained in colorature only awkwardly and uncertainly.

Even in the Wagner drama, that last extremity of dramatic style, there are many phrases calling for the ease and fluency of the colorature singer. What heavy-voiced soprano can carol the music of the Forest Bird in "Siegfried"? How do all the impersonators of Brünnhilde stumble over the first clarion peal of the "Hojotoho" unless their voices have been trained to the execution of trills and leaps. Even the mordent, which Wagner made a characteristic feature of his melody, cannot be sung cleanly by a singer who has no agility.

It is true that the modern singer need not be able to sing such passages as Faustina and Cuzzoni sang with amazing brilliancy, nor need she rival Jenny Lind or Patti. There is a wide field for the artist who elects to leave "Semiramide" and "Lucia" and their kind out of her calculations. But how much more elegant and gracious will be her delivery of a pure cantilena if she can sing the fiorituri of the florid rôles. What gave Lilli Lehmann her vast husbandry of resource but the fact that she was never in her greatest rôles taxing her technical resources? When she was singing Isolde, she had Violetta and Norma in reserve. They provided her with a fluent technic which made her "O sink' hernieder" touching in the sinuous curves of its delicious cantilena.

Observe the perfect command of every interval and every progression displayed in Madame Sembrich's song recitals. She is standing always on the firm foundation of a facility of execution far beyond anything demanded in the field of song literature. She is always within herself. She is never, as racing people say, extended.

It is impossible to overestimate the value of agility of voice. Hence every singer should strive to acquire a fluent colorature. There is only one way to get it, and that is by practice. The pianist acquires rapidity of finger by beginning with simple five finger exercises and advancing as fast as he conquers one form of agility to the next one. The singer has to do the same thing. There is no royal road to agility. Teachers who profess to know tricks by which a perfect trill or a flawless scale can be acquired in three lessons or four are charlatans, and they know they are.

There is an old story about Porpora and his famous pupil, Caffarelli, one of the wonderful male sopranists of the early eighteenth century. It is said that Porpora wrote on a single sheet of music paper all the feats that could be performed by the voice and set Caffarelli to work at them. After two years the discouraged student began to complain that he made no progress. Porpora reminded the youth that he had promised to do precisely as his teacher bade him. Caffarelli went back to his sheet of paper. To make the story short, Porpora is said to have kept him at it for six years, and then dismissed him with the words, "Go, my son, you are the greatest singer in the world."

In those days to be a great singer meant to have perfect breath control, absolute accuracy of intonation, full command of a sustained and beautiful cantilena, a perfect messa di voce and portamento, and ability to execute the most appalling difficulties in ornament. It has been well said that in technic the singers of to-day are tyros compared with those of the Caffarelli period. The passages which they sang with dazzling brilliancy would stagger almost any of our colorature artists.

It is not desirable, therefore, that the singer of our time should set out to acquire an agility which would enable him to rival the vocalists of Handel's operas. Yet he certainly ought to learn how to sing the music of those works, for that is the most admirable of all colorature song. It is the most musical, the most vocal and the most artistic. It unites genius in composition with a perfect knowledge of writing for the voice. One who can sing Handel fluently and expressively need have no fear of any technical difficulties in the music heard on the operatic stage to-day.

It is unnecessary, however, to confine one's self to Handel. There were fairly good masters before and after his time. Mozart, for example, provides opportunities for the study of florid music, and whatever he wrote commands the attention of the singer. Mozart was a greater inventor of melody than even Handel, and he knew well how to write for the voice. The grand airs of "Don Giovanni" are living evidence of his mastership. Turning to the German school, one finds the writers of the big dramatic bravura airs, such as "Abscheulicher" and "Ocean, Thou Mighty Monster." These airs demand splendor of tone, great power and volume, as well as agility. They should never be undertaken by singers who have not first learned how to sing Handel and Mozart.

Rossini, Donizetti and even Bellini provide good examples of the colorature style of the early nineteenth century, a style well adapted to the voice, but far less admirable in its musical qualities than the styles of Handel and Mozart. The singer should not neglect any of these masters. However, before the student can study the arias of the famous composers he must acquire the elements of agility.

Colorature singing is best learned from some one who has mastered it. Hints may be given in print, to be sure, just as they may in regard to almost anything else, but, after all, the teacher is the true guide to the acquirement of the ability to sing florid music. It may be said here, however, that the foundation of agility in vocal music is the same as that in instrumental performance, namely, the scale.

Short passages, constructed of successive notes of the scale, form the best elementary exercises. These passages should rest firmly on some one tone as a root from which the others are to be derived. In singing an ascending exercise, for example, the student should get firmly fixed in his mind the pitch of the tonic of the scale, which should form the starting point of the exercise.

Then if the passage to be used comprises five tones, ending with the dominant, he should get the pitch of the dominant thoroughly established in his mind. He might sing the interval several times from tonic to dominant to get the relative pitch firmly established, for it is vital to clean colorature execution that the intonation be accurate. If the intonation be imperfect, the colorature will always be slovenly, and wholly without brilliancy.

When the student has his ear perfectly attuned to the interval of the fifth from tonic up to dominant, he should sing the scale ascending through those five tones. Practice of this sort should never be rapid or loud. The passage should be sung piano and with a light touch, care being taken that each tone is clearly brought out and neither smeared over into the next nor separated from it by a noticeable stroke of the glottis.

After the student can sing this ascending passage with comparative fluency, he should sing the same notes in inverse order, descending. After he can execute both passages cleanly, he may essay an octave. In singing octave scales it is essential that the pupil should get the tonic, the dominant and the leading tone very firmly defined in his mental ear.

Lamperti gives an exercise in which the scale is sung very slowly with long holds on these tones. After singing the scale this way Lamperti's pupil is advised to sing it with comparative rapidity, lightly and cleanly. At the termination of the scale the student should sing an arpeggio of the four tones of the chord descending. This will hold him to the intervals of the chord. In practicing the scale of an octave descending the student should begin with the lower tonic and take the interval of an octave upward and then sing down the scale to the lower tonic again.

Lablache, Manuel Garcia, Panseron, Winter, Martini, Garaude, Manstein, Fétis and others recommend a systematic progress from vocalises* on

* "Vocalises" is a convenient term used by singing teachers for vocal exercises. It is derived from the Italian singers' technical word "vocalizzi."

two notes up to the octave. Garcia says: "Those who wish to sing scales or other passages without having begun on two, three or four notes risk failing to execute roulades." He holds that it is easier to sing a passage of two notes than one of three, and one of three than one of four, and that, therefore, the correct progress begins with two.

The exercise which he gives for two notes is simple. The student is required to sing, say, C and D below the clef in alternation, the first time in quarter notes, four to the measure, then in eighth notes and finally in sixteenth notes.

The exercise for three notes consists of the progression C, D, E, D, in quarter notes, then in eighth notes and then in sixteenth notes. Any teacher following out this idea can construct a series of progressive exercises for his pupils. These exercises are recommended by Lemaire and Lavoix as "an excellent gymnastic by which the voice will be rendered supple and agile." The "ah" sound is the most favorable for the majority of voices, though teachers will doubtless find cases in which some other vowel sound will better bring out the best qualities of tone in running passages and perhaps correct some faulty pose of the organs.

Lilli Lehmann believes in the practice of what she calls the "great scale" previous to all exercises in agility. The great scale is nothing more than the diatonic major scale divided into groups of long notes with pauses for breath. Doubtless an exercise of this sort would aid in warming up the voice and fixing the intonation.

After sufficient facility has been acquired in the execution of scale passages in fluent style, the pupil will need to take up the delivery of staccato passages. These are best suited to the high tones of the soprano voice, because of the delicate and neat execution which they demand. Detached or staccato tones are executed by attacking each with a stroke of the glottis and quitting it immediately after the attack.

Lemaire and Lavoix say: "These sounds, of very short duration, should be articulated with dryness and without length, with a moderate opening of the mouth, and perfectly detached from one another. The inspiration is cut short after each tone and is suspended; it is not correct to breathe, for a series of detached notes should be executed always with the same breath."

Chromatic scales offer difficulties of no small

kind to the teacher and the student. On the method of approaching them most of the old masters are agreed. They found from their extensive experience in instructing that it was necessary to fix firmly in the minds of their pupils the intonation of chromatic intervals before they permitted students to attack the chromatic scale.

They therefore devised a series of exercises constructed on the same principle as Garcia's series of two, three, four and more tones in the diatonic scale. For example, one exercise begins with C, D, C in the first measure, while the second consists of C, C sharp, D. These two measures were written in quarter notes and were intended to be sung slowly and carefully in order that the student should get the difference between the whole interval and the half interval clearly impressed on his mental ear.

Having sung C, C sharp, D correctly, the pupil next sings D, D flat, C. Finally he exercises on the ascending and descending series. This exercise, it will be noticed, covers the interval of a second. Next the pupil is permitted to exercise on the interval of a major third, always singing the interval itself before attacking the chromatic steps of which it is composed.

By a series of progressive exercises of this kind the student is carried forward till he sings a chromatic scale of an octave. Then comes the practice of increasing rapidity, beginning again with the interval of a second. This is the method of the French Conservatoire, which adapted it from the works of Garcia, Concone, Martini and others.

It is, or ought to be, clear to the reader that Garcia's exercise on two notes is the best possible preparation for the trill. The only way to learn how to trill is to practice singing the two tones of which a trill is made till one can sing them sufficiently rapidly.

The exercise must be proportioned to the pupil's respiration. It should be in short passages at the beginning. The student should let the breath pour itself out gently with perfect equality and without effort of either the chest or the larynx.

Tosi, Mancini and Hiller recommend beginning the study of the trill in the earliest lessons, working at it every day, but always a little at a time, without trying to make it too long and always stopping the exercise as soon as the effort makes itself felt in the larynx.

Other masters advocate postponing the study of the trill till the voice is fairly well placed. It must be borne in mind that in the days of such masters as Tosi and Mancini agility was a prime requisite in singing. To-day the study of colorature is rather a means than an end. Some of the masters of to-day do not insist on the practice of colorature. Giovanni Lamperti says, Where the pupil "has no natural gift do not waste time on colorature study." Again, he says of the trill: "Not every voice is suited for this embellishment; heavy voices may even be injured by purposeless trill practice." The present writer believes that trill study should begin when colorature is taken up, after tone control has made considerable progress.

Agility should be acquired by every singer. Some will naturally acquire it in a greater degree than others, but all can acquire it to some extent, and it is the foundation of ease and grace and fluency of delivery. It is an essential part of the beautiful old art of bel canto, upon which to-day singing must make its foundation.

10

Treatment of the Vowels

As EVERYONE WELL KNOWS, SONGS WITHOUT words are written only for instruments. Voices are required to sing music accompanied by text. Hence, we are now confronted with the problems of enunciation. Singers often find difficulty in producing a good quality of tone on certain vowels in certain parts of their scale. Again, they find some consonants obstructive to that smooth flow of tone which is essential to a beautiful legato style.

It is unquestionable that these obstacles have faced singers from the beginning of the study of the technics of their art. In spite of their recognition of these difficulties, the masters of music and vocal art have never ceased to demand of singers clean, correct and intelligible enunciation. Giulio Caccini in the preface to his "Nuove Musiche" (1601) declares that his experiments in writing vocal solos, then a new form of composition, were the result of his dissatisfaction with the contrapuntal masterpieces of the Church because they made the text unintelligible.

A little more than a century later we find Tosi writing thus: "Without a good pronunciation the singer robs the auditors of a great part of the charm which song receives from the words and excludes force and truth. If the words are not distinctly uttered one can find no difference between the human voice and the sound of a cornet or an oboe. Singers should not ignore the fact that it is the words which elevate them above instrumentalists."

France, which developed out of the pompous recitative of Lully her elegant and theatric declamation, has from Rameau's day to the present stood as a leader in the study of diction. Therefore we are not astonished to read the words of Gounod:

"There are two principal things to observe in pronunciation. It must be clear, neat, distinct, exact, that is to say, not permitting any uncertainty of the pronounced word to the ear. It must be expressive, that is to say, it must picture to the mind the sentiment expressed by the word itself. As to all that concerns clarity, neatness, exaction, pronunciation takes rather the title of articulation. Articulation has for its object to reproduce faithfully the exterior form of the word. All the rest is the business of pronunciation. It is this which imparts to the word the thought, the sentiment, the passion, in which it is enveloped. In a word, articulation has for its domain form or the intellectual element. Articulation gives neatness, pronunciation creates eloquence."

It is plain that Gounod by "pronunciation" meant vowel sounds, and that he had a clear conception of the value of pure and beautiful vocal color in their delivery. The difficulties which many singers have found in pronouncing correctly some vowels in the upper ranges of their scales have given rise to numberless theories as to the true method of securing a beautiful tone color.

All the systems have one ultimate object, namely, to enable singers to produce sounds which shall convey at least a hint of the real vowel to the auditor and at the same time be beautiful. Almost every teacher clings to the long established theory that it is not possible to sing certain vowel sounds honestly throughout one's compass and that therefore the trick technically termed "vocalization" must be learned.

If you cannot easily sing "ee" on a high note, you must learn how to pretend that you are singing it so as to deceive the ears of your hearers. If you cannot honestly sing "oo" at or about the place where your chest register meets your head register, you must acquire a method of simulating that vowel sound in that neighborhood.

Now, as long as the singer does this he will never get further than a poor imitation of the tone coloring which he seeks, however honestly and industriously, to obtain. The first students of artistic singing made no mistakes in these matters. In Zarlino's "Institutione Harmoniche" (1562) we find it commanded that the singer should make his voice conform to the sense of the text, that he should sing gayly those things gay and joyous, and gravely all serious words; that he should distinguish between sacred and secular styles, and finally that he should not change the sounds of the vowels, transforming "ah" into "o" or an "ee" into "a." How different this from the sort of mysterious instructions one reads in some of the contemporaneous treatises on the art of singing.

"It is important that the singer should understand that a certain modification of the vowel is indispensable to the perfect production of sound in certain parts of the voice. For instance, the vowel 'ee,' as pronounced in 'deep,' is favorable to the upper middle tones, but when it occurs in the lower middle register it should be modified to 'i' in 'dip,' and in the chest or thick register it should be still further modified to 'ü' as in the German 'grüss.' "

This passage appears in a work which is notable for its good sense in regard to most of the principles of singing. Lilli Lehmann, taking another view, advocates a continual mingling of vowel sounds. She holds that if the "ah" sound be used in perfect purity it produces a bright vocal color without depth, while if it be slightly modified toward "u" it results in a mellow, round and touching quality. But this is only another way of saying that the "ah" sound should be properly placed well forward where it is rich and solid, and not too far back where it becomes white and shallow.

That this is what Madame Lehmann had before her is still further shown by her advice to singers to keep the "u" sound always in mind, thus holding the vocal organs in position to give all the vowel sounds throughout the voice with equability. Let the reader say "u" and observe where the sound of that vowel naturally locates itself. He will perceive that a forward tone is what Madame Lehmann was seeking, though she took a roundabout way to convey her idea.

But there is something more in this department of singing than correct placing of the tone. In a large percentage of the cases in which singers find difficulty in singing some vowel sounds in certain parts of their voices the fault is partly in imperfect pronunciation of the vowels.

This is a difficulty which prevails especially among American singers. Most concert goers have observed with wonder the ease with which English tenors, Mr. Lloyd, Mr. Davies and others, sing English text and rise to their upper G and even A and B flat. Most Americans, on the other hand, are generally obliged to abandon all pretense of giving the vowels their real sounds above the clef.

There can be no doubt that the round and mellow English speech is the secret of the English singer's easy treatment of his vowels in song. The

Englishman of culture uses a good free tone in ordinary speech, and softens almost every vowel sound. Thus, when he comes to sing, his vowels lie well in his mouth.

All his life he has formed them in his mouth. He has never tried to force them back into the throat and violently to drag the palate or some other unconcerned organ into their formation.

Hence his vowels help him to a forward tone; they do not fight against it. In his every "o" and "i" and "e," for example, there is just a touch of Madame Lehmann's darkening "u," which softens the sounds, makes the tongue pliable in forming them, and preserves the singing form of the resonant hollow of the mouth.

What about the Americans? Only a very, very few of us speak English as the English do. We have our own "accent," as it is called. We are a nervous, eager, strident people. We know it, though we do not relish having foreigners tell us about it. We speak not mellowly, not with lax tongues and palates, but sharply, shrilly, with hardened mouth and with tones forced back upon the palate.

Our "ah" is almost an "a" as in "at." Our "a" as in "at" is a bleat. Our "ee" is as hard as hate and is squeezed out over tongues jammed resolutely against upper teeth. Our "i" is begun in the middle of the throat and ended almost at the lips. We strangulate two-thirds of our vowels and swallow half the other third.

Pure, round, sonorous tones are almost never heard in our daily speech. We hear much of the ease of singing in Italian because of the purity of the Italian vowel sounds; but suppose the Italians pronounced their vowel sounds as we pronounce most of ours, would it be easy to sing in Italian then? No, we must first learn the correct sounds of our vowels. We must cultivate beauty of tone in daily speech. We must learn that every vowel sound in the English tongue can be formed without interrupting the flow of a beautiful speaking tone.

When we have learned that, we shall be ready to perceive that it is quite possible to sing all the pure vowels without modification throughout the range of the voice. The whole bag of "vocalization" tricks can be thrown overboard. They are but a cumbrous method of begging the question. The question is not how can we modify so as to deceive the public ear those vowel sounds which we have already modified incorrectly in our daily speech, but how can we reform our pronunciation of the vowels so that they will be the roots of beautiful tones?

Here the reader will ask, "Did not many of the best masters of singing teach the modification of vowel sounds? Were not many of these masters Italians?" The answer is simple. It is true that many Italian masters have taught the tricks of vocalization, but the greatest masters have generally agreed that the text can be and ought to be sung correctly. Giovanni Lamperti says:

"The vowels 'i' ('ee') and French 'u' ('ü') are hard to sing on the high notes. We shall take no singer to task for changing the position of such words or for substituting others with more euphonious vowels—provided he possess the technical ability to vocalize the above-named vowels on the high tones. The pronunciation of the vowels having been sufficiently practiced in the solfeggi and vocalization, we need dwell no longer on their quantity (long or short), for a pure pronunciation, free from dialect and sharply articulated, is a prerequisite."

In other words, Lamperti points out the most difficult vowel sounds, and says he would forgive any singer for dodging them, but not for being unable to sing them. This is a fair presentation of the view held by the best masters. But transposition of words or substitution is not always practicable, and therefore Lamperti's belief that every singer should be able to deliver the difficult vowel sound on his high tones is a good one.

Wagner, who was by no means a mere theorist, held that the dramatic vitality of operatic declamation was largely founded on the life-giving quality which the color of the vowel sounds imparted to the singing tones. This is the theory which some of the most advanced students of vocal technics have taken up. It is not the office of vocal tone to color the vowel, but of the vowel sound to color the tone. The question is not how will you alter your vowels to suit your tone, but how will your pronunciation of vowel sounds enrich and liberate your tones?

Practice, continual practice, backed by careful

observation and patience, is the only royal road to pronunciation of the text in song. No hard and fast rules can be laid down. If the pupil has acquired a sure and trustworthy command of respiration, if he has learned the art of free and natural tone formation, all that he need do is to bear ever in mind that he must not sing his vowel sounds in such a way as to cause him to abandon his method of tone production.

He must seek for union of the perfect tone and the perfect vowel sound. The one will aid the other. When they are in conflict, which is rarely the case, they must be reconciled. They never are in conflict except in the high tones, and here every singer must find his own solution of the problems.

Perhaps it may be well for the student to bear in mind that in singing compound sounds, such as the diphthongs "ai" or "au," he should take advantage of the fact that the first half of the combination is "ah," and form his tone by dwelling on that and giving the second sound very little duration. So in singing the vowel sound represented by the long English "a," which has a touch of "e" at its end, the second sound must be brief.

Such solutions of the simpler difficulties will occur to every singer of intelligence. It will require more thought to find the best way of singing the modified vowels of French and German. Such a word, for instance, as "*perdu*" brings its own troubles to many a singer. Let him avoid the common French vice of forming the "u" right between the lips and thus turning tone into husky noise. The sound can be formed further back, retaining the normal position of the tongue and mouth, and thus allowing the tone to have a true vocal quality.

M. Plançon, for instance, sings the modified vowels of his native language without abandoning that noble sonority of tone which is one of the most admirable characteristics of his art.

David Frangçon-Davies, whose thoughtful and sensible book, entitled "The Singing of the Future," has already been often quoted in these pages, says that "right breathing can only be judged by right tone," and that "right tone can only be judged by the *summum bonum* of the singer, viz., pronunciation—pure, truthful pronunciation, in every part of the voice, high or low. The word with its atmosphere is the test. Pronounce with refinement, with the quick wit of rational and imaginative beings, and your tone will be right. Breathe so that you pronounce rightly and you breathe rightly." And he adds a footnote to caution the reader that by pure and truthful pronunciation he means something radically different from vocalized pronunciation.

The present writer is a relentless antagonist of the vocalization apparatus. He may not go as far as Frangçon-Davies in believing that right breathing induces correct pronunciation, but he is satisfied that the one aids the other, and that incorrect pronunciation of elementary vowel sounds has created the need for many of the tricks of vocalization, simply because the impure pronunciations twist the mouth and throat into positions inimical to the flow of free and beautiful tone.

The secret of treating the vowel sounds is this: pronounce beautifully and you will be able to sing the sounds without difficulty, except in one or two cases. These difficult sounds can be produced by keeping the throat and mouth free and easy. Think always of purity of tone, freedom of emission and control of breath. Do not think of how you can pull your mouth about so as to alter the sound a little and thus make it easier.

That will not make it easier, and it will surely render it ugly. Face the difficult sound honestly and sing it honestly, supporting it with a calm, steady air column and a reposeful position of the mouth and throat. You will in the end learn to sing it correctly and with a good tone, instead of incorrectly and with a poor tone.

The words of Gounod quoted in the early part of this chapter now take a deeper significance. The composer of "Faust" stood on the same ground as the composer of "Tristan und Isolde." "Pronunciation creates eloquence," said Gounod, and he echoed Wagner. Both agreed that much of the expressiveness of song lay in the color of the vowel sounds. Both had the demands of the poetic drama in view. Singers will do well to bear this in mind.

Treatment of the Consonants

IN HIS "MUSICAL EDUCATION AND VOCAL CULTURE," Albert Bach, the English teacher, says: "In Sanscrit the consonants are called vyongana—*i.e.*, plain revelation. The vowels are called svara—*i.e.*, sounds; and there is a proverb—'Be sparing with the vowels, says the tongue, and you will speak beautifully; honor the consonants and you will speak distinctly.' The consonants must always be uttered with exactness, but quickly, so that the continuity of the flowing tone may suffer as little interruption as possible. The attention paid to distinctness of pronunciation must never be carried so far as to prejudice the note sung."

The fault in this otherwise excellent advice is that it goes too far, and thereby betrays the author's want of insight into the true principles of pronunciation as related to singing. It is true that the consonants should be uttered exactly and also quickly, but it is not true that distinctness need ever work injury to the note sung. The problem which confronts the singer in dealing with consonants is how to enunciate distinctly and still preserve a flowing style of song. It is easy enough to acquire the declamatory manner in which the consonants are purposely allowed to interrupt the steady flow of tone, but to preserve the legato and still make every word clean-cut is what staggers most singers.

The secret of the whole thing lies first in the perfect purity of the vowel sounds and second in a free and untrammelled articulation. By keeping the vowel sounds pure and round the pose of the vocal organs in the formation of tone is preserved. When this pose is disturbed by bad vowel pronunciation, as it often is, the movements of the tongue and lips in forming consonants are exaggerated and thus the consonants become greater obstacles to singing than they naturally should be.

By free and untrammelled enunciation of the consonants is meant the articulation of them with no more movement of the enunciating organs than is absolutely essential. Most singers harden the muscles of the tongue and contort their lips in enunciating consonants in such a way that a steady flow of tone is quite out of the question. Furthermore, they do this while they are striving to acquire clearness.

It is the striving which does the damage. Singers should practice speaking in clear, round tones with clean-cut enunciation of the consonants and learn that it is possible to carry on a conversation thus without twisting the mouth into all sorts of shapes and pulling the tongue about so that the larynx cannot remain in a state of rest.

It is just as easy to enunciate in singing as in speaking. The purpose of every singer should be to carry from speaking into singing a simple, natural, free manner of enunciation. The action of the enunciating apparatus should be without effort. It should feel restful. The principal of perfect freedom from stiffness or restraint should prevail here as it does in tone production.

A few intelligent observations will enable any student to solve all problems of consonantal enunciation in singing. The question almost invariably asked is whether an attempt must be made to join the consonant to the vocal tone or not. Now, whether this is or is not to be done, nothing is to be gained by dwelling on the consonant. It should be enunciated clearly, but quickly, unless the singer desires, for some particular dramatic effect, to give it extraordinary prominence.

Some of the consonants have a certain quantity of vocal sound. These are l, m, n, r, w and y. The combination ng at the end of a word is also in this class. The letters r, w and y have a partial vocal sound which does not interfere with the flow of air through the mouth. The letters, l, m, n are likely to impart a nasal color to a tone if they are prolonged, because they force too much of the air blast into the nasal passage. This is especially the case with m. Hence these consonants should be enunciated quickly.

When any one of these consonants occurs in the middle of a word it does not stop the flow of tone at all, but slightly alters its color. The singer should be careful in singing such words to give the requisite quantity to a note by prolonging the vowel, not the consonantal sound. He should, for example, sing not "ham—m—m—mer," but "ha—a—a—mmer."

The consonants with which most singers have trouble are those which tempt us to guttural vocal sounds. These are b, p, d, t, g, j and ch. The trouble is that so many of us in our ordinary speech precede these consonants with a half formed vocal sound. We say as nearly as it can be expressed in type, "ub-bread," "up-poison," "ug-go," "uj-joy" instead of clean and simple "bread," "poison," "go," "joy."

Now, in singing we must wholly avoid these preliminary rumbles. We must cut out our b, t, p, etc., clearly and distinctly as consonants. Thus when we have to give them at the beginnings of words we shall not disturb the poise of the tone forming apparatus before the word itself is reached, but after the enunciation of the initial consonant we shall find the tone producers in free and comfortable position to perform their functions.

When one of these consonants occurs at the end of a word the singer need not concern himself as to whether there is a faint vocal tone imparted to it or not. His diction will certainly be more elegant if it is not, but if it should be, his enunciation will not thereby be made indistinct.

A fault not uncommon among public speakers should be avoided. In their anxiety to bring final consonants of this class out clearly speakers frequently add a syllable, transforming "head" into "head-uh" or "rob" into "rob-uh." Singers need hardly be told that such a practice is subversive of correctness in diction.

The labial and dental consonants are often badly treated, in spite of the fact that they are the easiest of all to manage. The consonants f, s, z and the diphthongs sh, th, wh, have no vocal qualities at all. Their sounds are separate from those produced by the vocal organs.

This fact suggests the correct treatment of them. They must be made entirely independent of the tones with which they are associated. If one of them occurs at the beginning of a word, it must be sounded clearly, but before the tone itself is attacked. The attack of the tone must follow instantly after the conclusion of the consonantal sound, so that there shall not be any interval between them.

Conversely, when one of these consonants occurs at the end of a word, the tone should be completed before the consonantal sound is made, but no interval should appear. When one of these sounds appears in the middle of a word, it is impossible to prevent a brief interval in the flow of tone, but the singer should always bear in mind that the consonant is not to be given duration. That quality is reserved for the vowel. The consonant must be made as short as possible. In this way the flow of tone will at least seem to the hearer to be smooth and continuous.

Any endeavor to push forward the vowel tone before the consonant is out of the way will result in straining. It will, as one writer says, "cause a muscular effort and produce tension in parts of the body, which will rob the vocal sound of beauty and deprive the singer of freedom."

When the singer has acquired a pure and round pronunciation of the vowel sounds and a clear and smooth enunciation of the consonants, he should give no little time to the practice of clear delivery of text. He will soon find that certain combinations bother him more than others. For example, how many public speakers always make a mess of such words as "rests" or "tests."

The combination "sts" is, in nine cases out of ten, transformed into a double s. This is wholly unnecessary. The cause of it is haste. The speaker does not take the time to form the three consecutive sounds. Now the singer is far more likely to hurry, because he will be anxious to carry his voice forward to the next vowel; but it is entirely unnecessary to do this. The consonantal sounds can be clearly enunciated without checking the flow of tone or destroying the atmosphere of the legato.

Suppose you are singing "Oh, rest in the Lord." The "st" in "rest" must be clearly enunciated or else the beauty of the text and the pathos of the passage will be destroyed. Now, when the cavity of the mouth is in shape for the short "e" in "rest" the tone may be properly prolonged on that vowel, and the "st" taken with the tip of the tongue gently and clearly, leaving the tongue in precisely the right position for the formation of short "i" in the next word.

In the practice of the delivery of text the singer should note all details of this kind and store them away in his mind for future use. This use should be that of study only. To suppose that a singer in the practice of his art must think always of all the rules is absurd. Study makes him master of the rules. It does not make them master of him. The pianist spends years in acquiring a correct position of the hands and fingers, but when he is playing he does not concentrate his mind on these matters. The violinist studies long and arduously to acquire an automatic command of the positions, but he does not have to center his thought upon them when he is interpreting Beethoven's concerto.

The singer's technic must in the course of time become automatic. The purpose of long study is to perfect an automatism which shall be absolutely correct. Then the singer can concentrate his mind on the higher features of technic, such as phrasing, style, dramatic expression. These things, too, are technical. There is a way to phrase and a way not to phrase. There is a way to sing lieder and another way to sing the music of Rossini. There is a way to be purely and nobly dramatic, and there is a way to be a charlatan, appealing to the ears of groundlings.

The earliest masters of vocal art were peremptory in their demands that the text should be clearly delivered. The theories of Peri and Caccini, the leaders of the movement which resulted in the establishment of opera, called for a perfect enuncia-tion. They were engaged in an attempt to recon-struct Italian dramatic music on the lines of the Greek drama, and they laid down as the basic tenet of their creed the law that the music should follow and embody the sentiment of the words. To sing such music so that the words would be incompre-hensible would have defeated their entire purpose.

But only a few years elapsed before musicians themselves saw that the endless recitative was not the ultimate perfection, nor even the fundamental material of an artistic lyric drama. The need for musical design speedly made itself felt, and the arioso recitative of Monteverde's "Arianna" was but the prelude to the rhythmic aria of Cavalli.

Once the aria, with its inevitable return to the first part, had been established as the solar light of opera, the fidelity to the text soon disappeared, and with it fled the regard for clear and beautiful enunciation. The Italian singers came to hold in high esteem their pure and sonorous vowels, because these furthered the production of good tones, and at the same time these singers began to slight the consonants simply because they found these sounds in the way and were unable to perceive any great merit in them.

With the development of dramatic music in France the demand for clear enunciation was revived, for the Frenchman had that natural inclination for the theater which aroused in him a desire to hear the speech of the actors, singing or speaking. This demand reacted upon the Italians, because they sought success in the French capital.

Again, the history of opera in Germany led toward the rehabilitation of clear diction. From the beginning the German loved the "singspiel," the opera with dialogue. He above all men desired to know what was going forward on the stage. He had no use for prolonged dialogues in recitative. He demanded that they should be in speech, and so they were even in Mozart's "Die Zauberflöte," Beethoven's "Fidelio" and Weber's "Der Freischütz."

The Italian dramatic school of the early nineteenth century was not slow to feel the influence which was spreading over Europe, and Rossini and his contemporaries wrote recitatives and arias of which the text was intended to be heard. It is true that they wrote others in which the words were of no importance, but in Italy as elsewhere the general trend was toward that dramatic verity which demanded that the words should be conveyed to the auditors.

With the full development of the lied of Schubert the imperative necessity for clear enunciation was made apparent to the entire musical world. The Wagnerian drama cried aloud for such enunciation. The result is that to-day no one questions the claims of the words of vocal music. On the contrary, the demand that they shall be clearly and beautifully enunciated is not to be avoided.

Of all singers in the world those of America sin most consistently in this matter. We have some singers who can enunciate, but the typical American singer cannot sing his own language so that an audience can understand him. Opera in English is a lamentable travesty. This is an unpalatable fact, but it ought not to be disregarded for that reason. On the contrary, every American student of the art of singing ought to give most careful attention to his pronunciation of the vowels and his enunciation of the consonants and aim to acquire a clear, beautiful and distinguished diction. That experienced teacher Madame Marchesi says:

"Do not fail to go over the text of your songs again and again and penetrate yourselves with their meaning. A singer with a moderately good voice who has mastered the significance of his words will always have the advantage over the possessor of a much finer instrument to whom they are a sealed message. Gounod was wont to say of a singer of the latter type, 'What a beautiful organ pipe!' "

12

Style and Recitative

THERE ARE MANY TEACHERS OF STYLE. SOME OF them appear to believe that style cannot exist without parade. The fact is that the term "style" is too loosely used. It ought to be accepted as signifying appropriateness. The manner of singing Mozart is not the manner of singing Puccini, nor will the manner suitable for Donizetti be found appropriate to the lyric dramas of Wagner.

Manner is not matter. The method of the singer is his matter, and that is always the same. There is only one right way to sing, in so far as the technics of the voice are meant, and that way is right for Scarlatti, for Handel, for Mozart, for Beethoven and for Wagner. The manner is altogether another thing.

In this department of style tradition plays a leading part, but the warning before given as to the trustworthiness of tradition applies here also. In the course of time the manner of singing, as handed

down from teacher to pupil, becomes imperceptibly remodeled. Teachers do not always live a
hundred years, after the fashion of Manual Garcia,
and even if they did it may be doubted whether
their earliest conceptions would not unconsciously
be changed by the progress of three-quarters of a
century. Garcia in his last years may firmly have
believed that he could reconstruct the manner of
singing Mozart which his father brought to America in 1825, but there is room for doubt about it.

The study of style may best be pursued by careful examination of the music to be sung, coupled
with thorough and intelligent reading of such contemporaneous writers as may be obtainable. If one
reads the comments of the contemporaries of the
famous singers of the eighteenth century he will
not be in the dark as to the salient traits of their
style.

They were invariably praised for the purity and
equality of their tone, their breath power, their
messa di voce, their portamento, their smooth and
beautiful execution of runs and other florid passages
and for their trills. We also find that they were not
without pathos, but it was the pathos of pure tone

and finished phrasing, not that of dramatic declamation.

We read similar comments on the singers of the seventeenth century, about whom the singers of today know absolutely nothing. Yet these vocalists laid the foundations of that Italian skill which made the singing schools of 1700 a landmark in the history of musical art.

From 1700 to the present time the records of singing are writ in large letters. There is no difficulty in learning how Farinelli, Caffarelli, Cuzzoni, Faustina and their contemporaries sang. Neither is it troublesome to learn all about the manner of Malibran, Grisi, Mario, Rubini, Tamburini, Ronconi, Lablanche and the others of that generation.

As for the music of the older composers, that is heard in plenty. Of course we do not hear performances of the entire operas, but we are frequently treated to recitatives and arias in the concert room. Furthermore, the operas of Mozart preserve for us the conversational recitative of the Italian opera buffa in its best form, and they also present to us the grand recitative of the opera seria, for in Donna Anna's discovery of the identity of her father's assassin we have a dramatic declamation of the highest Italian style.

With some of the Handelian oratorios, too, we have the old eighteenth century style preserved. The recitative preceding "Waft Her, Angels" in "Jephtha" is written in the grand style of the opera seria of the period. It will bear comparison with any recitative in such a work as Lulli's "Armide" or Rameau's "Hyppolite et Aricie."

In the delivery of recitatives there is abundant opportunity for every singer of opera or oratorio to display a knowledge of style. Nevertheless in no department of singing is greater ignorance of style disclosed. A little retrospect of the field may serve to revive some latent memories. The origin of all recitative must be sought in the stilo parlante or rappresentativo of the Florentine reformers who aimed to resuscitate the Greek drama and to substitute it for the polyphonic choral drama which at that time did inefficient service as festal entertainment. This original recitative was practically a literary, not a musical product. It was a form of intonation, not remotely associated with the ecclesiastic chant which suggested its outline and its style to the youthful adventurers into new fields.

Peri, who was associated with Caccini in the composition of the music of the first lyric drama, and who invariably gets all the glory, wrote a preface to "Euridice." In it he endeavored to explain his ideas about the proper way to write dramatic music.

He held that the movements of the voice through musical intervals should imitate those of the voice in speech. For calm or reflective passages the recitative should be fluent and smooth and should use only a small range of tone. For more agitated sentiments the intervals should be wider, the range greater and the movement more rapid.

This fundamental thought was easily expanded and ramified, so that the details of recitative soon became more elastic than they were in the hands of the first writers; but the fundamental principle remained the same. The speech was the dominant factor. Musical accent, as such, did not exist in this recitative. The accent and the emphasis were those of the text. There was no rhythm except that of the words. There was no musical phrasing. The textual phrase alone was observed.

Now let every student of the art of singing note that in three hundred years there has been less change in recitativo secco, the original species of lyric speech, than in any other form of music. What it was in the day of Monteverde, whose "Orfeo" was produced in 1608, it essentially is now. In those days recitativo secco was accompanied by a few chords played on the harpsichord. These chords were sounded between the phrases of the recitative and usually marked a resolution or a cadence in the harmony.

Melodic outline was shunned in this recitative because the musical phrase was not adapted to the parlando style. To permit the entrance of musical form the lyric stanza was needed, and hence until the middle of the seventeenth century, when the sharp demarcation between recitative and aria was reached, the lyric stanza was little used. Blank verse was the suitable form for the recitativo secco.

Certain idioms crept into the recitativo secco early in its history, and they are still there. Sequences of notes used for the conclusion of phrases of recitative came into existence with the practice of the earliest masters, and they have survived for the simple reason that they cannot be escaped without entering the domain of free melodic composition.

These phrases were built by men seeking to imitate the inflections of the voice in speech, and they can no more be removed from the language of opera and oratorio than the typical inflections of speech can be removed from the spoken drama. These phrases are to be found in the operas of Peri, Carissimi, Handel, Scarlatti, Mozart, Rossini, Donizetti, Verdi, Puccini, Weber and Wagner. They are also to be found in the oratorios of Bach, Spohr, Mendelssohn, Haydn, and Sir Edward Elgar.

Now these historical facts lead us to the primary law governing the delivery of recitativo secco. The first thought must be given to the text. The music is altogether a secondary consideration. The singer who examines the notes of a passage of recitativo secco and endeavors to determine how best they may be phrased and emitted is in error from the very outset.

The notes must be examined wholly in the light of the text. The phrasing must be that of the words. The accent must be that of the words. The emphasis must be that of the words. The singer who endeavors to make a cheap vocal effect on a high note in a piece of recitativo secco will in nine cases out of ten ruin the sense and, therefore, the eloquence of a fine passage.

On the other hand, the singer must not permit himself to regard the delivery of this species of recitative as a purely mechanical achievement. The imagination finds in the field of recitative ample scope for its play. The delivery of recitativo secco calls for histrionic ability, just as that of the dialogue of the spoken drama does.

To give this musical speech vivacity, convincing verisimilitude, poetic beauty, calls for insight, as well as sincerity. As Lamperti pertinently says, "the chief requirement of this vocal style is that the singer's imagination should be fired by the given situation."

Since this is true of recitativo secco, especially in its higher contemporaneous forms, it is still more desirable in the treatment of recitativo stromentato.

This is the more common variety of recitative in the lyric works of to-day. The harpsichord has disappeared from the instrumental force of the opera house. When the voice is supported simply by chords we hear the strings in passages where Mozart would have used the clavier of his day. Since Rossini set the fashion our masters write whole operas without strict secco recitative. The orchestra accompanies it all.

Wagner is the perfect embodiment of recitativo stromentato, because so much of his operas consists of more or less melodic dialogue, with only occasional flashes of sustained arioso form. The melodic fragment is his principal apparatus, and with it he nears the bulk of his lyric edifice. "Lohengrin" is especially rich in examples of the modern recitativo stromentato coupled with phrases of the old secco, supported in this opera by orchestral chords. Wagner utilizes cadences which were invented by Peri side by side with elaborate musical speech couched in intervals which would have made the early Italians gasp.

The delivery of recitativo stromentato requires careful preparation. The question for the singer to decide in every instance is how much of the passage before him demands strict tempo and how much calls for the free style of the secco. A mingling of the free and the strict style will be found in nearly all extended passages of recitativo stromentato.

Much here depends upon the composer. The earliest writers were less inexorable in their demands that singers should be bound to the beat of the measure than the moderns are. Their recitativo stromentato differed but little from their recitativo secco. It was slower in tempo and it had some orchestral phrases scattered through it. Later, in what may, from our point of view, be called the middle period of opera, the stromentato recitative approached nearer to the arioso and the orchestral accompaniment became more varied.

Even here the vocal phrases frequently stood by themselves, and the orchestral passages were placed in the intervals between them, so that the voice part could be sung ad libitum and the orchestral phrase played with similar freedom. This is the most common form of recitativo stromentato. All the modern composers use it, for its application to all possible situations in the lyric drama renders it of universal value.

But the musicians of to-day more frequently compose recitativo stromentato in strict tempo. The orchestral support flows forward in a ceaseless stream of melody, and the voice must enter and finish on the beat. Otherwise confusion is sure to arise. Wagner is insistent in his demand that his recitative be sung precisely as written and in perfect tempo.

To many long passages in the works of Verdi, Puccini and the latter-day Italians and to many also in the lyric productions of the Frenchmen this demand of Wagner applies with great pertinence. What the singer of recitativo stromentato must invariably do is to examine the voice part in all its relations to the accompaniment in order to ascertain just where strict musical requirements exist and just where a liberty approaching that of the secco may be found. And through it all he must preserve the true conception of recitative, which is speech in song.

At this point the student of singing will ask, "How much of this applies to the treatment of oratorio recitatives? Surely you are not going to lay down the same rules of style for opera and oratorio?" Perhaps the best answer to this is found in a passage in Dr. Spitta's "Life of Bach."

"The recitative was in its origin a dramatic form of art, and its function is to facilitate the presentment of a transitory incident either by narrative or dialogue. Hence the important point is what is said in singing, and not what is sung in the saying; in other words, the meaning conveyed rather than the melody which is engrafted on it. Still it had an eminently musical side, and it must soon have been detected that with the means at its disposal and an impassioned text it could rise to a high pitch of pathos and impressiveness—nay, all the more so from being devoid of all equalizing uniformity.

"In consequence of this it was, on the other hand, peculiarly fitted to prepare the hearer, by exciting and attuning his attention (musically), for a composition presenting itself in a more complete and symmetrical form [namely, an aria].

"From the former point of view it could have no application in church music, and even in the latter no immediate justification, for it is impossible to say that the self-assertive display of personal passion is appropriate to the church.

"Hence the dramatic factor was set aside in the words, while the composers absorbed the musical element unchanged into church music. They treated recitative exactly as in opera, as speaking in a singing voice, a kind of chant, with here and there a stronger musical accent, as the poetry admitted."

This is an adequate and safely guiding account of the character and purpose of the earlier recitations; but it is not applicable to those of a later period. Some of the highly dramatic recitations of such works as Mendelssohn's "Elijah" demand vocal style quite as animated and declamatory as those of Saint-Saëns's "Samson et Dalila."

In short, an oratorio singer is bound to have command of all styles of recitative, for this method of speech in song is liberally employed by oratorio composers, who have utilized all its resources and all its varieties, from the most primitive recitativo secco to the opulent modern recitativo stromentato, or endless vocal melody.

The oratorio singer, however, must never forget

the distinction between "dramatic" and "theatric." The oratorio demands unbending dignity of style. It is a pity that the students of singing who aspire to eminence in this department of their art cannot have a course of training in the music of Lulli and Rameau. Though these were French opera composers, their recitatives demand a broad, noble, even pompous style, coupled with a perfect enunciation of the text, and the study of this style would, with a little toning down, provide an excellent preparation for oratorio.

The dignity and breadth of these old recitatives were essentially dramatic, but not theatric, as the recitatives of Italian operas of the eighteenth and nineteenth centuries so often were. Admirable as many of the improvements of Rossini were, his recitatives too often degenerate into mere points of vocal display, designed wholly for the opera house.

Later Italian writers have followed in the flowery path of vocal dalliance till the purity of a distinguished and invaluable branch of the lyric art has apparently been permanently defiled. For many writers of oratorios in these nervous modern times have adopted the phraseology of the Italian opera, and all the way from Gounod's "Redemption" to Tinel's "St. Franciscus" and thence even to Perosi's "Lazarus" we hear the theatric spoutings of "Semiramide" and "Möse in Egitto."

The singer is to a certain extent helpless when confronted with these passages. He must sing what is written. But he can preserve his self-respect by sacrificing the opportunities for personal display to a sincere consideration of the text. Let him not forget, even though the composer does, that "the point is what is said in singing, and not what is sung in the saying." This is the essential law of all recitative up to the point at which arioso begins. By keeping it ever in mind a singer is not likely often to go wrong.

The study of recitative style is sadly neglected in these days of eagerness to rush before the public. Teachers of style and repertoire ought to compel their pupils to take thorough instruction in it, for it is one of the fundamentals of vocal interpretation. It is the root from which all our operatic and oratorio singing sprang. For that reason alone it ought to be studied; but that is not the only reason.

It might perhaps be going too far to say that the correct delivery of recitative is the key to all proper interpretation, but it is not too much to declare that without it perfect style is not attainable. In the modern song, for instance, such as the lieder of Strauss and Wolf, the intimacy of text and music is such that only the philosophy of the old recitative can supply the key to a correct analysis of it.

The key to the dialogue of Wagner's "Tristan und Isolde" is the recitative of Mozart and the dramatic scena of Beethoven and Weber, that wonderful compound of recitativo, arioso, cantilena and dramatic bravura. The open sesame to the treasures of Elgar's "Dream of Gerontius" and "Apostles" must be sought in the recitatives of Bach and Handel.

This suggests the advisability of a final caution. The conception of recitative as speech in song must never so befog the singer's mind as to obscure the fact that it is still song. Recitative is to be sung, not shouted, cackled or barked. Identification of musical accent and emphasis with those of the text does not mean effacement.

The rank heresies of Bayreuth, emanating from the extraordinary mind of Cosima Wagner, and fostered in a score of German theaters from which the art of beautiful singing has for many years been an outcast, have made the Wagnerian drama the hotbed of bad recitative delivery.

Instead of the broad and elastic form of declamation designed by Wagner, a declamation embracing all the elements of musical speech from the cut and dried phrases of the old secco to the splendid eloquence of modern dramatic arioso, we have a nondescript thing, compounded of brittle, formless staccato and vociferous shouting. This thing should be wiped out of existence. It is neither art nor music.

13

The Lyric in Style

THE STUDY OF STYLE IN SINGING CANNOT STOP WITH attention to recitative. While it is true that the worst offenders are those singers who ruin all the declamatory parts of modern operas by ignorance of the fundamental principles of recitative, there are many more singers who destroy the designed effect of their arias or lieder by incorrect style. The offenders in the department of recitative wander further from the truth, but in pure melodic singing wanderers are more numerous.

This is especially true in these days of song recital. In the opera house certain traditions are respected. Some of the traditional rules are indisputably good, while others are at least questionable; but on the concert platform everyone is a law unto himself. Singers vie with one another in differences of style and interpretation. Madame Cantando sings Strauss after the manner of Milan, and Mademoiselle Chant sings Schumann according to the theory of the Boulevardes, while Frau Singspiel delivers herself of "Caro mio ben" in the manner of Bayreuth.

Each contends that the other is wrong. Each proclaims that hers is the only true and authoritative style. All the world wonders. No one is quite certain of anything, except that there are more ways of singing a song than of cooking a goose. The critics vainly thunder. No one pays any attention to them. The glorified vocalist has her little army of worshipers, and in the religion of musician worship there is neither conversion nor apostasy.

The question of interpretation may in some cases be debatable. It is not thus in as many instances as the singers would have us believe. Your true artist who cannot sing a certain passage in the right manner without disclosing some defect of voice, is very ingenious in preparing arguments to demonstrate that her wrong way is the true way. Still for the sake of temporary comfort let us assume that there may usually be differences of opinion as to the correct interpretations of songs. Granting that it is so, there is still no room for wide divergence of belief as to style.

Style is general; interpretation is particular. Style is the character of a period or a school or a master. Interpretation is the disclosure of an individuality. Style may embrace all the songs of a single composer, though it seldom does; but interpretation can apply only to one at a time.

In order to construct a correct style it is essential first to reconstruct the period to which the music before us belongs. When an orchestral conductor endeavors to electrify us by reading Mozart's "Jupiter" symphony as if it had hissed from the burning pen of Tschaikowsky, he commits a radical error. He tries to impart to the composition a character which no composer of Mozart's time conceived. When a singer attempts to make Mozart's arias more "dramatic" by singing them as if they had been written by Puccini, he sins in precisely the same manner.

The first thing a singer must do in studying an aria or a song is to get a correct conception of the content of the work itself. Without that, true interpretation is quite impossible. The next thing to do is to examine the music in the light of the period to which it belongs. The final thing is to analyze the music in the light of the known artistic aims of the composer.

To know the period the singer must be acquainted with the history of his art. If one is to sing an aria of Alessandro Scarlatti correctly, he must be familiar with the general conditions of operatic composition in that master's time, with the aims of the composer himself and with the state and resources of the art of singing.

Very few singers know anything about the state of singing in the latter part of the seventeenth century. Fewer still have any knowledge of the progress made in the art in the middle or early part of that century. Yet there is no period in the history of singing so interesting as this one. A very brief glance into it will satisfy the artist that there were vocal giants in those days. The operas of the latter half of the seventeenth century bristled with technical feats. Every singer had to be a vocal acrobat of the highest order. On the other hand, the cantilena of that day demanded exquisite purity of tone, perfect command of messa di voce and portamento, a genuine legato style and great finish in phrasing and nuance.

This period paved the way for that of Handel and Hasse, the period of the extraordinary vocal virtuosi who were graduated from the schools of Pistocchi, Bernacchi, Porpora and their contemporaries. The testimony of those who heard these famous singers is that they sang with a marvelous command of all the resources of the art of bel canto.

They were not specialists. The operas of their day were not constructed in such a manner as to call for one dramatic and one lyric soprano, one dramatic contralto, one tenor robusto, one baritone and one basso cantante. All the singers were sopranos, contraltos, and tenors, with an occasional bass.

The baritone voice was not used in the opera at all. Male rôles were often sung by men with soprano voices, and in the same opera you will sometimes find a male soprano singing one male part and a female soprano singing another. All the music was in the same style. Everyone in an opera was entitled to at least one aria di bravura, and all singers excelled in both sustained melodies and sparkling fiorituri. Techniques were at their apogee. It was the golden age of the art of singing.

The singer who takes up an aria of this period must be prepared to give it a large amount of his time and attention. He must refine and refine till he recalls Kipling's description of Robert Louis Stevenson as a man who made most delicate mosaics in words and filed out to the finish of a hair. There can be no rough spots in a correctly prepared aria of the Handelian time. The cantilena must flow like a broad river, the bravura like a sunlit fountain.

Let no singer fall into the foolish error of supposing that there was no expression in the singing of the Handelian era. All the testimony is to the contrary. We are told of wonderful achievements by Raff, Senesino, Caffarelli and their compeers in moving people to tears. All the contemporary comments speak of the excellence in pathos of this and that artist.

The fact is significant. It is invariably the pathos of the singer that is praised. No description of tragic fury or majestic wrath is ever found in the accounts of Mancini, and other writers of his time. This, together with the constant insistence on the perfection of vocal techniques, should show clearly the correct style of the music these artists sang. The broader sentimental passages were either contemplative or melancholy. In the bravura there was a certain amount of assertiveness, but no such attempts at tragic delineation as we find later in the music of "Norma."

Hence it follows that any singer who endeavors to impart forcible verbal accent to the arias of Handel's day, in the hope of making them more potently dramatic, goes diametrically contrary to the spirit of the music and the correct manner of singing. The textual parts of these arias must be treated smoothly. Clearness of enunciation is certainly desirable, but it is undeniable that the composers and the singers were but little concerned about it when they came to the ornamental passage work designed wholly for the exhibition of vocal facility.

If the modern singer's conscience troubles him at all about the slaughter of words in these old arias, let him comfort himself by an honest essay to set forth the words so that the hearer can get hold of them at least once. For since these words are sure to be repeated, the singer may perhaps be forgiven if at their second appearance he sacrifices sense to sound. That, apparently, was the practice of the greatest singers the world has ever known.

It is probably quite hopeless to make a plea for the abolition of the cheap and vulgar vibrato in the delivery of these old airs. It is indeed painful to hear "Caro mio ben" sung with a French opera vibrato, which robs it of half its noble simplicity. It is said that the vibrato was introduced by Rubini. At any rate, it was new to the singers of his day, and had not at that time been heard in the memory of man. There is no account of its use in the writings of the contemporaries of Caffarelli and Farinelli. On the contrary, the master singers of their day are praised for the steadiness of their tones and the perfect smoothness of their style.

It is evident, therefore, that the vibrato is a trick invented after their day. It certainly is quite out of place in the music of their period. But whereas Rubini used the vibrato from time to time for the creation of what he regarded as a dramatic effect, almost every singer of to-day tries from the beginning to acquire a habitual vibrato, to be used at all times without regard to fitness.

Some of our singers have so successfully cultivated this trick that they have developed it into a tremolo of generous proportions. It would be interesting to know what Porpora or Fedi would have thought of a twentieth century tremolo, especially when introduced in an aria by Carissimi.

The stages of early vocal style may not inaptly be likened to the three varieties of ancient architecture—Doric, Ionic and Corinthian. The Doric period is that of the founders of opera and oratorio, when vocal composition went no further than recitative and arioso. The Ionic style is that of the operatic masters of the seventeenth century, in which melodic beauty and a limited amount of expression were joined with graceful and opulent exfoliations of vocal arabesque. The third style is that of the Handelian era, which, like the Corinthian architecture, gathered up all that was best of the other two and added to it a characteristic ornament of its own, thus crowning all with a beauty fashioned by the development of culture.

The old style of architecture contains nothing

Gothic. No more does the old style of singing. The change comes after Mozart. To sing Mozart one must sing. He must not shout or declaim or rant. Always he must sing, just as if he were interpreting the music of Handel or Scarlatti. For the recitatives he may utilize a much broader accentuation, but for the arias he must find it possible to introduce the tragic accent without departing from the pure bel canto.

This problem has been successfully solved in our own day by such singers as Lehmann and Nordica. It can be solved by any singer who has given any attention to what the French call the grand style. In the majestic arias of Rameau and Gluck, even in the rather pompous deliverances of Méhul, Spontini and Cherubini the singer of to-day should seek some of the elements of his Mozart style.

True, they followed Mozart, but they were much closer to him than the Italians ever were. Rameau, building upon the foundations laid by Lulli, determined for all time the character of French dramatic singing. He insisted upon the absorption of the spirit of the text in the treatment of the music. He was the father of that distinguished and elegant diction which is still one of the glories of French lyric art.

No student of singing can afford to neglect a thorough examination of the French opera in the days of its inception. Let any student of modern Italian opera music take up such a number as the "Enfin est il ma puissance" of Lulli's "Armide," or that beautiful air, "Tristes apprêts pâles flambeaux," in Rameau's "Castor et Pollux," and he will at once perceive wherein the Gallic masters of the elder time attained a certain grandeur of style which their Italian contemporaries never reached.

The Italian music is the more passionate, the more elastic. The French is the more aristocratic. It is just this aristocracy of manner that every student of vocal art must attain in order to add to his style that polish which he can never acquire from a narrow adherence to the field of Italian opera. A singer thoroughly trained in the French grand style and afterward in the German dramatic manner would put to shame the feeble attempts at Schubert's "Die Allmacht" or Beethoven's "Die Himmel ruhmen," founded wholly on a combination of Italian and Teutonic training.

By an artistic fusing of all the elements of Italian, French and German vocal art, which were defined before the era of Mozart, the singer may at last enter the kingdom of the marvelous boy. He who can adequately sing Mozart is a mastersinger. Perhaps nature may have denied him the robustness of voice essential to the latest combinations of solo and orchestra, but their style, at any rate, will hold for him no insuperable difficulties. He can triumphantly paraphrase Monte Cristo rising from the sea and exclaim: "The riches of Mozart! The world is mine!"

The competent singer of Mozart is ready for Rossini, Meyerbeer, Bellini, Donizetti, Ponchielli, Verdi and the contemporaneous writers. All that is superimposed on the music of Mozart (considered wholly from the point of vocal style) by these writers is a large and frank theatricalism. With Rossini entered the vocal *tour de force*, and with that began the demand for the Big Tone, the curse of to-day's singing.

It is not the growth and development of the modern operatic orchestra that has made the need for the Big Tone. It is the degradation of public taste by a deliberate pandering to vulgar appetite. As Frangçon-Davies has truthfully said, the voices often drown the orchestra, and he asks how we should like to hear actors bellow Shakespeare at us as singers bellow Verdi.

The problem for the opera singer of to-day to solve is how to unite a pure, mellow tone with the highly emphasized declamatory style necessary for modern operas. In nine cases out of ten singers overdo the accentuation in the Italian operas of the early nineteenth century. It wearies the ear and insults the intelligence to hear the sempiternal "Addios" turned into "Add-d-d-Dio," so that legato becomes spiccato and the stage is showered with shattered phrases.

This sort of offense in style is the result of a reflex action caused by a mistaken notion about the proper manner of singing the opera of to-day. The singer who seeks for a sure guide to the correct manner of singing contemporaneous opera will find it in the proposition that an appeal to the intelligence of the audience must be made before that to the senses.

Before the Big Tone, for which the shouters of "bravo" are always waiting, must come the immersion of self in the poetic content of the text, the identification of self with the character. The artist must bear in mind that the lyric drama of to-day rests upon the theory of Wagner, which transformed mere singing into that puissant organic union of melody and word which he called "word tone speech." Communication, not tickling of the ear by sound, is the purpose of the entire lyric art of this era.

The materials for the vocal style of to-day are provided in the works of the earliest Italians, Peri, Caccini and Monteverde, in those of the early Frenchmen, Lulli and Rameau, in those of Gluck, and, finally, in those of Mozart. After Mozart, Beethoven and Weber. But what are "Ocean, thou mighty monster" and "Abscheulicher" but combinations and amplifications of "Don Ottavio, son morta" and "Non mi dir"?

The foolish assertions of ill-equipped vocalists that Wagner demands a technique and a style not to

be acquired from the study of the old masters have been laughed to scorn by the preach-
ings and the practice of such artists as Lehmann, Brandt, Fischer, Ternina, Nordica, Jean
de Reszke and a host of others who were trained
in the old music.

The bawling of some early Wagnerian singers
echoes through the opera houses of Germany to-
day simply because the impersonators of Wagner's
characters are not singers at all in the true sense of
the term. They can no more sing Mozart than they
can sing Wagner. If they could sing the former
they could sing the latter, and perfect style would
be within their reach.

Be not deceived. Singers like Caruso cultivate the
Big Tone quite as industriously as the Germans.
The Italians are following the downward path that
leads to mere noise.

Of course the public applauds. The public always
applauds anything that fills it with astonishment.
The acrobatic feat meets with swifter recognition
than the finish of exquisite art. On this point Tosi
spoke long ago these pithy words: "An audience
that applauds what is blamable cannot justify faults

by its ignorance; it is the singer's part to set it right."

What a blessing it would be if the lyric artists of to-day would unite in one determined effort to give to the stage the pure and elevated style which ought to be its glory. The public would not be long in discerning its superiority over the popular manner of vocal mouthing.

All that has been said in regard to operatic art applies with equal pertinence to oratorio and the song. The modern art song is "word tone speech" of the most subtle variety. The singer who would sing lieder well must bury himself in the texture of the tone-poem and reproduce it for his hearers.

If he will do that he will find the correct style; but with too many singers the temptation to sacrifice the contour of the phrase or the sense of the word to the opportunity for some petty piece of vocal display destroys the whole. To this must be added what has been said before in the course of these papers, that the pressing need of covering up some radical defect in vocal techniques quite as often works for the destruction of the singer's best effort.

Technique, technique, technique! That comes first. The Corinthian columns must rest on a firm foundation or they will fall, and great will be the fall thereof. When the foundations are laid, musicianship and cultivated taste must be backed by sound knowledge of periods and individual composers before the study of particular compositions will give the singer insight into the traits of style.

14

Wagner-Singing

FOR YEARS ONE OF THE MOST FORMIDABLE OB-
stacles in the way of an immediate appreciation of
the Wagnerian music drama was the atrocious
manner in which its music was sung. I am here
confronted by a lion in the path, a vicious, snarling
lion of evil tradition, fed fat in the mews of Wahn-
fried itself. The manner in which the music of
Wagner has been sung in the past and is still sung
by the authority of Bayreuth is fundamentally incorrect; and I hope here and now to establish that
truth.

Why does the typical German singer of the
music of Wagner bark, cough, or sneeze the notes
instead of producing them in a normal manner?
Why is it regarded by so large a part of the German people as absolutely wicked to *sing* the music
of Wagner? It is true that there are Germans who
do really sing this music, but they are always confronted with wagging heads in their own land.

There is believed to be something radically wrong with them because they permit the voice parts of the Wagner music dramas to be revealed in their native beauty. In the benighted country in which I live we listen to such singing with joy. For we have at last come out of the wilderness in which we were aforetime lost, and have learned that the highest achievement of the old Italian art of singing is the delivery of Wagner's music as he, poor man, dreamed it, but rarely heard it.

Fifteen years ago the writer of this volume was derided, because he had said that Wagner never intended that his music should be delivered as the German singers of that day were delivering it. He had declared that if what Lilli Lehmann and Emil Fischer did was right (and even the Germans in New York praised them), then what Alvary and Elmblad and others of that sort did was all wrong. In more recent years he was still making the same argument, holding that if Ernst van Dyck was right in his method of singing Wagner, then Jean de Reszke was wrong. Fifteen years ago there was hardly one to agree with me; now everyone says, "Why, of course; that's what we always said."

Heaven help me, I am no Columbus. I never could make an egg stand upright. But I did read my Wagner, and I knew that the master would have given much if he could have found a Jean de Reszke to introduce his *Parsifal*, and a Ternina or a Nordica to make known his *Isolde*.

The theory of Wagner declamation as held in Germany, and most of all as proclaimed at the present time in Bayreuth, is radically incorrect. It is not Wagner's theory, and even if it were, it is opposed to the laws of vocal interpretation, and must therefore fail to accomplish the purpose for which it is striving. What is that purpose? The interpretation of text by sung tones. It is a plain fact that Wagner threw aside forever the old Italian theory that the text of an opera was merely a peg on which to hang pretty tunes. That is so familiar to the musical world that it need not be discussed here. The Wagnerian theory of music drama included the use of music as a means of expression, and that only. The employment of music as a means of expression made it absolutely essential that every word of the text should be intelligible to the auditor. For since it was no longer to be the pleasure of the hearer simply to listen to tunes played on voices, as they might be on instruments, but to pay the closest attention to the speech of the actors in order that the significance of a drama might be grasped, it was incumbent on the performer to deliver the text clearly, using the music just as he would the inflections of the voice in speaking to bring out the meaning of the sentences.

From this premise the school of so-called Wagner singers has developed a theory of Wagnerian declamation, which calls for the most clean-cut treatment of the consonants. With this there should be no quarrel, did it not also include such a use of the vowel sounds that the delivery of those pure, sustained musical tones which constitute song becomes impossible. It is at this point that I find myself compelled to part company with the genuine Bayreuth style of Wagner singing. I do not believe that Wagner wrote the beautiful voice parts of his music dramas with the intention of hearing them cackled in the Bayreuth staccato, as practiced by such eminent dispensers with vocal art as Messrs. van Dyck and Kraus.

The reason why I do not believe that this is the

right way to sing Wagner is that Wagner said it
was not. It has always been my firm opinion that
if any man who ever lived knew just what he
wished, that man was Richard Wagner. There was
nothing for which he wished more fervently than
an eloquent delivery of his music, and he knew
in what way eloquence was to be attained.

He knew that the first duty was that of the
composer. Unless the music was so written that the
musical accent should be identical with that of the
text, every effort of the singer properly to phrase
the music would end only in obscuring the intel-
ligibility of the words. He therefore devoted himself with heart and soul to setting his texts in such
a way that the poetic and musical phrasing and accentuation should be organically united.* That
being done, it was necessary only that the singer
should sing the notes precisely as they were written, without any liberties, and the text could be
clearly and poetically enunciated. When he set out
to do this in the early part of his career, he had
to contend with the indolence of the German

* He did not always succeed. There are more than a few instances of bad declamation in Wagner's works. But these are
exceptions to the ruling practice.

singers, to whom recitative had long meant "laisser-aller" in singing. Writing to Liszt on Sept. 8, 1850, he said:

"Nowhere in the score of my 'Lohengrin' have I written above a vocal phrase the word 'recitative'; the singers ought not to know that there are any recitatives in it; on the other hand, I have been so intent upon weighing and indicating the verbal emphasis of the speech so surely and so distinctly, that the singers need only sing the notes, exactly according to their value in the given tempo, in order to get purely by that means the declamatory expression."

This is one of the earliest statements of Wagner's wishes in regard to the manner in which his declamation should be treated. It is all the more significant because in "Tristan und Isolde," the drama in which the worst offenses are committed by singers, the music is purely melodious, and therefore to be governed by the rules of style applicable to that of "Lohengrin." Now, in seeming contrast to the passage quoted, let me adduce another, taken from the essay entitled "A Glance at the German Opera Stage of To-day" (Prose Works, W. Ashton Ellis's translation, Vol. V.): "My advice to friendly disposed conductors of opera might therefore be summed up as follows: If you otherwise are good musicians, in opera pay heed to nothing but what is happening on the stage, be it the monologue of a singer, or a general action; let it be your prime endeavor that this scene, so infinitely intensified and spiritualized by association with its music, shall acquire the 'utmost distinctness': if you bring that distinctness about, rest assured that you at like time have found the proper tempo and correct expression for the orchestra."

Here again we have convincing proof that Wagner did not regard distinctness in the outline of the scene as synonymous with a destruction of beauty of musical movement or loss of melodic contour. On the other hand, he held that the two things were inseparable. On the one hand he urges the singer to sing the notes precisely as they are written, in order that he may, as it were unconsciously, attain the right declamatory effect; and on the other he tells conductors that, by working in perfect harmony with the singer in producing perfect clearness, he will reach the correct movement of the music.

The present theory as to the proper method of singing the declamatory music of Wagner has grown out of a misconception of the way in which he desired to have the verbal rhythm, the declamatory accent, enforced. He abandoned as unsuited to the musical form which he wished to employ in his dramas the verse forms familiar to the prosody of German as well as English. He could not write his endless melody if he permitted the text to prescribe the rhythm and the sectional divisions of the music. He says himself that in order to escape this mastery of word over musical setting, he adopted the iterative verse, the staff rime, which he used exclusively in "The Ring." His purpose in doing this he has made perfectly clear to us. He did it, not that the singer might fall upon the iterated consonant or vowel attacks with all his enunciative force, but that the iterations might make their own rhythmic effect when the singer was strictly attending to his business of singing. It was taken for granted as a part of Wagner's plan, that the singer of his music should be one who could enunciate. For without a distinct proclamation of the text the whole Wagnerian scheme of an organic union of the arts tributary to the drama must fall to the ground. Read what Wagner himself says about this "Staff Rime":

"In Stabreim the kindred speech-roots are fitted to one another in such a way that, just as they sound alike to the physical ear, they also knit like objects into one collective image in which the Feeling may utter its conclusions about them. Their sensuously cognizable resemblance they win either from a kinship of the vowel sounds, especially when these stand open in front, without any initial consonant; or from the sameness of this initial consonant itself, which characterizes the likeness as one belonging peculiarly to the object; or again, from the sameness of the terminal consonant that closes up the root behind (as an assonance), provided the individualizing force of the world lies in that terminal." As illustrations of what he means, Wagner gives the combinations, "Erb' und eigen"; "Immer und ewig"; "Ross und Reiter"; "Froh und frei"; "Hand und Mund"; "Recht und Pflicht."*

Again, "To impart a feeling with utmost plainness, the poet has already ranged his row of words into a musical bar, according to their spoken ac-

* "Opera and Drama," Part II, chap. vi.

cents, and has sought by the consonantal Stabreim
to bring them to the Feeling's understanding in an
easier and more sensuous form; he will still more
completely facilitate this understanding, if he takes
the vowels of the accented root-words, as earlier
their consonants, and knits them also into such a
rime as will most definitely open up their understanding to the Feeling. An understanding of the
vowel, however, is not based upon its superficial
analogy with the riming vowel of another root,
but, since all the vowels are primarily akin to one
another, it is based on the disclosing of this Ur-
kinship through giving full value to the vowel's
emotional content by means of Musical Tone. The
vowel itself is nothing but a tone condensed: its
specific manifestation is determined through its
turning toward the outer surface of the Feeling's
'body'; which latter—as we have said—displays to
the 'eye' of Hearing the mirrored image of the outward object that has acted on it. The object's effect
on the body-of-Feeling itself is manifested by the
vowel through a direct utterance of feeling along
the nearest path, thus expanding the individuality
it has acquired from without into the universality

of pure emotion; and this takes place in the Musical Tone."*

It would be impossible to give a fuller explanation of the nature and purpose of the staff rime than that found in the first of these extracts, while the second contains one of the finest lessons in the philosophy of singing ever written. I marvel that the so-called disciples of Wagner have the audacity to treat his music as they do in the face of these authoritative words. He begins by telling us that he places a special value on the elementary relationship of all vowel sounds, especially when not preceded by consonants, or, in other words, when most favorably situated for the production by a singer of a pure and vital musical tone. Secondly, he proclaims his belief in the influence of this elementary relationship of the vowel sounds when treated in such a broad vocal style. The vowel sound as delivered to the consciousness of the listener in a pure musical tone becomes an emotional power second to none. It can expand its individuality into "the universality of pure emotion." And this, he tells us, "takes place in the Musical Tone."

* "Opera and Drama," Part III, chap. ii, W. Ashton Ellis's translation.

But he also tells us that the poet has previously arranged his words in a musical bar "according to their spoken accents." Here we have a full demonstration of the endurance of the principle which he proclaimed when he wrote to Liszt about the manner of singing the recitatives in "Lohengrin." The poet has placed the words in musical order with due recognition of their accentual value. It now becomes the business of the singer to sing them exactly as they are written, to enunciate the consonants distinctly, but still more to preserve that fundamental emotional power of the pure vowel sound which is only to be conveyed to the hearer as musical tone. And that is the very kernel of the philosophy of singing. It is what the oldest and best Italian teachers taught; it is what the best of those now living teach. It is in accordance with the practice of the greatest living singers, all of whom enunciate distinctly, but without forgetting that the tone is identical with the vowel sound, and that in this fact lies the secret of emotional influence in song.

Two things have combined to obscure these facts about Wagner's theories of dramatic song. At the time when he first became a recognized power in the operatic world, the singers were all engaged in the performance of works in which music was not a means of expression, but the sole end to be sought. Consequently they devoted their entire vocal skill to the production of a pure and lovely singing tone, without much consideration of the words of the text. Consonants which were found to interfere with the flow of tone were slurred over, or omitted. Vowel sounds which were inconvenient for any particular singer were altered to suit the favorite position of his tongue.

It is not difficult to imagine the struggles of the mere tone-producers of that period, when they were suddenly called upon to enunciate the words of the text, and to treat the opera as a form of poetic drama in which the public was to find the musical sounds only a means of expression. The result was bad tone formation, untuneful singing, vocal contortions of the most painful sort, and a public convinced that all this was in the nature of the music of Wagner. In the year of grace 1888, when the musical editor of the *New York Times* said that Wagner could be and ought to be sung with the same beauty of style as Donizetti, many estimable persons regarded him with deep sorrow and some kindly pity for his unfortunate condition. Since they have heard Jean de Reszke sing Tristan, they have come to think that while he perhaps did not know what he was talking about, Wagner at any rate knew what he was writing. In 1889 I said in the *New York Times*:

"Signor Saccharini might sing the music of Siegfried without a single error in method or vocal style, and yet fail to move an audience as much as Herr Wachsend, who outraged his glottis with every note, and constructed his phrases with the delicacy of a musical blacksmith. But because Herr Wachsend is so fine a dramatic performer, we are not to forget that at every appearance he strews the stage with the *disjecta membra* of the lyric art. Singing is a very important part of the opera, even of the Wagnerian music drama. 'Nothung! Nothung! neidlisches Schwert' can be sung strictly in tune and with the aid of all the resources of the most perfect vocal method, without the sacrifice of one shade of its magnificent dramatic power. And people who pay for the expensive privilege of listening to operatic performances have a perfect right to demand that it shall be."

Time and the man came to demonstrate the truth of these words, derided as they were at the hour of their appearance by those who now echo them. Singers who possess the real old Italian method, not the false one practiced all over Europe by half-trained singers in Wagner's early days, have proved that when Wagner's music is sung with opulent beauty of tone and with a perfect diction, it rises to heights of beauty and eloquence which the first exponents of it never attained. Heinrich Vogl was a true artist in most senses, but his Tristan was no such moving interpretation as Jean de Reszke's. Albert Niemann's Tristan was marvelous, but its marvel lay chiefly in the triumph of the man's dramatic power over his native inability to deliver Wagner's text to the public as Wagner wrote it. For in the Wagner drama the text consists of words and music welded together into a perfect form of dramatic speech. Niemann could not sing the music of Tristan. We saw him act, and gathered as much of the music as we could from the orchestra. It was magnificent; but it was not Wagner.

The second of the two things which have combined to obscure the truth about Wagner's theory of dramatic singing is the constant publication of false theories loosely thrown together by the German-taught Wagner singers as explanations of their own inability. Mr. Ernst van Dyck, in an interview published in the *Pall Mall Gazette* a few years ago, gave to the public his theory of the proper method of singing the music of Wagner. This theory was no other than that taught at Bayreuth at the present time by the distinguished relict of the composer. Its chief tenet is that in order to convey the illusion of a musical dialogue in the declamatory voice parts of the Wagner dramas, the legato must be abandoned, the pure fluent, round musical tone set aside, and the consonants delivered with the fullest possible insistence on their value, while the vowel sounds are treated with regard only for their conversational characters, and with none for their availability as tone producers.

How completely false this theory is to the thought of Wagner, is demonstrated by the passages quoted from "Opera and Drama." Its results were most easily observed in the singing of Mr. van Dyck, a consummate dramatic performer. He was wont to deliver the operatic text of Wagner in a hard, brittle staccato, in a dry tone without resonance and almost wholly devoid of singing quality. And German singers, who could not sing properly, have for years been singing Wagner in some way similar to this, and declaring that Wagner should not be sung in any other way. Poor Wagner! What would he not have given to hear the memorable performances of "Tristan und Isolde" at the Metropolitan Opera House in the winter of 1898-99! Isolde, Lilli Lehmann; Brangœne, Marie Brema; Tristan, Jean de Reszke; Kurvenal, Anton van Rooy; King Mark, Edouard de Reszke; Melot, Lempriere Pringle; the Shepherd, Mr. Meffert, and the Sailor, Mr. Meux. An audience of nearly five thousand persons listened to the first matinée performance of the work by this cast; and Marcella Sembrich, with whom I sat through the second act, said to me at the fall of the curtain, "Did you notice how absorbed the people were? Not even a cough was heard! Wonderful!" And this same Marcella Sembrich, the most accomplished coloratura singer in the world since the decline of Madame Patti's exceptional powers, agreed with me that there was only one right way to sing and that way was right for both Rossini and Wagner. And she demonstrated the truth by singing Eva in "Die Meistersinger" with ravishing beauty of tone and a perfect embodiment of the character. Lillian Nordica is as great in "Il Trovatore" as she is in "Gotterdämmerung," and Milka Ternina sings the essentially Italian Tosca as dramatically as she does Isolde. Jean de Reszke sang Faust and Tristan with equal beauty, and all the great singers of to-day agree that Wagner's music is perfectly singable, and that it is to be sung best by following the old Italian laws of singing.

15

The Singer's Musicianship

FÉTIS IN WRITING OF GARAT, THE FAMOUS FRENCH tenor, said: "An air, a duet, according to this great singer, did not consist in a succession of well-performed or even well-expressed phrases; he wanted a plan, a gradual progress, which led to great effects at the proper moment, when the excitement had reached its climax. He was rarely understood when discussing his art, he spoke of the plan of a vocal piece, and musicians themselves were persuaded that his ideas were somewhat exaggerated on this subject; but when he joined example to precept and to demonstrate his theory sang an air with the different colorings which he could give to it, they then comprehended how much of reflection and study were necessary to arrive at perfection in an art which at the first view seems destined only to procure enjoyment for the ear."

If this means anything it means that at a time when most singers were fixing their minds upon the perfection of those details which belong entirely to the department of vocal technique, Garat was rising above the surface and surveying the field of song from the point of view of the musician. Fétis indicates that he was a master of style, and that his mastery came from his grasp of the entire form of a vocal number.

This is the secret of ultimate perfection of style. One may have a perfect tone attack, a beautiful legato, a ravishing portamento, a noble messa di voce and an elastic fluency of delivery, yet sing ineffectively. If the singer bestows all his thought on the perfection of each phrase as an individual entity he will never sing eloquently, though here and there he may rise to heights of extraordinary beauty.

There must be a plan, as Garat called it, which is but another word for design. The singer must grasp his aria or his recitative in its entirety, and he must also perceive clearly its relation to all that precedes and all that follows it. Only in this way can he arrive at a proper conception of the delivery of his music, for only thus can he determine the distribution of vocal effects.

Now the correct distribution of vocal effects gives us what we call style; but it gives us something more than that, for upon it depends largely the interpretative eloquence of the singer's delivery. It is impossible to interpret an aria or a lied eloquently if the vocal effects are out of balance. The style and the interpretation usually go hand in hand. It is not possible, for example, to sing eloquently the recitative of Handel with a Wagnerian style, nor can the music of Mozart be treated in the same manner as that of Richard Strauss.

Correct style and interpretation rest partly upon traditions, but tradition is by no means a trustworthy guide. Traditions are but imperfectly transmitted from generation to generation. Lineal descent in vocal art has provided the great fathers of bel canto with some strange children. No one can make the doughnuts as mother made them; no one can sing Handel and Hasse as Farinelli and Boschi did.

There is a safer ground for style than tradition. That is the ground of musicianship. Singers should belong to the universal brotherhood of musicians, but as a rule they do not. They are the most obstinately one-sided of all practitioners of musical art. It is known to all who observe the doings of the musical world that the violinists all go to violin recitals, but almost never to piano or song recitals. The pianists all flock to hear the other pianists, and 'cellists turn out only when a noted 'cello virtuoso appears. So the singers go only to hear singers.

One does occasionally see a pianist at an orchestral concert or a violinist at the opera, but the singer never goes to hear anything but singing. That is the rule. The exceptions are few, and they are also notable. Now, this is all wrong. Singers should go to hear all sorts of music in order that they themselves may be thoroughly musical. Neither the poet who never reads prose nor the prose writer who never reads poetry can sound all the depths of his native tongue.

There is not a clarinet player of solo ability who cannot give hints to a singer. There is not a pianist of virtuoso rank who cannot offer him suggestions about dynamics and tone color. But all this is still in the domain of techniques. What the singer can get at the orchestral or chamber music concert is an acquaintance with musical architecture. He can gain an insight into the significance of the larger forms and in time acquire a conception of those broader principles of musical design which he ought to know in order to construct the plan of a rôle.

Every singer ought to add to his course of technical study a curriculum of general musical information. First and foremost he ought to acquire some measure of ability to play upon an instrument. Naturally his choice will prefer the piano, for this instrument can be utilized in the study of his own branch of art. The mistake of most singers is that they never use their pianos for anything else. They learn to strum out accompaniments and there they stop.

This is not enough. The singer should learn to play some piano music. He need not become a virtuoso, for that would demand too much of his intellectual force and of his time; but the broadening of his musical conceptions by intimate personal acquaintance with some forms of melody other than those suited to the voice will prove of incalculable benefit to him. It is a field which should not be neglected, but which usually and altogether too generally is.

The singer should know the principles of musical form. How many of them do? How many of them can analyze the simplest aria and state with the certainty of absolute knowledge where its phrases begin and end, how many phrases there are in a section, how they are balanced, and how the sections are formed into periods? Yet without such knowledge these singers will not hesitate to prepare an air, arrange their phrasing and their dynamic effects and preen themselves on the musical quality of their plan. It is true that in occasional cases natural dramatic or musical instinct leads such singers along the true path, but in more cases it does not. This is especially likely to be the case when the singer enters an entirely strange field. Some opera singers who have essayed lieder with sorrowful results would have advanced much farther toward the light if they had known the laws of musical design.

The singer should study harmony. Perhaps in the early days of the last century this might not have been essential, but that time is far behind us.

The development of harmony has been more rapid in the last seventy-five years than at any other period in the history of musical art. The harmonic structures of Beethoven and Weber are simple as compared with those of Wagner, and still more so when placed beside those of the contemporaneous school of distortionists. It matters not what we may believe as to the value of such methods of composition as those of the latter-day Frenchmen, we cannot, as practitioners of the art of music, ignore them. We are bound to learn the new things.

The singer of to-day must not be troubled by the strange intervals of Strauss and Debussy. He must know precisely what they are, why they are, and whither they lead. He must have his ear attuned and his intelligence practiced in the modulations of the new idea. What threw the operatic world into confusion on the appearance of Wagner? What made singers say this new music was unsingable? Its demands upon the voice? Nonsense! Its demands upon the singer's musicianship caused the trouble. The old simple diatonic progressions, the stock phraseology of song, were laid aside for a new harmonic diction, and the singers could not intone the unfamiliar intervals.

A knowledge of harmony will enable a singer to understand the new progressions. The emotional restlessness of the contemporaneous style is built largely of postponed resolutions of chords. Let the singer grasp that and he will find that the strange orchestral accompaniments will not throw him off his musical balance.

Every singer ought to be acquainted with the history of music, and especially of his own branch of the art. Very few know anything about these subjects, but for the development of correctness in style it is essential that the singer should know the general character of the music of the period to which the composition before him belongs, the particular character of the vocal style and technic of that period, and the individual aims and artistic ideals of the composer of the music.

It seems as if this ought to go without saying, but the truth is that while a few intelligent singers are quite ready to admit that the practice of an instrument is a good thing, and some others do not deny that it would be well to know something about harmony, very, very few indeed profess to have read the history of their art.

It is unfortunate that the English reader is forced to go unsatisfied in the study of the history of vocal art. He can sate himself with histories of opera, oratorio and the song, but the historical consideration of the art of singing has been sadly neglected by English writers.

However, most singers read French, German and Italian, and in these languages they can find information of great value. For the average student who wishes to acquire a bird's eye view of the subject there is nothing better than "Le Chant," by Lemaire and Lavoix. It is a pity that the work is out of print, but copies are still to be had by those who are willing to take the trouble to search for them. A large part of the work is devoted to the technics of singing, but more than a third is historical.

Another admirable book is Hugo Goldschmidt's "Die Italienische Gesangsmethode des XVII. Jahrhunderts." This is a contemporaneous work, and it makes a careful and complete examination into the vocal technic of the seventeenth century, beginning with the "Nuove Musiche" of Caccini. As the singers of this century developed the method which the great masters of 1700, Pistocchi, Porpora, Redi and the rest, taught to Farinelli, Caffarelli, Cuzzoni, Faustina, Gizziello, Senesino and their contemporaries, it follows that the seventeenth century method is the foundation of all artistic singing.

It is aside from the purpose of this book to furnish a list of works relating to the history of vocal art. Those who desire them will have no difficulty in finding them in French, German and Italian. That any large number of singers or students of singing could be induced to embark upon a serious examination of the history of their art after reading anything merely giving good reasons why they should do so is altogether too much to expect.

It may seem wholly unnecessary to urge singers to learn vocal sight reading, but those who are acquainted with the astonishing ignorance of a large number of vocalists will know that it is not. It is no foolish jest of the newspapers that many opera singers have to learn their rôles by ear because they cannot read music. Others who can read music have never learned the art of vocal sight reading, and hence are obliged to sit down before a piano and pick out their parts note by note on that instrument, and in this primitive fashion commit them to memory.

Every singer should be a master of vocal sight reading. A page of music should be to him as the page of a novel is to a reader of language. This branch of the musical art puts the finish to the musicianship of the singer. With a knowledge of form and harmony the sight reader can grasp the music of a vocal score at once. Without any one of these three the vocalist is musically ungrounded and is never certain of his footing.

I may be pardoned at this point for inviting the reader's attention to one singer who has all the qualifications demanded in this chapter. It not infrequently happens that superficial opera-goers ask why Madame Sembrich receives so much critical praise in spite of the indisputable fact that she is no longer in the bloom of her years nor the springtime of her voice.

Her exquisite art is entirely lost upon those who have no knowledge of its qualities. The truth is that

Madame Sembrich enjoys a unique superiority by reason of her thorough musicianship. She began her career as a pianist and next became a violinist. She was an accomplished virtuoso on both instruments and learned the fundamental principles of music from the point of view of the instrumental musician. When she discovered that she had a voice she took up the study of singing.

But she was already an excellent musician, and for years she kept up the practice of both piano and violin. Her sight reading is swift and accurate. She knows harmony and modern music does not trouble her. All her singing is instinct with musicianship. Her phrasing is both dramatic and musical. Her feeling for rhythm is exquisite. Her treatment of recitative is that of a singer who has played Beethoven and Chopin, and who perceives the musical sense wedded to the declamation. Her knowledge of style is perfect.

But enough. The point is that Madame Sembrich is a musician of high scholarship, and this knowledge, added to her fine perceptions and cultivated taste, gives her singing a peculiar and lasting charm for those who value refined and captivating art above the mere physical products of younger and more vigorous throats.

In an experience of years this writer has seen hundreds of singers who ruined their most ambitious attempts through want of the musical knowledge needed to carry out their wishes. He has yet to see the singer who destroyed the precious gift of temperament and voice through excess of scholarship.

Lilli Lehmann says: "When we wish to study a rôle or a song we have first to master the intellectual content of the work."

Every student of singing should take to heart these words from the greatest tragic soprano of our time. The intellectual content of a vocal work is both literary and musical, and the musical portion consists in melody, harmony and rhythm. The accompaniment, which comprises the harmonic background, is just as important to the student as the voice part. To plan the delivery of an aria, as Garat did, the singer must grasp all that came from the mind of the composer.

PART II
A Lifetime of Reviewing

The Nineteenth Century's Greatest Singers

November, 1896

WHEN THE LIST OF GREAT SINGERS IN THE LAST century is scanned the first name to appear in large letters is Maria Malibran, the famous daughter of Manuel Garcia. She came to the United States with her father in 1825. Though she was not beautiful, she had a mobile countenance and the pictorial expressiveness of genius.

Her mezzo-soprano voice was not naturally of the highest type. It had been extended in range by arduous study, so that it was weak in the middle of its two and a half octaves and powerful at either end. This was the secret of her marvelous leaping cadenzas, for by ranging from top to bottom of her voice she concealed much of the weakness of her middle tones. But she had real genius as an executant, almost reaching the originality of a composer. Her dramatic ability was small. The versatility of this extraordinary singer may be inferred from the fact that she sang with equal merit Amina in "La Sonnambula" and Leonora in "Fidelio." Malibran's greatest rival in the early years of the nineteenth century was unquestionably Pasta, who triumphed by her conquest of an intractable voice. Her method was beautiful, her delivery rich in eloquence, and her dramatic delineation superior to that of any of her contemporary prima donnas.

Tradition, however, has been less kind to these two artists than to the beautiful and inspiring Giulia Grisi. Probably the one fact that this most lovely of sopranos became the wife of Giuseppe Mario, the most captivating of tenors, has served to keep alive romantic memories in the minds of those who like to think that operatic artists are made of richer clay than other humans. Then, too, she had a long career, and reigned over audiences for nearly thirty years. She sang in the United States in 1854, and died in 1869.

Grisi's voice extended two octaves, from C to C, and was ravishing in its natural beauty. She could sing most exquisitely in slow and moderate passages, and again, emitting the full splendor of her tones, could rouse an audience in tragic scenes. Her Norma was noted for its grandeur and her Lucrezia Borgia for its passion. She was a dramatic soprano of the first rank, and was noted for being always in the forefront of companies composed of other artists of equal ability. She sang many seasons in the company of Giambattista Rubini, Giuseppe Mario, Giorgio Ronconi, Louis Lablache, Antonio Tamburini, and other artists of that class, but always shone brilliantly.

Wilhelmina Schröder-Devrient, Wagner's original Adriano, Senta, and Venus, was a contemporary of Grisi. She excelled in impassioned acting rather than in her singing, which was never of a high type. In later life her desire to shine as a lyric actress led her into extravagances of movement. Jenny Lind also sang in those days, but even to this time the echoes of her American "boom" exaggerate her importance. She was the possessor of a wonderful facility in execution and of much beauty of style in sustained music; but she was no such genius as Malibran, Pasta, or Grisi. On the concert stage she was unquestionably at her best.

Teresa Tietjens, who visited this country in 1875, enjoyed here and in London a popularity greater than she had on the European continent. She was a dramatic soprano of real force and intelligence, and her interpretations of such parts as Donna Anna, Leonora, and Valentine would be welcomed in these narrow times when great dramatic singers are so few.

Christine Nilsson, who came to this country in the early seventies, was what Chorley calls a first-rate singer of the second class. With a good voice and style, she had moderate dramatic temperament and a good deal of assurance. She was a member of the first company that sang in the Metropolitan Opera House, in 1883-1884. Two seasons later she faded almost out of memory before the new glories of Lilli Lehmann, who, taking her all in all, was the greatest dramatic soprano of our time.

Trained in the old school, Mme. Lehmann could sing admirably such rôles as Violetta in "La Traviata" and Filina in "Mignon," yet she rose to the splendid heights of Brünnhilde and Isolde. No one who heard it will ever forget her touching Sieglinde, her passionate Venus, her noble Valentine, her grand Donna Anna, or her tender Amelia in Verdi's "Masked Ball." Her magnificent natural voice, her dramatic intensity, her musical intelligence, and her imposing beauty combined to place her at the head of her class.

Of all singers of florid music in our time, the most dazzling was Adelina Patti, who made her début in New York in 1859. Mme. Patti was probably the most faultless deliverer of tones that ever trod the stage. Her luxuriant soprano voice had a peculiarly velvety quality, and her singing of simple airs, such as "Home, Sweet Home" and "The Last Rose of Summer," moved every hearer by the richness of its tone-color and the finish of its style. On the other hand, in the delivery of such ornate music as that of Rossini's "Semiramide" she has never been equaled in our time. No other singer commanded such a salary, and it was given to her entirely because the public was willing to pay any price to hear her. But she had no gift for dramatic parts.

Contemporary opera-goers, too, have had the good fortune to hear a singer of the older Italian operas who preserves the style and traditions of their school—Mme. Sembrich. Her musical skill and her vocal mastership have best been shown in such parts as Susanna, Rosina, Amina, Adina, Gilda, and Lucia. Like Mme. Lehmann, too, she has attained the highest rank as a song-recitalist.

The nineteenth century produced many contraltos, but only three who could be awarded places in the first rank. These were Marietta Alboni, Benedetta Pisaroni, and Annie Louise Cary. Pisaroni belonged to the earliest years of the century. She was very ugly, with a face badly pitted by smallpox; but her noble voice and superb style commanded instant praise from the best critics, though she was not always to the taste of the less observant public.

Marietta Alboni was Rossini's only pupil in singing. She was a supreme artist, and after laying Paris and London at her feet she toured the United States in 1853, with large success. She retired from the stage in 1866, chiefly because she had grown too stout. Her voice was one of glorious quality, and she was a singer *par excellence.*

Annie Louise Cary, retired from the stage in

1882, in the zenith of her splendor. She had a magnificent voice of great range, and her delivery was characterized by vocal skill and dramatic eloquence. Her Amneris in "Aïda" has never been equaled. She was also most admirable as Leonora in "La Favorita," and achieved triumphs in other important contralto rôles.

Contraltos of minor merit were Sofia Scalchi, whose facility in florid music blinded the public to her numerous offenses against good taste, and to her inequality of tone, and Zelia Trebelli, who was really a mezzo-soprano, with a forcible rather than an elegant style. Earlier in the century Marietta Brambilla was one of the popular contraltos in London, but she belonged to the vanguard of the second rank.

Two great tenors flourished in the early years of the century, Giambattista Rubini and Giuseppe Mario. The former died in 1854, the latter in 1883. Mario was Rubini's successor in the famous company already mentioned. Rubini was a genuinely great singer, possessed of a ravishing voice and a finished technique. But he was not a true operatic artist. He made his impressions by the singing of certain arias, not by the impersonation of characters. He walked through half his opera to save himself for some air, but then he sang like a god. His style may be conceived from the fact that he was the greatest representative of Bellini's heroes.

The English critic, Chorley, who was an admirer of Mario, declared that this most adored of all tenors was in his singing merely an amateur. He was possessed of a captivating voice and personality, but he was not a thoroughly trained vocalist. On the other hand, he was a superb impersonator of operatic heroes. His acting, especially in scenes of love-making, was intensely fervid. He was magnificent in the fourth act of "Les Huguenots." He was irresistible in the delivery of sentimental romances. Moreover, he wore something of a halo as the hero of a romantic career, for he was a nobleman and a cavalry officer in the King of Sardinia's army when he threw up his commission in order to become a singer.

Rubini resembled more closely the vocalists of the eighteenth century, who sang and did not act. Mario belonged to the epoch when acting and singing joined hands in operatic delineation. He was a combination of Italo Campanini and Joseph Capoul, without the former's vocal finesse. It was late in his career that he visited America—in 1854, the year of Rubini's death. He had a tremendous repertoire, including all the operas of Rossini, Bellini, Donizetti, and Verdi that were staged in his day.

The elder days held too many tenors for extended mention here. But we must not omit the names of Duprez, who conquered Paris with his somber tones in "William Tell," "Les Huguenots," "La Juive," and similar works; Tamberlik, who had a name for a time in works of this same kind; Theodor Wachtel, whose brilliant lyric voice pleased New York in the early seventies, and whose high C is still recalled by lovers of flights above the staff; and Sims Reeves, who delighted England for nearly half a century.

In the latter half of the century the names of Campanini, Tamagno, and Jean de Reszke claim mention. Caruso is of the present and the future, and Bonci, exquisite artist as he is, is yet a newcomer in America. Italo Campanini enjoyed his highest repute in the United States. He was never so adored in England or on the Continent. His pure resonant tones, which he could modulate to the sweetest *mezza voce*, closely approached Caruso's in beauty and power, though they were less mellow. He was far and away a broader artist than his successor, for he was equally great in Don Ottavio, Don José, Faust, Rhadames, Otello, and Edgardo. Even his Lohengrin was admirable, though it was Italian rather than Wagnerian. His Don José was overwhelming, while his Faust fell short only of Jean de Reszke's in elegance and charm.

Of Jean de Reszke it is difficult to write with judicial poise. Not gifted with a remarkable voice, he was past master of the art of singing. The elegance, the finish, the gracefulness of his style were heightened by the unfailing poetry, passion, and intelligence of his interpretations. He was at home in every school, a master in every field. He sang with equal perfection Raoul in "Les Huguenots" and John of Leyden in "Le Prophète," Faust and Tristan, Romeo and Siegfried, Rhadames and Werther.

His singular insight into the genius of every

school of music was one of the traits of his art which raised him above his contemporaries. His Rhadames, without losing the distinction of French training, was in spirit thoroughly Italian; while his Siegfried, preserving the finish of the Gallic stage and the vocal purity of the older styles, was thoroughly German and essentially Wagnerian. M. de Reszke was not a great actor, but he carried the power of interpretation by singing to heights of greatest eloquence. He was the master singer of the last half of the nineteenth century, and his successor has not been found.

Francesco Tamagno had what Maurel called the "unique voice of all the world." It was a magnificent *tenore robusto*, reaching high C sharp, and full of a pealing quality that overcame, if it did not move, the hearer. Tamagno was the original Otello in Verdi's opera, and his interpretation of the jealous Moor was one of the masterpieces of the modern stage. Only Salvini's could vie with it in poignant despair or in puissant passion.

Two celebrated barytones adorned the early years of the nineteenth century. These were An-

tonio Tamburini and Giorgio Ronconi. Both of
these singers belonged at times to that brilliant con-
stellation which included Rubini, Mario, Grisi,
Malibran, and Viardot. Tamburini had a gorgeous
voice of two octaves, sang with finish and warmth,
was engaging in appearance, and was a capital actor. Ronconi, who succeeded him in the constella-
tion, as Mario succeeded Rubini, was quite his
equal as an artist, and his superior in some respects.
Ronconi's voice was small in extent, poor in natural
quality, and hard to keep on the pitch. But such
were the vigor and eloquence of his expression and
the potency of his acting that he earned for himself
a reputation as great as that enjoyed by any other
singer of his day.

Manuel Garcia (born 1775, died 1832) was not
so great a singer as either of these, but he was an
operatic genius nevertheless. He sang well, acted
well, composed tolerably, taught admirably, and
managed successfully. It was he who introduced
Italian opera in New York, in 1825, with a company largely composed of members of his own family. He taught his distinguished daughters, Malibran
and Viardot, as well as his son and namesake, Man-

uel. The second Manuel Garcia, after a career of some distinction as a barytone singer, also became a noted teacher, the most famous of his pupils being Jenny Lind. He died in London only last year, at the age of one hundred and one.

The famous barytone of the middle of the century was Jean Baptiste Faure, who wrote that perennially abused song, "The Palms." He was at his best in such rôles as De Nevers in "Les Huguenots," Don Giovanni, Hamlet, and Mephistopheles. He was probably the best Mephistopheles that the operatic stage has known. Maurel, who was heard here in recent years in his incomparable impersonation of Falstaff, was a visitor to this country in the seventies, when he shone more as a singer and less as an actor. Barytones of the caliber of Tamburini and Ronconi have not been known to audiences of the last quarter of a century.

Undoubtedly the greatest of all basses was Louis Lablache, who made his début in 1812 and retired in 1852. His voice was a noble organ of two octaves, from E to E, and his singing was superb in every rôle that he undertook. He was without ques-

tion the greatest of all Leporellos in Mozart's "Don
Giovanni," but his powers were not confined to
humorous rôles. He was equally successful as the
doge in "Marino Falieri" and the Puritan captain in
"I Puritani." He was a man of immense proportions
and of imposing action. If the accounts of his contemporaries are correct, we have never beheld his
equal.

In the seventies, Karl Formes, a German bass,
had a high reputation, but it rested chiefly on the
possession of a huge voice and a tireless vigor. He
sang without polish and frequently out of tune, as
many other basses have done. A better singer was
Giovanni Nanetti, who came with Campanini and
his associates in the seventies. There was little
warmth in Nanetti's style, but his voice was smooth
and sonorous and his style was polished. In such
rôles as the Ramfis in "Aïda" (he was the original
here) he was excellent.

In England, France, and the United States the
best-known basses of the concluding years of the
nineteenth century were Delmas, of the Paris
Grand Opéra, Edouard de Reszke, the younger

brother of Jean, and Pol Plançon. Delmas, with his suave style, has not yet been heard in this country. He is a *basso cantante*, and some notion of his ability may be gathered from the fact that he has succeeded in pleasing some American hearers by his Hans Sachs in "Die Meistersinger."

It is hardly necessary to speak at length of Edouard de Reszke and Plançon. The former, who sang in America with his brother for a dozen seasons, triumphed largely by reason of his immense voice and his vigorous style, while the latter, who is still a favorite here, is distinguished for the smooth richness of his tone and the elegance of his delivery.

2

Emma Calvé

December 6, 1896

IN THE SEASON OF 1892-3 THERE WERE NO PER-
formances of grand opera in the Metropolitan
Opera House, because the interior of the building
had been destroyed by fire. In the Summer of 1893
the work of reconstruction was begun, and under
the energetic direction of John B. Schoeffel it was
completed, in spite of all predictions to the contrary, in time for the opening on Nov. 27. The
favorites of two years earlier returned to us, and
we heard "Faust," with Eames, Scalchi, the de
Reszkes, and Lassalle in the cast. In the period of
darkness at the Opera House rumors often came to
us of a dramatic soprano, a Frenchwoman, beautiful with a strange, magnetic beauty, and gifted with
the fire of dramatic genius. We had heard so many
rumors of that kind that we were chary of belief.
The Atlantic cable had so long been the tool of the

press agent and the impresario that it had earned distrust. Yet this Frenchwoman, Emma Calvé, had sung in England, and apathetic London had been warmed to enthusiasm. But, then, had not London sent us the glorification of the Ravogli sisters? So we waited and went to the second performance of the season of 1893-4 with steeled nerves.

It was on the night of Nov. 29, 1893, that we first learned to know Santuzza in "Cavalleria Rusticana." On Dec. 20 Mme. Calvé taught us the meaning of Carmen. She sang Suzel, in Mascagni's "L'Amico Fritz," on Jan. 10, 1894, but the opera was not popular. "Carmen" was given thirteen times that season, and at each performance the receipts were in the neighborhood of $10,000. The public of New York never paid a greater tribute to one woman's genius. Toward the close of the season there were dissensions among the leading women of the company, and it became noised abroad that Mme. Calvé would not return to America. The news caused profound regret, and when she appeared in a scene from "Carmen" in the farewell performance of selections on April 27, she was made the object of an especial demonstration, and was compelled to make a little speech in French. She said:

"I shall never forget that to the American public I owe the greatest success of my artistic career. I hope that I am not saying good-by, but only au revoir."

Mme. Calvé did not sing to us the following season, but she returned a year later and made her reappearance at the Metropolitan on Nov. 20, 1895, in "Carmen." On Dec. 4 she made her first appearance here as Ophelia in M. Ambroise Thomas's "Hamlet," and demonstrated that her abilities as a singer pure and simple had been underrated. On Dec. 11 she interpreted the rôle of Anita in Massenet's "La Navarraise," a one-act opera written especially for her. She also sang Marguerite in Boïto's "Mefistofele" Jan. 14 last. This completes the list of parts in which Mme. Calvé has exhibited her abilities to the American public. There have been desires frequently expressed to enjoy further revelations of her powers in other rôles. Some believe that she would be a remarkable Marguerite in Gounod's "Faust." These are of the number of those who find no limit to the possibilities of Mme.

Calvé's art. Others would prefer to have her confine herself to the narrower list and wider range of highly emotional rôles upon whose complexity of feeling she might better expend the splendid resources of her temperament. It remains, however, a fact that no artist who has appeared before New York audiences has so "got the start of the majestic world" without the use of a large répertoire. The name of Calvé is in the public mind indissolubly united with Carmen and Santuzza, and the impresario of the Metropolitan Opera House, M. Maurice Grau, naturally gives the public what it demands. But it will not be possible to circumscribe the genius of Emma Calvé. She has expressed herself as weary of Carmen and eager to conquer new worlds. She will explore and she will discover. Whatever she does, she will not fail.

Many pretty stories are told of her methods. Perhaps most of them are apocryphal. It is said that she went to Spain and spent much time in studying the Spanish gypsies at short range. She herself has sanctioned this story by permitting it to stand uncontradicted. The story, indeed, is to her credit. It shows that she went out to see whether there was anything in a Spanish gypsy that might help her to make an illusion for her public. In all human probability she found nothing. Certainly there is nothing of the coarse and cheap nomad of the peninsula in her Carmen. She did better when she spent some of her days and nights in the study of Prosper Merimée's story. There she found a complete, concrete personality. But Calvé's Carmen is a creature of her own imagination. Frequently she is the exhalation of a passing mood. This Carmen is in the main the result of study and artistic composition; but sometimes she is only a pouting Carmen and at other times she is as stormy and as fathomless as are the seven seas. But, after all, if one goes often to study the impersonation he realizes that it is always in the mass the same Carmen. There is a difference only in detail. It is a better Carmen always when there is a Don José of equal note, for Mme. Calvé requires the restraint of an art equal to her own to prevent her from giving free rein to the impulse of the moment. That she is the greatest Carmen that ever trod the stage is indisputable. Her dramatic temperament is overwhelming and her means of expression is beautiful and eloquent.

But let us all remember that Mme. Calvé is not simply a lyric actress. She is a singer, and within her field a great one. Her voice is not one of the notable organs of operatic history, but it is a very good one, and has the loveliness of a distinct musical individuality. The very quality of her voice is in itself an embodiment of her warm and magnetic personality. And Mme. Calvé possesses in a marked degree the admirable faculty of coloring her tones to meet the emotion of the words. Listen to her singing in the second act of "Carmen." Note how the quality of tone changes when she ceases to storm at Don José and begs him to fly with her to the gypsy camp. There you will find an art of song that lies far beyond the methods of the schools.

The story goes that in her Santuzza Mme. Calvé is simply a careful imitator of Eleanora Duse. It would be no discredit to the singer to make a model of so great an actress, and it is probably true that Calvé has adopted all of the Italian woman's ideas that are suitable to an operatic impersonation. But there the adoption must end. An operatic impersonation is vastly different from a theatrical one, and the limits put upon operatic acting by the demands of singing, such things as rests, entrances, tempi, and the requirements of breathing quite escape the thoughtless observer. Mme. Calvé could not slavishly imitate Duse's Santuzza, no matter how earnestly she might strive to do so. The thousand details of business, gesture, facial expression, and by-play must be sacrificed upon the altar of song. It therefore becomes necessary for the operatic artist to compose her characterization from a new point of view, and those who cannot perceive the potent originality of Mme. Calvé's Santuzza must be led astray by preconceptions. Fully two-thirds of the dramatic effect of her performance is wrought by her delivery of the music. The rest is accessory, forcefully pictorial accessory, if you will, but after all only annotative of the subject matter.

Mme. Calvé's Ophelia is one of the master creations of the lyric stage. Of course her great triumph in the part was reached in the mad scene, which had been used as a piece of vocal fireworks in the concert room so often that its dramatic possibilities were not known. Mme. Calvé showed us that this mad scene was one of the opportunities of a dramatic singer's career. The technical difficulties she overcame in a manner which proved that as a vocalist pure and simple she had few equals. But her conquest was in imbuing every measure with emotional eloquence, while she accompanied her song with look and action suited to the word. In short, it is true that Mme. Calvé is a great actress; but what we are in danger of forgetting is that she does most of her acting with her voice, and that she is first, last, and all the time a singer.

3
Changes in Singing

February 8, 1903

THE REVIVAL OF VERDI'S "ERNANI" AT THE METRO-
politan Opera House curiously enough chanced to
come just at the time when the stockholders of that
institution were confronted with the possibility of
having to find a new impresario. Some of the problems before the future director of the fortunes of
opera in this town were discussed in this place a
week ago. The reader may perchance remember
that one of the difficulties noted as lying in the
path was the scarcity of singers of the kind now
to be found at the Metropolitan.

The revival of "Ernani" has pointed out with
peculiar force the weakness of the contemporaneous
school of singing in the delivery of the older music,
which demanded perfect purity of style. In this
old-fashioned sort of music, which nurtured the
famous coterie of singers of the Italian Theatre in

Paris only one of the cast heard in Verdi's opera at the Metropolitan seemed to be at home. We think we live in a period of wonderful singers, but how weak and poor some of them sounded when they had to stand still and sing, when they could not disguise their vocal poverty by rushing about the stage, by exploding in stentorian declamation, and waving their semaphoric arms in the circumambient air.

Think of that little band of artists of the Italians. There were Maria Felicita Malibran and Giulia Grisi, sopranos; Giovanni Rubini, Antonio Tamburini and Giuseppe Mario, tenors; Giorgio Ronconi and Luigi Lablache, baritones. Where do we find their kind now? We count upon our fingers Patti, now in the sere and yellow; Sembrich, still in possession of her glorious powers, and Melba, thrilling the Australians and throwing her aged father into hysterics. Where are our tenors of the brilliant Tamburini style or of the melting Mario manner, the Mario who with a tenor note could charm a soul in purgatory? As any rate, Bulwer said he could, and he ought to have known.

In the two performances of "Ernani" given at

the Metropolitan the admired tenor of the Italians of this town demonstrated utter inability to reproduce the atmosphere of the music. He sang earnestly and when he had an opportunity to hurl a top note at the gallery he did it with abandon. His compatriots accorded him the precious meed of bravi, without which a tenor's life is but an empty delusion. But can it be said that he touched any heart? Was there anything melting in the character of his tone, anything persuasive in the nature of his delivery? Where were the velvety smoothness of voice, the clarion quality of the peal of the high register, the perfect gradation of the range from piano to forte, which went to make the merely mechanical exercise of the old time tenor's voice a delight?

Again take the case of Mr. Scotti, who is a better singer than most of the other men in the Metropolitan company. How he, too, failed to fit his manner to the music of "Ernani." He shattered many of his phrases into fragments with ejaculatory delivery acquired in the interpretation of the declamatory operas of the modern Italian school. The truth is that neither Mr. Scotti nor Mr. de Marchi is acquainted with the old traditions of the opera of his native land. They belong exclusively to the present, are trained in the present and cannot get back to the past, no matter how hard they may try.

Yet the testimony of every great singer of modern times is that in the kingdom of song one must become as a little child before he can hope for salvation. He must go back to the principles which were codified by the great masters, Pistocchi and Bernacchi at the end of the seventeenth century. He must learn to sing as the famous pupils of their school sang. The first of all models must be Caffarelli, Farinelli, Nicolini, Senesino, Cuzzoni, Gizziello, Faustina Hasse. It is very doubtful whether most of our contemporaneous vocal celebrities ever heard of them.

The reason why singers must begin where they began is this: Little or no acting was required of them; but they were compelled to sing. The laws discovered by their teachers lie at the fountain of all singing. In order that they might sing perfectly these artists refused to do things which would interfere with their production of a beautiful tone, their exquisite phrasing and their marvelously delicate nuancing in recitative passages. The result was that the characteristics of their school came to be beauty of tone, command of breath, accuracy of intonation, smooth agility in the delivery of rapid music, finished treatment of trills and leaps, and, in short, perfection in the fundamental technics of song. In this department the school was the greatest the world has ever seen.

The laws and practice of singing as made by this school descended to the second school—that which was represented by the singers of the Italian theatre in Paris—by the visitors who came to New York in the primitive days of Palmo's and the Astor place opera houses. That there were poor singers among these visitors goes without saying. The leaders of the Italian vocal art at that time, however, were the forbears of Patti and Sembrich and Melba. The changes in the art of song were largely brought about through altered conditions and through developments in the musical drama itself.

It is not to be denied that the demands of the singers of the school of Caffarelli and Farinelli led to an utter subversion of the true principles of the lyric drama as set forth by Peri in his preface to the first Italian opera. The public learned to expect and to desire to see singers drop all pretense of dramatic verity while singing one of the great arias. The public asked for nothing but perfect singing, and preferred that to all else. Hence came insatiable singer worship and with it the inordinate vanity and princely domination of the lords of song.

The issue of this condition soon crystallized in the rules which the singers set down for the composers. Writers of music were regarded simply as tailors whose business it was to fit the vocal aristocracy with garments of glory. The singers proclaimed that each one of them was entitled in every opera to one entrance air and one agility air. No two airs of the same character might be heard in succession, even though sung by different singers. All the women singers were sopranos and all the men tenors, with the admission of an occasional bass. Three women and three men were allotted as the proper number for an opera. No barytones were employed; they were a later French innovation. Duets were permitted, but not quartets. The order of succession of arias, duets, ensembles, &c.,

was all laid down by the lordly singers, and the composers had to write in accordance with their commands. The star system of the present day fades into pallid insignificance in comparison with the blaze of those hours of vocal dawn, when every singer in turn drove the chariot of the sun.

Such were the days of Handel. The influence of that time lived through the period of Rossini, Bellini and Donizetti. It was dominant in the labors of those men, though the teachings of the stilted dramatic school of France, the propaganda of Lully and Rameau, had begun to have their effect on Italian composition. The Italian opera became more dramatic. Recitativo secco gave way to recitativo stromentato. The expressive powers of the orchestra were more freely used. Less attention was paid to providing singers with pure cantabile passages and larger demands were made upon their combined powers of action and delivery.

Yet the idea of a stoppage of the full activity of the movement of the scene for the singing of important set numbers did not by any means disappear. It was still felt that the vital element of the opera was music in some variety of the aria form and that for the most effective presentation of that music something must always be sacrificed. Hence we find in the older works such intervals in the dramatic movement as those made for the delivery of "Casta diva," "O Giorno d'Orrore" and "Chi mi frena." A significant variation of the old aria made in this period was the dramatic scena, and its characteristics sum up the nature of the advance made by the school. Vocal delivery was still the chief end, but a larger measure of tragic utterance was required, and it was to be had even at the sacrifice of some of the more artificial beauties of the older school.

The recent Italian composers have sought to contend against the growing influence of the elegant and pictorial lyric drama of France on the one hand and that of the introspective and philosophical German school on the other by importing into their works something of the outward traits of both. Boïto led the way when he injected the subtleties of Goethe's speculative thought into the text of his "Mefistofele," and Verdi joined forces with him when he essayed to combine the essentials of dramatic verity with the pictorial panorama of a Meyerbeer and the orchestra tintings of a Berlioz in his "Aïda."

In their endeavors to remodel modern declamation to suit the demands of the reconstructed lyric drama, later Italians have deprived it of much of the spontaneous musical fluency with which two centuries and a half of practice founded on a study of the capabilities of the voice had equipped it. In striving for a lyric equivalent of speech they have to a large extent forgotten musical cantilena. Verdi, indeed, has shown well how the two things can be reconciled; but usually other Italian composers have simply oscillated between the one and the other and have therefore asked of their interpreters a fusion of styles, which has ended in confusion.

The singers who have been trained exclusively in the delivery of the works of these recent writers cannot deal successfully with compositions of the Rossini and Donizetti periods, nor with the early works of Verdi, which are of the same school. They fail to discriminate between the nature of the arioso or recitatives of the earlier works and the strenuous declamation of the later ones. Even if they did make the discrimination they would only deepen the pit into which they would fall through their want of mastery of a perfect legato style of singing. A singer cannot sing in the perfectly smooth flowing manner of the old school all at once just because he perceives that the music before him ought to be sung that way. He must be trained to it from the beginning, and the training is a long and laborious process.

Without this training there can be no lasting or high success in the field of vocal art. The foundation of the bel canto is the ability to sing legato. The foundation of all singing is the legato. It is just as essential to the delivery of Siegfried's forge song as it is to that of "Salut demeure" in "Faust."

Why? Because it was the beginning of the art of song. The singers of the Pistocchi and Bernacchi school did not sing as they did only because they did not know anything else, but because they had to know that before they could know more. The laws of tone production, of breath management, of phrase making, of sustaining the flow of breath and sound, had to be thoroughly explored before the details of dramatic accentuation and textual nuancing could be laid on. These things had to be discovered first, just as the fathers of music had to exhaust twelve centuries in formulating the laws of polyphony before modern music was ready to advance beyond the *a capella* counterpoint of the medieval Church.

On a reduced scale the singer who wishes to succeed in all kinds of vocal work must follow the course of history. He must first master the fundamental laws of vocal art, formulated by the early Italian schools of singing. Then he may come down the centuries a step and acquaint himself with the processes of the secondary schools, in which declamatory accentuation was laid like a veneer above the solid foundation of the true legato.

He does not have to take a lifetime to do this, for what his predecessors discovered now lies ready to his hand. It takes a long time to add the sum of any science, but when the addition is made, the answer may be compressed into a few figures. A single volume may contain the records of what explorers took hundreds of years to discover. But neither can it all be mastered in a hasty year or two of study. The training of the vocal organs is after all a process requiring time and care, and these are just the requisites which students neglect. Haste, haste—that is the pernicious element in modern study of vocal art.

When teachers tell their pupils that they should take several years to study the fundamental laws of singing, the pupils always think that the instructors are simply trying to keep them for the sake of the fees. No doubt this is true in some cases, but as a rule the teachers are right. It must be a student of exceptional gifts who is fit to appear in public with less than five years of study, and the ordinary pupil needs several more years. There was a solid foundation of truth in the old story that Porpora kept Caffarelli six years at work on what he had written on four pages of music paper. When the weary and disheartened student was ready to abandon all hope of ever passing that first lesson, Porpora said to him: "Go, my son, you are the greatest singer in Europe." The teacher had written down all the elements of the art, but how long it took to master them! And to-day we find one of the world's great singers, Lilli Lehmann, cataloguing the traits of good singing in her recently published book and asking how these are to be attained. She answers her question thus:

"Through natural gifts, among which I reckon the possession of sound organs and a well-favored body; through study, guided by an excellent teacher, who can sing well himself—study that must be kept up for at least six years, without counting the preliminary work."

How did Lilli Lehmann come to be a great interpreter of the Brünnhildes and Isolde? By such preparation and by first learning to sing the old-fashioned music. She began with Mozart and made her second début as Violetta in Verdi's "La Traviata," and even as late as 1891 could sing acceptably Filina in "Mignon." Lillian Nordica began also with Violetta, and she can sing it yet. Why does not Mme. Sembrich sing great dramatic rôles? She can sing their music, but not with sufficient power. She has not a dramatic soprano voice, and to attempt such rôles would be to outrage nature and destroy the gifts of heaven. But all singing rests on the same foundations. Let lovers and students of the art not forget that.

4
Mme. Tetrazzini's Violetta

January 16, 1908

MME. LUISA TETRAZZINI MADE HER FIRST APPEAR-
ance in this city last night at the Manhattan Opera
House, singing the music of Violetta Valéry in
Verdi's opera "La Traviata." By reason of the
cabled reports of the extraordinary stir caused by
her recent performances in London public curiosity
here had been stimulated to the verge of excitement
and the theatre was occupied to the limit of its generous capacity by a nervous, eager, bustling throng.
Like all New York first night audiences this as-
semblage contained a very large element with its
decision formed before the curtain rose, so that
Mme. Tetrazzini upon the instant of her appearance was acclaimed as a Patti might have been. No
disinterested and uninformed spectator would have
supposed that these people had never before heard
the woman and did not know as yet whether she
was a fact or a mere phantasm of the cable.

Mme. Tetrazzini came to New York under the most trying of all conditions, silly and extravagant overpraise. Of her brilliant success with the populace in London there can be no question. But how could American students of operatic records know whether history had not repeated itself with startling fidelity? When "La Traviata" was first performed in the English capital in the '50s, the exponent of Violetta's glorifying passion and redeeming consumption was Piccolomini. London went quite mad about her. People fought with one another for places in the opera house. Seats were sold at exorbitant prices.

Yet it is a matter of record that Piccolomini had a small voice and smaller ability as a singer. Her most potent charms appear to have been unbridled assurance and a beautiful pronunciation of Italian. When Borzo arrived in London the next season and sang Violetta without extravagance, with purity of taste and style and with artistic repose the amiable Britons awoke from their dream.

Those who know the London of to-day are aware that it is not incapable of entering into a new Piccolomini delusion. Those who remember that the great Piccolomini furore had its inception in press agent tricks, even inclusive of broken contracts, have naturally waited to hear Mme. Tetrazzini before deciding that all memories of colorature art and pure bel canto were to be effaced and a new standard set up for people who measure merit not by its approach to the ideal but by its superiority over what they have already known.

The claims set up for Mme. Tetrazzini by her San Francisco admirers were that if she ever came to New York she would drive Melba and Sembrich into unending seclusion. Similar predictions have recently been set afloat in West Thirty-fourth Street. Such talk does no real artist any good. It arouses the hostility of the partisans; it creates profound distrust in the minds of the impartial.

In the case of Mme. Tetrazzini it can be said that after last night's hearing it did grave injustice to a singer who has certain well-defined claims to popularity. The audience, ready as it was with the unfailing reception, was moved to vigorous and prolonged applause at the conclusion of the first act.

The cheers and the other glad noises could not have been greater had all memories been obliterated and the new singer's delivery accepted as the gospel of a new art. Even those industrious journals which take it to be their duty to create excitement when there is none must be hard put to it to overdraw the demonstration of last night's audience after the banquet scene.

That there was a most ominous silence after the duet with Germont in the second act may have been due to real interest in the art of delivering simple cantabile music with repose, finish and pathos or to disappointment at the absence of more feats of coloratura.

Like the traditional Violettas of old time Mme. Tetrazzini does not appear to be in any immediate danger of wasting away with consumption. Her figure is well nourished and her face is as round as the silver moon. But she is a woman of pleasing appearance for all that, and her smile is both generous and frequent. Her countenance cannot fairly be called mobile or sensitive, but for the workaday conventions of opera world it will suffice. And after all the singing is the thing.

Mme. Tetrazzini has a fresh, clear voice of pure soprano quality and of sufficient range, though other rôles must perhaps disclose its furthest flights above the staff. The perfectly unworn condition and youthful timbre of this voice are its largest charms, and to these must be added a splendid richness in the upper range. Indeed, the best part of the voice as heard last evening was from the G above the staff to the high C. The B flat in "Sempre Libera" was a tone of which any singer might have been proud. The high D in the same number was by no means so good, and the high E flat which the singer took in ending the scene was a head tone of thin quality and refused to stay on the pitch.

In colorature Mme. Tetrazzini quite justified much that had been written about her. She sang staccato with consummate ease, though not with the approved method of breathing. Her method is merely to check the flow between tones instead of lightly attacking each note separately. But the effect which she produces, that of detached notes rather than of strict staccato, is charming. Of her shake less can be said in praise. It was neither clear in emission nor steady, and the interval was surely at least open to question.

Descending scales she sang beautifully, with perfect smoothness and clean articulation. Her transformation of the plain scale in the opening cadenza of "Sempre libera" into a chromatic scale, though a departure from the letter of the score, was not at all out of taste, and its execution fully sustained its right to existence.

The ascending scales in the same number were sung in a manner which would not be tolerated by any reputable teacher in a pupil of a year's standing. They began with a tremulous and throaty *voce bianca* and ended in a sweep into a full medium, with the chest resonance carried up to a preposterous height.

The most notable shortcoming of Mme. Tetrazzini's singing as revealed last night was her extraordinary emission of her lower medium notes. These were all sung with a pinched glottis and with a color so pallid and a tremolo so pronounced that they were often not a bad imitation of the wailing of a cross infant. This style of tone production she carried into most of her recitative, till she seemed to be inclined to think that Violetta ought to show that fondness for "baby talk" which is sometimes accepted as a charm among her kind.

In cantilena the new soprano fell furthest below the demands of supreme vocal art. Her cantabile was uneven in tone quality, the breaks between her medium and her upper notes coming out most unpleasantly and her tricks of phrasing in short and spasmodic groups, with breath taken capriciously and without consideration of either text or music, were serious blots upon her delivery. For example, in beginning "Ah, fors e lui," she deliberately made a phrase after the u, and, taking a leisurely breath, introduced the i as if it belonged to the next word.

The continued employment of cold color in cantabile quite removed the possibility of pathos from "Non sapete," while a pitiless description of her infantile delivery of "Dite alla giovine" would read like cruelty. One of the neatest pieces of singing she did was her "Ah, se cio e ver," in which the staccato effect previously mentioned and some crisply executed diminutions in short phrase were excellent.

It is altogether probable that Mme. Tetrazzini will have a larger measure of real success when she sings the embroidered mad scene of "Lucia." Greater commendation from the public than it accorded her last night she can hardly expect. Her principal associates in the performance were Messrs. Bassi and Ancona, of whom the latter in his "Di Provenza" contributed a smooth and well considered piece of singing.

The record must be completed with the note that Mr. Hammerstein appeared on the stage to receive his share of the gratulation of the night and that several prima donnas of distinction assisted the lay members of the audience in applauding the newcomer. Mr. Campanini, the brother-in-law of the débutante, conducted.

5

The Conception of the Ideal Tone

December 20, 1908

A MAN NAMED TAYLOR HAS STARTED ONCE MORE
the interminable discussion about the teaching of
the art of singing. He has written a book called
"The Psychology of Singing," in which he begins
by noting that everyone is wrong. That is to say,
everyone now living is wrong. The dead masters
who used to occupy themselves with turning out
such singers as Tesi, Faustina, Caffarelli, Farinelli
and Senesino were perfectly right, and the reason
they were right was that they did not focus the
attention of their pupils on the vocal mechanism,
but on the idealization of tone.

Mr. Taylor is going to have a very pleasant time.
He will hear of things to his disadvantage from
the inventor of the "umbrella method" and from
other inventors of equally valuable short roads to
correct tone production. He will be called "vil-
lain" and other pet names by singing teachers who

confound their pupils with directions as to how to operate their cyoroid cartilages and their epiglottises and their palates. Nevertheless some people are going to sit up and take notice of what he has written, and it will do them good.

It would do many opera singers good if they would take to heart Mr. Taylor's thoughts on the office of the æsthetic powers in conceiving the beautiful tone. One of the most lamentable deficiencies of to-day's singing is the absence of a high ideal of tone. The majority of singers are seeking not quality but quantity. They desire to overpower, not move their hearers; and for the eagerness to accomplish this entirely worthless end we are chiefly indebted to the salvos of applause which ring through the opera houses when any singer emits an enormous sound, particularly if at the same time it is of high pitch. As touching upon this topic a letter to this writer seems at this point to be pertinent.

A few days ago *The Sun* had occasion to note a lapse of memory on the part of Maria Labia while she was singing the rôle of Santuzza at the Manhattan. At the same time mention was made of the fact that she had deliberately altered one or two phrases for the convenience of her voice. Apropos of this matter comes a somewhat heated letter from a music lover whose name seems to have a familiar sound. Thus he indites:

What? The alterations in Mme. Labia's Santuzza are due to lapse of memory? No, sir. She often declamates because she has not the voice to sing Santuzza as written by Mascagni. Here is why this great dramatic soprano never sang in Italy except in concerts. When we dagos want to see actresses we go to see Duse, Di Lorenzo, Mimi Agulia, &c.; when we want to see beautiful women and legs in silk tights we go to the vaudeville. But when we go to the opera we want to hear, first of all, voice, voice and voice. Other gifts are subordinate to that.

Please learn this: We dagos call dramatic sopranos those —indeed very few if any at present—who have voices to cope the dramatic situation created by the composer. We do not call dramatic sopranos singers who can declamate and act well. That's the question. Please excuse my English because I am a dago.   G. BALDASSARINI.

This is one of the frankest and most satisfying declarations of the operatic faith of the Italians of this city that has ever been given by anyone. Voice, voice, voice, and everything else subordinate to that. Indeed that is true. That explains why the exquisite vocal art of Bonci is wasted on his compatriots. He cannot make sound enough to please them. They would rather hear the reverberations of Mr. Zenatello's hard unsympathetic tones, because they are bigger and more brilliant.

What makes the enthusiasm of the railbirds at the Metropolitan when Caruso sings? Is it a fine perception of the perfect pose of his moderato, the effortless projection of the pure and vital tone of the middle register, or the "dramatic climax," which for these hearers comes only with a vocal *tour de force?*

This is a matter that leaves little or no room for discussion. When Mr. Baldassarini laments the failure of Miss Labia's voice to meet the dramatic situation designed by a composer he clearly means that the soprano cannot construct a crescendo of huge proportions; that, in plain English, she cannot scream loudly enough to penetrate to the marrow of a true Italian appreciation.

As to her rank in Italy, that is a matter which need not be discussed here. Possibly some of the younger Italians in this city will live long enough to learn that the rank of singers in their native land does not concern us. American artistic opinion is not manufactured in Italy, and it is by American opinion that these singers will have to be judged here. Not all the shoutings of the old guard behind the rail can make us believe a singer to be an artist when we know we are hearing nothing but voice, voice, voice.

Meanwhile this particular observer of musical doings begs leave to assure Mr. Baldassarini that Maria Labia would without doubt be found a highly acceptable singer in Italy, for dramatic sopranos, even of the type he describes, are extremely scarce there at the present time. It seems a great pity that Italians, with their lamentable prejudices against singers of other nationalities, should also be dissatisfied with one of their own people, simply because she cannot make a tone sufficiently piercing.

The impressionistic reader is respectfully requested not to construe these remarks as the proclamation of an opinion that Labia is a greater singer than Melba. The Australian prima donna is in the late summer of her glory, and she is still, as she always has been, a model for young students of vocal technic. In the first place Mme. Melba never screams. She never tries to force her voice to proportions not given to it by nature. She sings always within her limits and that is one reason why her tones are so rich, so smooth, so mellow.

It would be worth much time and money to a host of the young singers of this town if they would take one lesson a week by simply listening to Melba. This woman has an ideal conception of tone. She is seeking all the time for a pure, velvety, luscious quality—not for a huge volume. Secondly, she makes her exquisitely conceived tone carry by the rational process of focussing it correctly and floating it out to her hearers on the surface of a thin, steady, solid column of breath.

Gentle reader, did you ever nurse a particularly succulent piece of candy between the tip of your tongue and the hard roof of your mouth? Yes? Well, the next time you are listening to those succulent tones of Melba just think of them as vocal candy and of her as nursing them in that manner. This will come pretty near to indicating to you the spot where she focusses those wonderful tones.

Of course she does not think about that. What she thinks about is the quality. Her whole heart and soul were wrapped up in that quality till it became automatic with her. Now it comes in answer to her demand for a vehicle for the communication of her musical thought. That's the way a woman like Melba sings. She is not worrying about the operations of her palate or the back of her tongue.

If Mme. Tetrazzini had ever in her interesting life cherished a high ideal of tone, nothing under the canopy could have induced her to retain in her scale those pallid baby sounds which she is in the habit of producing in her lower range, especially in recitative. If she had ever had a high ideal of tone she would not have fallen into the habit of making violent transitions from her lower infant tones to full and sometimes forced tones in the upper middle register. Lovers of beauty in singing are startled and disappointed by such vocal tricks, although they inevitably gain the applause of those highly intelligent listeners who worship voice, voice and voice. The value of their applause may be measured by the fidelity with which they have clung to their idol of last season.

What is the matter with Geraldine Farrar? It is said that her health is far from good and that the defects in her singing this season are due to her want of physical power to support tone. This is what the irreverent might call nonsense. If Miss Farrar is in poor health and suffering from physical weakness she can support short and moderate tones perfectly, but perhaps not long and large ones. When she becomes tired, when her small stock of physical strength is exhausted, she will have either to cut her phrases or to sag from the pitch. But it is not inevitable that this must happen from the moment she appears on the stage. The truth is that in the last recent performance of "Carmen" Miss Farrar sang with sufficient power, but she did not sing her intervals correctly.

The true cause of Miss Farrar's faults are two. One of them is an unjust conception of tone. Largeness, power, brilliancy, are what this young woman has sought instead of mellowness, liquidity and perfect pose. But this writer is not disposed to lay much stress on Miss Farrar's shortcomings this season, for the excellent reason that she is not enjoying artistic repose. Among the other jarring elements in the present disturbed state of the Metropolitan Opera House caustic remarks upon the singing of some of the artists by the musical director are not the least.

Miss Farrar is said to have been a mark of especial consideration.

Richard Martin is the name of a young American tenor in the Metropolitan Opera House company. When he made his first appearance here everyone was pleased with his voice, for it is a real tenor and of most excellent quality. But Mr. Martin speedily disclosed the fact that he had enjoyed very little stage experience, and furthermore that he had almost no vocal resource.

This season he has had opportunity to show that he has been making progress. Owing to the failure of the amusing Quarti, Mr. Martin was called upon to study the rôle of Cavaradossi in "Tosca" in a few days. He mastered the music, but it was regarded as a foregone conclusion that he would sing it in a cold and perfunctory style. It was therefore an agreeable surprise last Saturday night to find that he had discovered his temperament. To be sure it is not a big temperament, but it is a lot better than none at all.

In the air beginning with the recitative "E lucevan le stelle" in Act III, Mr. Martin roused his audience to enthusiasm, and he did it by the legitimate expression. The secret of this achievement lay in the simple fact that he had acquired sufficient freedom of voice to lay aside restrictive circumspection in the delivery of tones and abandon himself to the sentiment of the scene. That one piece of singing gave promise for young Mr. Martin's future. There is hope for his ultimate success.

Mr. Hammerstein deserves gratitude for introducing to this public a tenor who possesses a lovely voice and a good ideal of tone. This is Mr. Constantino. He is a typical Italian tenor of the lyric variety, and his emotional flights are not lofty, but there is so much excellence in his tones that he is certain to become a favorite with the Manhattan audiences.

The shrewd Manhattan impresario has not been so successful in introducing such singers as Mme. Doria and Mme. Mariska-Aldrich. But the latter of these is suffering chiefly from inexperience. What she will eventually be cannot now be foretold. The highest development of the artist is the result of long self-study and criticism.

What a singer can do, but seldom is willing to

do, was demonstrated last week by Emma Trentini. When she sang Musetta she shrieked through the entire second act and transformed the little Bohemian into a musical as well as a temperamental cat. This is quite unnecessary. The impersonation of a vixen does not demand vixenish singing. Miss Trentini almost persuaded some of her hearers that this was her only way of singing, whereas on Wednesday night she proved that it was not.

On that evening she sang Antonia in the final act of Offenbach's "Les Contes d'Hoffmann." This is a rôle requiring sympathetic tone and fluent delivery. A hard or dark tone would so alter the expressional character of the music as to render null the most intelligent effort at interpretation—as the word is usually understood. Miss Trentini displayed a certain musical instinct in her treatment of the part, for she sang without forcing her tones and with an unusually mellow timbre.

It may be doubted whether this achievement was so much the result of artistic conception as of a certain natural dramatic instinct. That it worked for good in the impersonation is just now the point. It is equally worth noting that what Miss Trentini did from instinct can be done by an accomplished singer from intention.

Once a singer has acquired a perfect pose of tone, or, as it is commonly worded, has got the voice correctly placed, she can sing her tones in any way she chooses. If she needs a white tone she can produce it. If she needs a dark tone it is hers at will. A singer who cannot color her tones loses invaluable aid in the field of dramatic interpretation.

Singers are sometimes discouraged by the failure of the public to appreciate the delicacies of their art. But the public is not an expert and never will be. The few who perceive the excellences of the art of the singer rejoice at every evidence of insight into their mysteries. The general public enjoys only the total result. Ninety times out of ninety-one it lays down faults in singing to the natural character of the organ, and when the singing is beautiful it exclaims "Oh, what a beautiful voice!"

This, however, is a matter about which the singer need not concern himself. Was it not a tremendous triumph for Jean de Reszke with a voice of moderate beauty to convince the world that he was its greatest tenor? That indeed was a conquest of high art which every young singer might well yearn to emulate.

6

Pauline Viardot

May 22, 1910

THE DEATH ON WEDNESDAY OF PAULINE VIARDOT removed from the ranks of the living the last of the great coterie of singers which made the early half of the last century famous in the history of vocal art. She was first a pupil of her eminent father, who died in 1832. An extraordinary man was the elder Garcia. Rossini wrote the rôle of Almaviva for him and brought the first opera company to the city in 1825 and produced "Il Barbiere di Siviglia." The company included his son, Manuel Garcia, who lived to be more than a hundred years old, together with Angrisani, De Risch, Mme. Barbieri and Maria Garcia, later to be adored throughout the musical world as the matchless Malibran.

The elder Garcia wrote seventeen Spanish operas, nineteen Italian and seven French. It was in 1823 that he founded in London the celebrated Garcia school of singing, which was continued by his son. The elder Garcia's most noted pupils were his two wonderful daughters, Malibran and Pauline Viardot, his son Manuel, Mmes. Rimbault, Ruiz-Garcia, Favelli, Adolphe Nourrit (once the tenor idol of Paris) and Geraldy. The younger Manuel Garcia was the teacher of Jenny Lind.

Pauline Garcia was born in Paris July 18, 1821. As soon as her inclinations began to disclose themselves her parents hardly knew what to do with her, for she seemed to have talent for everything, though that for portrait painting appeared to be one of the strongest. When she was a child of about four she took lessons on the piano in this city from Marcos Vega. At the age of 8 after visiting Mexico with her father she became his accompanist in his teaching. While thus engaged she imbibed her first knowledge of the principles of good singing. Her mother gave her systematic instruction, but her father also kept her busy. He wrote parts for her in little operas performed at home. She confessed in after years that they contained difficulties much greater than any she had since met. Her piano studies were serious. For a time she was a pupil of Liszt; a real, not an advertised pupil.

After her father's death she made her vocal début in Brussels in 1837 with De Beriot, the distinguished violinist and second husband of Malibran, and afterward went on a concert tour with him. One of her feats at that time was the singing of a vocal composition called the "Cadenza del Diavolo," built on Tartini's violin variations, "Il Trillo del Diavolo." When she made her début in London in 1839 in "Otello" (Rossini's) the amateurs favored her because she was something like her distinguished sister Malibran. Some of them, however, discovered that she had individuality. Her dazzling bravura later captured the public and her popular success was then assured.

In the autumn she was engaged by Louis Viardot, impresario of the Théâtre Lyrique, Paris, and there she became one of the group of famous singers whose glory shines undimmed on the pages of vocal history. Among her companions were Giudetta Grisi, Persiani, the great tenor Rubini and the unequalled bass Lablache.

She became Mme. Viardot in 1840, and then went on tour in Italy, Spain, Germany, Russia and England. Her successes were triumphal. She returned to Paris in 1849 for Meyerbeer's production of "Le Prophète." The composer had chosen her to create the rôle of Fides. Moscheles wrote that "she was the life and soul of the opera, which owed to her at least half of its great success."

Mme. Viardot sang Fides not less than 200 times in various parts of Europe and carved so deeply the lines of the rôle that the mother of John of Leyden, as we of to-day know her, is the art work of this consummate artist. Mme. Viardot divided her principal labors between London and the Théâtre Lyrique of Paris from 1848 to 1858.

In 1859 came the great revival of Gluck's "Orfeo." The work had not been heard in Paris for thirty years. The score originally presented the rôle of Orfeo as written for the celebrated sopranist Guadagni, but Gluck subsequently transposed the part for Legros, the noted haut contre.

In doing this he made certain concessions in the way of ornamental notes and other traits out of keeping with the character of the rôle. The restoration of 1849 was made by Berlioz, and in this production Mme. Garcia, who reproduced the primitive effects with much skill, achieved what Clement and Larousse call "un succès d'enthousiasme, le plus grand peut-étre de sa carière théâtrale."

The success of this revival led to the preparation for 1861 of "Alceste." Berlioz had some hesitation in arranging this work, because of the perceptible failing of Mme. Viardot's voice and because he regarded the rôle itself as "well nigh inaccessible." Yet so admirable was her vocal art and so beautiful her interpretation that she was received with acclamations.

Those who wish to know what a mezzo-soprano of those times could sing (her voice ranged from low C to high F!) are commended to a view of her répertoire. It contained Desdemona (in Rossini's "Otello"), Cenerentola, Rosina, Norma, Arsace (in "Semiramide"), Camille (in "Orazzi e Curiazzi," Cimarosa), Amina, Romeo (in Bellini's "Montecchi e Capuletti"), Lucia, Maria di Rohan, Ninette, Leonora (in Donizetti's "Favorita"), Azucena, Donna Anna, Zerlina, Rahel, Iphigenie, Alice, Isabelle, Valentine, Fides and Orfeo.

Mme. Viardot settled in 1863 in Baden and after that appeared no more in opera. She was sometimes heard in concert. She devoted herself to composition. She wrote several short operas to librettos by Turgénieff and had them performed in her private theater by her pupils. One of her works, "Der letzte Zauberer," book by Richard Pohl, was publicly given in Weimar, Riga and Carlsruhe.

The Franco-Prussian war compelled her as a Frenchman's wife to leave Germany, and she returned to Paris, where she dwelt till the end. She taught singing and was for a time one of the professors at the Conservatoire. Among her pupils she numbered Marianne Brandt, the great mezzo-soprano who was one of the original Kundry impersonators at Bayreuth under the direction of Wagner and who is well remembered by older New York opera-goers. She was one of the company of German singers engaged by Dr. Leopold Damrosch for the season of 1884-85 at the Metropolitan Opera House and made her début in a memorable performance of "Fidelio" on November 19 of that season. She was here afterward in the Stanton régime and sang under Seidl and Walter Damrosch. Mme. Orgeni, who long enjoyed an international reputation as a teacher, was also a pupil of Viardot.

It should not be forgotten that the gifted daughter of Garcia wrote some charming songs and that the transcriptions of Chopin mazurkas which Jenny Lind used to sing with so much effect were made by this artist. Robert Schumann knew her well and dedicated to her the beautiful Liederkreis, opus 24.

Mme. Viardot was the owner of the original score of Mozart's "Don Giovanni" till she gave it to the library of the Grand Opéra. She also had the manuscript of Bach's cantata "Schmücke dich," of Mendelssohn's 42d Psalm and a scherzo by Beethoven.

To grasp the character of Pauline Viardot's art is not quite possible for us, who never heard her sing, never saw her slight frame shaken with the storm of passionate emotion nor felt the flame of her splendid eyes piercing us. George Sand and Liszt both wrote glowingly of her, and there is a beautiful and judicious record in the "Thirty Years' Recollections" of Henry Chorley, the distinguished English critic. Chorley expresses his regret that the first appearances of Mme. Viardot in London were not well planned. She sang first Desdemona in Rossini's "Otello."

The woman looked older than she was, and the voice, according to this astute critic, could never have sounded young. The maturity of adult feeling was in it. The girl was ill at ease, yet she convinced everyone that the stage was her home.

"Incomplete in its completeness" Chorley calls this first achievement, yet everyone knew that a new mistress of lyric art had arrived. When after several years she reappeared in London she had to live up to a reputation earned on the Continent, yet she appeared in "La Sonnambula." Unfortunately all London adored Persiani and Jenny Lind in Amina. Chorley says it was Lind's best part, which indicates just what sort of a singer the incomparable Jenny must have been.

Viardot was nervous. Her voice, always rebellious, refused perfect obedience; but she was not dismissed without commendation from the uncertain London public. She sang again, this time in "Les Huguenots." Her authority in the treatment of the music of Valentine was such that even the famous Grisi followed her style.

Again she sang her great rôle, Fides, in "Le Prophete," and Chorley declared her greatness.

"The intrinsic merits of this opera," he says, "will be discussed elsewhere, but here it must be repeated that our artist could set on the scene a homely burgher woman, with only maternal love and devotion to give her interest, and could so harmonize the improbabilities of a violent and gloomy story and of music much too forced as to make the world for a while accept it for its composer's masterpiece."

Chorley makes special note of what he calls her originating faculty, which appears to us to be a fine musicianship impelling her to discern the expressional value of neglected music. This is indicated by the fact that she brought out the recitative of Jezebel in Mendelssohn's "Elijah" in such a manner that its hitherto unnoticed excellence was made patent to all hearers. Chorley regarded as further evidence of this originating power her reconstruction of the rôle of Orfeo, in which her success was "beyond any triumph which the most sanguine and enthusiastic lover of the ancients could have anticipated." Farther on in the same admirable article he says:

"It may be doubted whether such a perfect rep-

resentative of Orpheus ever trod the stage as Mme.
Viardot. The part, originally written for an artificial Italian contralto, was subsequently transposed
to suit a high tenor French voice. That either
Guadagni or Legros could have satisfied the eye
may also be doubted. The Frenchman, we know,
was affected and grimacing in his action. As personated by Mme. Viardot it left nothing to desire."

Grace, simplicity and appropriateness were in
every pose and gesture. Her acting must have been
irresistible, for Chorley speaks of it in almost rapturous phrase. "The slight yet childish youth, with
the yearning that maketh the heart sick, question-
ing the white groups of shadows that moved slowly
through the Elysian fields, without finding his beloved one; the wondrous thrill of ecstasy which
spoke in every fiber of the frame, in the lip quiver-
ing with a smile of rapture too great to bear, in the
eye humid with delight, as it had been wet with
grief, at the moment of recognition and of granted
prayer—these things may have been dreamed of, but
assuredly they were never expressed before."

In the critic's comment on her singing we get a
good conception of her manner. "The peculiar

quality of Mme. Viardot's voice, its unevenness, its occasional harshness and feebleness—consistent with tones of the gentlest sweetness—was turned by her to account with rare felicity as giving the variety of light and shade to every word of soliloquy, to every appeal of dialogue. A more perfect and honeyed voice might have recalled the woman too often to fit with the idea of the youth. Her musical handling of so peculiar an instrument will take place in the highest annals of art."

Read and ponder that, all ye who believe that singing is *vox et preterea nihil*. But let Chorley continue:

"After the mournful woefulness of the opening scenes the kindling of hope and courage when *Love* points the way to the rescue were expressed by her as by one whom reverence had tied fast, but who felt that its law gave freedom to the believer. Her bravura at the end of the first act (the interpolation of which was sanctioned by Gluck, though the music is Bertoni's or Guadagni's—at all events not his own) showed the artist to be supreme in another light, in that grandeur of execution belonging to the old school, rapidly becoming a lost art. The

torrents of roulades, the chains of notes, unmean-
ing in themselves, were flung out with such exactness, limitless volubility and majesty as to convert
what is essentially a commonplace piece of parade
into one of those displays of passionate enthusiasm
to which nothing less florid could give scope."

The air to which Chorley refers was used in the
performance of "Orfeo" at the Metropolitan Opera
House last winter. It was written by Bertoni, not
by Guadagni. What the English critic says about
the character of Viardot's bravura bears out the regrets so often made in these columns, that the colorature singer of to-day does not know the secrets
of the overwhelming bravura artists of the past.
Could you for an instant apply to the delivery of
Tetrazzini or Melba the description of "exactness,
limitless volubility and majesty"? Certainly the
thought of majesty is far away. It is because we
have no truly dramatic bravura that we have no
adequate personator of Norma.

Pauline Viardot was the last link to connect us
actively with the remarkable generation of singers
which preceded that of Patti, Nilsson and Annie
Louise Carey. Sims Reeves sometimes sang in Lon-

don among these stars, but the names of Grisi,
Mario, Steffanone, Persiani, Alboni, Roconi, Tamberlik, Susini, Lablache and all the rest of that
splendid society of stars belong to history.

Mme. Viardot is not even a memory to the present race of operagoers, but her art may perhaps live
in some measure in the teaching of her pupils, who
should be able to hand down to their students some
of the secrets of the "grand style" so admired by the
cognoscenti of "the thirties."

7

The Present and the Past

February 26, 1911

SOME READERS OF THIS DEPARTMENT OF *The Sun*
have written recently to its editor asking him
whether he believed that there were no great singers
now living, whether he thought that all the good
singers were embalmed in histories, whether he believed that the method of singing taught by the
early Italian masters could be applied to the music
of to-day and whether he would not be kind enough
to point out what singers of to-day had perfect
methods.

This constitutes what our transatlantic cousins
might call "a tall order." Yet much of the ground
can be cleared by the proposition of a single belief
cherished by this writer: The singers of the early
eighteenth century would have to acquire a totally
new style in order to sing the operatic music of
to-day, but they would not have to learn a new
technique.

Mr. Caruso would have to acquire a new style to sing the music of Handel, but he would perhaps have very little to add to his present technique. Just how much facility he possesses in the delivery of florid music it is impossible to tell, as we have not heard him sing any of it; but his voice is so well posed, his tone production so free and natural and his voice so flexible in nuance that there is every reason to suppose that he can sing florid music well.

The famous operatic artists of the early eighteenth century were distinguished for their perfect tone production, their easy mastery of rapid passages, their exquisite treatment of the pure legato and their tenderness of expression in pathetic arias. These are the fundamental elements of good singing.

They must be acquired before the singer is competent to deliver the more declamatory compositions of contemporaneous masters. It is not merely an opinion of this writer that the singers of to-day do not thoroughly ground themselves in these fundamentals. It is a fact. Teachers of singing all over the world testify to it. They declare that their pupils are unwilling to spend the time to go through the old courses of study. They refuse to apply themselves to such things as the vocalises of Concone. They demand that after a few preparatory lessons in tone placing they be put to work on repertoire. They expect to graduate from the studio in about two years. People who are not in touch with the profession of music cannot know the real conditions.

These singers are no more fit to enter upon a professional career than a pianist who has not mastered scale playing or a violinist who is not sure of all the positions. The singer has the advantage of the instrumental performer in that he carries his charm within himself. An untrained voice which has been skillfully coached in certain rôles may earn its possessor a swift and easy success. It is this that the singers desire.

Many of these half trained singers are capable of giving interesting operatic impersonations for the simple reason that they distract attention from their vocal defects by a display of dramatic temperament or clever stage business. Furthermore some of these half trained singers have real musical instincts and sing with much interpretative eloquence.

What the writer of this department of *The Sun* regrets is the sad loss of opportunity among just such singers. They are content with half way things. They are satisfied with the easily obtained applause of the opera house crowd, of which the discriminating part is naturally the minority. They make no progress. They never reach the limit of their own possibilities. And whenever they are called upon to sing music demanding for its proper execution skill in the fundamentals of song they fail to reach the standard of excellence which has been accepted by connoisseurs ever since singing was recognized as a fine art.

The Sun's musical chronicler has often regretted that he could not gratify more operagoers by rhapsodizing as they do about certain beautiful personalities. But musical criticism has no very great concern with personalities except as disclosed in musical art. When they evade musical art and seek to influence the public by other means it is the unpleasant duty of the critic to call attention to that fact. It is his business to prevent, so far as is in his very limited power, public adoration of false gods.

The argument put forward at the present day

is that the study of singing in the old fashion is no longer necessary, because the style of the music is altogether different. This argument rests upon a confusion of ideas. The character of the music to be sung has no bearing whatever upon the manner in which the singer should be trained in the technics of his art. When a young man sets out to become a pianist he does not study along certain lines for the express purpose of becoming a Chopin player. He applies himself to the general technic of the piano and when he has mastered it he possesses the mechanical means with which to play anything.

In singing the truth is quite the same. The vocal artist must first acquire the general technics of singing, and these are in certain sense mechanical. The technic of the singer rests first of all on the perfect formation of tone, the equalization of the scale from top to bottom of the voice, the management of the breath so that the tone shall be properly fed and the training of the vocal organs to attack with readiness and certainty any possible succession of notes in either quick or slow time.

When the singer has mastered these elements of technic he is prepared to sing any music from that of Handel to that of Richard Strauss. All that comes after the mastering of the technic is musicianship and style. Singers used to have great difficulty with the music of Wagner, not because it was unsingable but because their ears had never been trained to Wagner's harmonic conceptions. Singers will laugh at you if you tell them in these days that Wagner is unsingable. Some singers have voices unsuited to Wagner's music, but even they are equal to its technical demands. If anyone supposes that Mr. Caruso cannot sing the notes of Tristan or Parsifal he is mistaken. But the style would be foreign to him.

When *The Sun's* chronicler of musical doings laments the lack of thorough vocal training in the ranks of opera singers he is doing only what hundreds of old time opera-goers are doing. He is lamenting the want of adequate technic, not the absence of beautiful voices, gifted natures and splendid theatrical talents.

But this writer must be excused from attempting to enumerate the sheep and the goats. Nothing can be gained by such a proceeding. No one would be any wiser than he is now. Those who do not know well-founded singing when they hear it cannot be taught to do so by a newspaper article.

There is one other point to which reference may be made, because it really needs a little clearing up. Whenever a critic expresses regret for the "good old times" he is accused of inability to live in the present. He is getting old, they say, and he is sour. He looks at all things through green spectacles, and he suffers from "indigestion." Oh, indigestion, what things are done in thy name! If it were not for you Geraldine Farrar's Juliette—but she does not look as if she suffered from indigestion.

The present writer would like to speak a word for his brethren, but that would be presumptuous. He will venture only to say that if they are old they do not know it and if they are unhappy they are the best aggregation of actors he has ever seen. They should be engaged for the New Theatre. They would cheer it up. As for himself, this writer can only say that he is getting younger every year and that he finds the present charged with keenest interest to its very lips. But none the less he is satisfied that it is a period of musical transition and that perhaps after he has passed beyond the consideration of earthly problems the experimental labors of D'Indy, Strauss, Debussy, Reger and the rest will lead to new and noble things in musical art.

Singing too will not pause, and the recognition of the immortality of its fundamental principles will come again about the same time as the perception that music cannot be composed without regard for the basic laws of design. New forms, new manners, new styles and even new methods will come with new creative minds; but since the Greeks first built their scales of two like tetrachords the law of balance and rhythmic distribution of parts in music has reigned and it will continue to do so.

But musical art has not pursued the way of progress like a stream flowing through a valley. It has advanced rather like the rising tide in waves, each rolling forward and receding, but continually moving further and further forward. Writers on music many times now far back in history have lamented the "good old days," and the utterances of these are pointed out as evidence that critics have always made the same sort of complaint. As matter of fact nothing of the sort is true. All that the real student of history has to do is compare the comments with the facts.

For example, one reads Mancini and finds him complaining about the decadence of vocal art in his day. But history shows us that there was a decadence just at that time (about 1796). When you read Chorley (fifty years later) you find him penning enthusiastic praises of famous singers of his time. You do not read any lamentations about the older days. Investigation shows that Chorley was right. The era of Malibran, Grisi, Rubini, Mario, Ronconi, Tamburini and Lablache was one in which the critical commentator could bask in the sunshine of delight.

A pursuit of this method of inquiry will very quickly satisfy the student that critics have not always been a sour brood, grumbling at what is and lamenting the absence of what is not. They have from time to time bewailed the decadence of their periods and usually with good reason. The inevitable reaction has caused the next generation of critics to sing pæans of glorification simply because there was something to glorify. But no one mentions these critics.

And in conclusion one final word about that dearly beloved old bugbear indigestion. Of all the comfortable and prosperous knights of the trencher known to this writer there are none to excel his brethren of the gray goose quill. They all eat with unction and smoke their after dinner cigars with satisfaction. One or two of them have a little gout, to be sure; but what would you? Can men feast all their lives on the riches of music and not grow gouty? Fie upon you, uncharitable reader! Dost think there shall be no more cakes and ale?

The Sun's chronicler of musical doings is writing this beside a window into which the splendid sunshine streams in almost intolerable glory. The sky is of that soft yet brilliant cobalt, veiled in tender gray, which is seen only in the Western world. A sweet breeze is blowing out of the inviting south. A thousand varicolored flags are dancing to its Aeolian music. It is very, very good to be alive. There may be unfortunate creatures who suffer from indigestion, but they must dwell in some other sphere. This one is filled with delight. Beauty is everywhere and life feeds upon it.

The Need of a Standard in Voice Production

January, 1913

FERREIN'S TREATISE ON THE VOCAL ORGANS WAS published in 1741. But it was more than half a century later that his ideas appeared to have any general influence. In the first thirty years of the nineteenth century several works on the same subject were put forth. Not, however, till Garcia invented the laryngoscope, in 1855, was there any real scientific application of the study of physiology to singing. Since that time the growth of vocal science has been large, and methods of investigation of the formation of the singing tone have advanced far beyond the fondest dreams of Garcia.

Cerone, a Spaniard, published in 1613 his *Il Melopeo*, a treatise on the rules of singing. In it we learn that at this period chest and head registers were recognized, that the classification of voices according to their timbers had been made, that emission of tone had been studied and reduced to a system, and that style and hygiene of the voice were both considerations in the daily curriculum of the studios. Lest we permit ourselves to be astonished we must recall the historical fact that Pope Sylvester founded singing schools in 1314, and that the church music was taken out of the hands of the congregation and placed in those of a trained choir as early as 367. In Cerone's day all the vocal ornaments performed by Tetrazzini were familiar to such famous singers as Victoria Archilei and Leonora Baroni. In fact, the whole foundation of the so-called "Italian method" had been laid. The codification of its laws was completed in the course of the seventeenth century, and when the great schools of 1700 were sending forth such famous singers as Farinelli, Caffarelli, Cuzzoni and Faustina, everything was known about singing that is known now—except the physiological laws. Of those, nothing whatever had been discovered, yet these schools produced the greatest singers the world has ever heard.

Now what is the matter? Is the physiological basis of singing of no practical value to the singing teacher? In the time of Porpora, Leo, Redi, and the other eminent teachers of the early eighteenth century the empirical method of instruction was the only basis of vocal art. Let us, if you please, call it the suggestive method. Its fundamental principles are set forth in Tosi's treatise. To allow the voice to flow freely without nasality and without throat constriction was the prime requisite. This was taught by example and by helping the pupil to acquire mental conceptions of the required tone. He was shown that the most important of all things for him to accomplish was perfect freedom. He must never let his throat or his nose interfere. Which, of course, meant that he must never shut off any of his resonance chambers or exert any muscular effort antagonistic to a perfectly normal condition of the organs. This empirical, psychological or suggestive method of teaching was the exclusive basis of vocal art up to the time when the physicians began to publish their descriptions of the tone-forming organs. During the years when the empirical method was employed, apt pupils acquired a vocal method so excellent as to enable them to conquer the world. Shall we, therefore, say that the revelation of scientific knowledge of tone-formation has worked injury to vocal art? For we know that ideal tone-production is excessively rare among the singers of to-day.

The fault is assuredly not to be laid at the door of science, for the progress of science makes truth clearer. It is undeniable that up to the present we have not acquired a complete body of indisputable scientific laws, for the doctors do not yet agree. We cannot hesitate, however, to declare that among the differences as to details which are found in the publications of voice investigators we have yet to find any final demonstration of basic error in the musical conception of tone acquired by the first great masters of song.

What is it then, that is wrong? I decline to assume the responsibility of deciding. But while for some centuries the psychological or suggestive method of teaching was the only one in use, there has not been a time when the scientific or physiological basis has been exclusive. I will venture to express my belief that it never can become the exclusive basis, but no educated man will deny that its acquired facts demand recognition by voice teachers. The only certain knowledge is that which is capable of scientific demonstration.

Every scientist will agree that an accurate and informing terminology is a first desideratum of knowledge. It is there, I think, that the chasm between the teacher and the physicist remains as wide as it was in the beginning. Too many vocal teachers have been alarmed at the apparent intricacy of the physiology of the organs of tone. They have perhaps looked timidly into some of the simpler treatises, such as Sir Morell Mackenzie's "Hygiene of the Voice," have gathered a few uncertain ideas, and have forthwith endeavored to apply them to their practice.

They have struggled vainly to reconcile their construction of the meaning of the time-honored figurative terminology of their profession with some scientific facts set forth by physicians. They have had a stock of names, such as chest and head registers, invented in the childhood of voice study in order to designate ideas conveniently which could not then be designated scientifically. They have tried to make these terms square with physiological theories. They sometimes inform their pupils that head-tones find their entire resonance in the frontal sinus and chest-tones in the lower pharynx. Some have even located tones in the sphenoidal sinus. I take it for granted that no laryngologist within the sound of my voice believes that any beautiful and correct singing-tone can be produced without a harmonious operation of all the resonating cavities.

The pupil who forms a picture of his highest tones as vibrating in the topmost resonance chambers sometimes arrives at a notion that these chambers are directly concerned in establishing the pitch of the tone, and thus we find not only some students, but also some teachers, talking learnedly about throwing the upper tones up into the head in order to get them at all. Such ideas rest upon insufficient scientific information and upon a worn-out and misleading terminology. It is pretty generally accepted in these days that pitch is determined at the seat of tone formation, the larynx, and that the resonating cavities are not creators, but qualifiers.

It seems to me that the path out of the wilderness must be opened by the coöperation of scientific investigators of tone-formation. It is for them to formulate the vital facts and to present them in language which will clear away all confusion of terms and consequent confusion of ideas. Every singing teacher ought to be thoroughly acquainted with the physiological basis of voice instruction. Every medical student of vocal organism should recognize the boundaries which separate the physiological laws from the psychological. In this way a general and authoritative science might be built up, and upon it a correct method of teaching tone-production. An end would be put to the ridiculous claims of those teachers who assert that they have a method different from any other and therefore far better. The real value of the teacher would be determined by his skill in teaching established truths, not by his assurance in boasting.

This blissful state can be attained only by a closer union between teachers of the gentle art of voice production and physicians and other scientists who make a special study of the operation of the vocal organs. The radical evil of vocal teaching at this time is the endeavor of singing teachers who do not understand the physiology of the throat to make their pupils get results by the voluntary movement of certain muscles. It is susceptible of scientific demonstration, unless I am utterly mistaken, that many essential muscles in the formation of tone are involuntary muscles and cannot be directed by the will.

But there are many other muscles which can be directed by it and which can be brought to bear on the organs of the throat in such a way as to interfere with normal tone-formation. And it is these muscles which some teachers are causing their pupils to operate incorrectly, to the enormous detriment of their singing.

Exposure of this evil lies within the province of the scientific investigator. But the teacher must be sufficiently fond of the truth and not too devoted to his own ill-grounded claims to originality to accept a scientific fact when it is held up before his eyes.

I may perhaps be pardoned if in closing I refer to my own calling. The exigencies of daily newspaper writing preclude the possibility of detailed or scientific voice analysis; but it is my humble opinion that the generalizations which constitute the vast bulk of newspaper comment might, without great difficulty, be brought into closer harmony with scientific truth and by precisely the same means as teaching should be.

9

Mme. Galli-Curci

February 2, 1918

THE REVELATION OF THE GIFTS AND ACCOMPLISH-
ments of Amelita Galli-Curci having been triumphantly performed, the world of opera resumes its
peaceful progress. It is a great pity that so richly
endowed, cultivated and gracious a woman should
have been heralded as if she were a new breakfast
food or a freak in vaudeville. But it seems that even
opera must now sometimes be delivered over to
agitators who treat it as if it were not an art, but a
newly invented intoxicant.

If Mme. Galli-Curci had come into New York
without the previous publication of an astonishing
variety of rumors and rhapsodies, her artistic success would have been precisely the same. But she
might not have been received by an audience whose
verdict was apparently formed before it entered
the theater and which received her with screams
and waving of handkerchiefs before she had sung
a note.

People sitting in the neighborhood of *The Sun's*
representative were in a state of excitement amazing
to witness. One woman, well dressed and bearing
the marks of a comfortable station in life, leaped up
and down in her seat and incoherently shouted:
"Whee! Whee! Whee!"

Well, despite the calm and unimpassioned accounts which appeared in some of the newspapers
the next morning, the records of their own files
will prove that there was far greater hysteria over
the début of Tetrazzini. On that memorable occasion women also waved handkerchiefs and
screamed, and men threw their hats into the air,
people leaped upon their seats and cheered, and
there was a scene bordering on pandemonium.
Eight months later a dead calm prevailed upon
those once turbulent seas and within two years it
became difficult to induce people to go to hear
Tetrazzini.

All of which is here recounted merely to expose
the worthlessness of réclame. When Adelina Patti
made her debut at the Academy of Music in 1859,
singing Lucia, the leading music critic of this town
wrote one-third of a column about her. Incidentally
he remarked with judicial calm that one of the rare

stars that infrequently illuminated the lyric heavens
had surely appeared. Patti did not fade away in two
or three years but had a career of some forty seasons.

Prophecy is no part of musical comment, but
there is ground for hope that Mme. Galli-Curci will
not be a passing meteor but a fixed star. She has
sound merits, substantial voice and art and a personal charm. Many tales have been told about her
almost miraculous gifts. It is said that she never
studied vocal technique. The story is improbable
but not impossible. But if she never "studied voice,"
as the musicians express it, then she is certainly a
good musician, for her conception of tone is just
and her treatment of phrase and melodic line most
fastidious.

To most opera-goers the beginning and the middle and the end of all singing is voice. It rarely occurs to them that by bad treatment the tones of a
beautiful voice can be deprived of their character.
Mme. Galli-Curci has a very beautiful voice, one
which has a flute-like color throughout, but which
excels the flute in the richness of its upper scale. It is
a well equalized voice, with a fine welding of regis-

ters. It is a voice of abundant power, but the singer with rare wisdom permits it to flow normally and does not force it. It is a voice of unsurpassed elasticity, lending itself readily to gradations of power, which its owner employs with most delicate musical skill and admirable taste.

In the delivery of sustained melodic phrases Mme. Galli-Curci shows that she is genuinely musical. Her cantilena is that of a real artist. Her coloratura is continent, well arranged and executed with perfect grace. There is no attempt at mere fireworks. Mme. Galli-Curci apparently is not bent upon performing feats to amaze her hearers, but seems rather to aim at displaying a purely decorative pattern of exquisite beauty and finish. If her future performances confirm this impression the present writer will have lively confidence in her permanent popularity.

Singers who astonish, amaze, astound, come and go. Their lives are brief and exciting. Each has his little bag of tricks. You go the first time and are almost dazed. You go the second time and lo! you hear the same feats again. You are astonished. You go the third time and out come the old "stunts" once more. You are now calm and observant. You go the fourth time and once more hear the now wearisome prestidigitation. You do not go the fifth time. You take a long rest before you try it again and when you do you mentally exclaim: "Would that she might learn a new trick!"

The singers who keep our affection year after year, as Sembrich and Melba did, as Caruso does, have something more than vocal acrobatics to offer. They sing music to us, not "stunts." Mme. Galli-Curci seems to be of a mind to do likewise, and for that we should all be grateful, for if she clings to true musical ideals she will be able to give us delight for years to come.

Naturally many people insist on comparison of the new prima donna with other famous singers. But comparisons have no value at all. It is necessary first of all to prove that the singer with whom you compare a newcomer was perfect or almost so. This cannot be done. There has never been a perfect singer. Every one of the famous birds of song, male and female, has had some faults.

Some of the most celebrated operatic impersonators have had recalcitrant voices, laborious methods and imperfect general equipment, but have mastered the public by sheer force of interpretative genius. Only a few have approached the mechanical equality of a fine instrument.

On the other hand, there is a tendency to overrate the achievements of the latest arrival by the employment of comparisons based on lack of information or on pure ignorance. A woman sitting within hearing of *The Sun* recorder on the evening of Mme. Galli-Curci's début, exclaimed, "There has been nothing like it since Patti!" If she was referring, as I believe she was, to the enthusiasm over the new revelation, it should be recalled that Patti made her début in 1859. If she meant the voice and art of the new singer, then one understands that when the divine Adelina last sang here, an old and decrepit shadow of herself, the young woman who spoke of her on Monday evening was about 10 years of age.

Mme. Galli-Curci is too fine and sincere an artist to need bolstering up by ill-grounded comparisons. The present generation of opera-goers can gather no information from vague statements that her voice has some of the quality of Patti's, that her tenderness of expression resembles that of Gerster, that she seems to be a musician just as Sembrich is, or that she makes a crescendo trill much as Melba did when she first came.

Meanwhile, it is worthy of note that the operatic public still loves a colorature singer. All that has been accomplished in the various reformations of the lyric drama can be temporarily overthrown in a moment by the caroling of a florid singer. We solemnly make our profession of faith in the dramatic verities, and vow that the opera is but a higher form of the poetic play; but let some composer present to us an insane heroine who trips about the stage scattering trills and staccati as she goes and we dismiss all thoughts of high art except that which dwells in the same regions as a high E flat.

The reign of the virtuoso will probably never end, and, indeed, so long as we do not permit virtuosity to enslave us there is no good reason why it should. But it would be a grave error for opera-

goers to regard Mme. Galli-Curci as a mere presti-
digitator of scales and juggler of trills. She is an
artist of feeling and taste and she sings a remarkably
good cantilena which has beauty and tenderness
to commend it.

10

Adelina Patti

October 5, 1919

THE YOUNGER GENERATIONS OF OPERA-GOERS WILL probably smile at the grave faces of their fathers and grandfathers who say in hushed accents, "So Patti is dead." The children little realize what the passing of a Patti means to the fathers. If the morning prints suddenly announced the last hour of Geraldine Farrar they would perceive a distinct personal relation and a ground for genuine sorrow. But Patti is to them nothing but a name enshrined in ancient history.

Without doubt most young enthusiasts find themselves secretly convinced that this much praised Patti was not quite as good a singer as their own adored Galli-Curci. Nor will they be moved by the testimony of those who have heard both. Others who remember Melba in her prime will be equally certain that she was greater than Patti, while still others will say: "They may talk as they please about the Divine Adelina, but I am sure she was never as fine as Sembrich."

All of which is as old as art and even older. It is as old as humanity. When Albert Niemann declared it to be his belief that Patti was the greatest singer that ever lived he was doing just what these others do. That which was present before him obscured all else. He had heard Patti. He never heard Agujari or Catalani. He had only read about them.

Yet when a singer passes away it is natural that even the younger opera lovers should say in the classic speech of their time, "Was she so very wonderful?" And then the prosy old historian is forced to ask, "What do you understand by wonderful?"

Perhaps after all it is the correct word, for let it once be accepted that a singer is a supreme exponent of florid music and all that the world asks of her is that she astonish it. Patti's "Home, Sweet Home," was very pretty and so was her "Suanee Ribber," but as a matter of fact Christine Nilsson sang both with far more tenderness, while in the voice of Etelka Gerster there was a note of feeling which excelled Patti's in some of her best rôles, such as Violetta, Amina and Lucia.

On the other hand Ilma di Murska could perform feats of agility which Patti would never have ventured to attempt. Why was Patti ranked so high, then? Because of her unique combination of voice, technique and taste.

Of course Patti was a colorature singer because she could sing colorature rôles such as Rosina, Lucia and Semiramide, incomparably. Her Martha was bewitching. But she shone with equal splendor in the rôle of Violetta in "La Traviata," a rôle commonly classed as colorature, whereas it ceases to be such after its first scene. Yet there lies the pit into which many an aspiring young singer has heavily, indeed fatally, fallen.

But the rôle has its charm for singers. Christine Nilsson selected it for her Parisian début, yet she is remembered better as Mignon and even Elsa. Lillian Nordica began with it and never abandoned it even after she had become a Brunnhilde and Isolde. Lilli Lehmann took it to heart early in her career. In the summer of 1907 the writer called on the great singer at her home just outside of Berlin. He inquired whether she would pass the summer at her habitual retreat in Tyrol.

"Yes," she replied; "but first I must fill an engagement of three nights in Ischl."

"And what will you sing?"

A beautiful and yet somewhat roguish smile broke across her noble face as she said in half-whispered accents:

"Violetta."

Still later at Salzburg she sang Donna Anna according to Mr. Scotti and Miss Farrar, who were in the cast, as no other living woman could. But to return to Violetta. The vocal tests of the rôle are "Ah, fors e lui" and "Sempre libera," which are the component parts of the brilliant finale of the first act, "Dite alla Giovine" in act two, the finale of the ballroom scene, and in the last scene "Addio del passato" and the duet "Parigi, O cara." Of these only "Sempre libera" demands mastery of colorature. The others are essentially lyric and ask for a perfect cantilena and the ability to express a tender if not profound pathos. That the pathos became heart moving when Sembrich sang the rôle was due to the supreme musicianship of the artist and to the peculiar qualities of that voice which could so thrill in Schumann's cycle, "Woman's Life and Love."

Patti's name will stand on the pages of musical history as that of a singer in whom luscious beauty of voice, admirable facility in florid music and exquisite, ravishing beauty in pure cantilena were happily united. Without this union she would not have been the matchless Patti. Who remembers the mere vocal acrobats? The world has its madness about them while they last, but only the truly great singers earn the somewhat doubtful immortality of history. People have gone exceeding daft over Mme. Tetrazzini, and yet Bernardine Hamaekers, one of the wonders of Paris opera from 1857 to 1870, surpassed her in some of her own specialties.

It is recorded by historians that Bernardine sang a trill in "Caro nome" lasting one minute by the watch. But Bernardine had attractions beyond her trill. Dukes bought her diamonds and nobles built her palaces. She was very popular.

About the time she was retiring Emma Calvé made her début at the Grand Opera as Marguerite and she was the best exponent of that rôle the present writer ever heard. Also she sang Ophelia in Ambroise Thomas's "Hamlet," with a mad scene of dazzling brilliancy. Yet she is best remembered as Carmen and Santuzza.

Patti's fame will undoubtedly rest largely on the technical perfection of her singing. There have been very many famous colorature sopranos beginning with Vittoria Archilei, the Euridice in Peri's opera of that name, in 1600. There were also Francesca Caccini, Leonora Baroni, the Lulli girls, and later Cuzzoni and Faustina. But we have pretty accurate accounts of their vocal feats, their cantilena, their cadenzas and their shortcomings. By a process of careful comparison we are forced to believe that Patti possessed most of their merits and almost none of their faults.

In an article in *Munsey's Magazine* for November, 1907, the present writer referred to this matter, saying:

"Agujari and Catalani had more extraordinary voices, but the former had little else, while the latter failed wholly in simple and plaintive melodies. Pasta and Grisi excelled Patti in the splendor of their dramatic powers, but neither could equal her in the flawless emission of tones. Malibran, the great daughter of Manuel Garcia, had a style which was marred by questionable taste in ornament.

"Doubtless Patti's greatest rival in facility and elegance was Jenny Lind, but Patti's voice was more extensive, more rich and more thoroughly equalized. Mme. Patti executed all the dazzling cadenzas of her rôles with consummate ease, exquisite taste and a perfect quality of tone. She sang sentimental numbers, such as 'Ah, fors e lui' in 'Traviata,' faultlessly. Her Zerlina in 'Don Giovanni,' Rosina in 'Il Barbiere' and Martha in Flotow's opera will doubtless remain the models of vocal ease, abandon and spontaneity, and the highest embodiments of elegant and vivacious comedy in the domain of opera."

In the same article the writer expressed regret that the famous soprano was one of the last representatives of a school of singing that was slowly dying out. Fortunately there have been some indications in recent years that pure singing, as distinguished from so called "interpretation" without the foundations of technique, is still regarded as worth while. The adulation of Mme. Tetrazzini and Mme. Galli-Curci shows that the public is still ready to enthrone the singer.

It is true that lack of perfect examples has permitted a depreciation in public taste and that much very bad singing is now mistaken for art; but let half a dozen real singers appear above the horizon and all this will quickly be changed. It is no new incident in comedy that the valet is mistaken for the nobleman till the real lord appears upon the scene.

Doubtless some of the younger readers of this department of *The Sun* would with interest steep their spirits in a detailed comparison of Mme. Patti with the reigning "queens of song." The writer can discern no great profit in such a comparison. If, for instance, he assures these readers that their adored Galli-Curci is not worthy to be discussed beside Patti they must at once dismiss him as an old fogy who has lost the zest of life. Then might arise even some adorers of Mme. Barrientos to present her claims, and to them the writer would be forced to bring the still greater shock of his conviction that Mabel Garrison is a better singer than the Spaniard.

No, the method of criticism by comparison, even at its best, is unsatisfactory. All one can do is to paraphrase Kipling and declare that Patti was Patti and when you have said that you have but come to the beginnings of knowledge. It is more encouraging for us to contemplate the future and to cherish the hope that the ardent pursuit of high vocal ideals may once more become general. No one wishes to hear a violin badly played, with a rough quality of tone, a scratchy bow, false intonation and a slovenly style, even though it be true (which is disputable) that the violin is the most expressive instrument. Yet people go to the opera and listen to just such treatment of beautiful natural voices and applaud rapturously. The cure for this is in the power of the singers. Let them sing, if not as well as Patti, as near to it as they can.

11

Enrico Caruso

August 3, 1921

ENRICO CARUSO WILL BE ACCORDED A PLACE IN THE list of the great tenors of operatic history. He will be mentioned in the future as Crivelli, Rubini and Mario are now. His voice was originally purely lyriç, a smooth, mellow, sonorous but not heavy voice, but beyond all question the most beautiful tenor heard by any living operagoer. His early successes in New York were in lyric rôles in such operas as "La Boheme," "Tosca," "L'Elisir d'Amore," "La Gioconda," with occasional excursions into the more dramatic realms of "Aida." In those days his voice had the charm of a velvety mellowness coupled with richness and sustained equality quite incomparable.

When the years have made the perspective clearer the most sensitive among music lovers will recall his delivery of the great arias "Cielo e mar" and "Furtiva Lagrima" as the loftiest flights of his lyric genius. His ambition, however, was to shine in more heroic parts and in the course of a few years he developed that powerful medium register which he used with such brilliant declamatory effect in "Samson and Delila" and "La Juive" and "Le Prophete." In doing this he sacrificed something of the transparent purity of tone which was one of the most beautiful traits of his earlier singing. He acquired a new manner of attack, more vigorous and explosive, but lost nothing of the pealing brilliancy of his high tones. Sometimes, too, he was impelled, if not compelled, to undertake parts foreign to his gifts and methods, but to such parts he gave a devotion and an unselfish artistic effort which should never be forgotten. Let those who think of Caruso as a victor in easy triumphs recall his achievement in Charpentier's "Julien."

The famous tenor's voice was not unusual in range. It extended through the typical two octaves from C to C and in his earlier days was almost perfectly equalized, but in recent years there appeared a marked difference between the upper and lower octaves. The character of this unique voice was due partly to a perfect balance of the vocal muscles given by nature and largely to a technique which was admirable in its ease and freedom. Caruso had also a remarkable lung capacity, excellently controlled and this enabled him to sing extraordinarily long phrases with fine sustaining power.

No other tenor remembered by living opera-goers had so beautiful a voice. No other had a better technic. But in range of conception, in ability to dramatize ideas and emotions with the voice, in power to give interpretations complete illusion, some others excelled him. In sincerity, in fervor, in devotion to his art, he was the peer of any opera singer in history. His growth in dramatic skill was observed with deep interest by all music lovers in the years of his New York activities. He was an indifferent actor and a supreme singer when he came here. He finished his career a singer less flawless, but an operatic interpreter who commanded the respect and sympathy of the severest critics, even when they could not credit him with triumphant success.

Mr. Caruso made his début here in the consulship of Heinrich Conried, who knew very little about opera, but who was an experienced theatrical manager and a trained actor. Conried may or may not have perceived that in the new tenor he had a singer of unusual quality, but he saw at once that Mr. Caruso had not the vaguest notions of stage dress.

When the great tenor revealed himself to New York he wore clothes that did not fit him; that were made of very poor materials; that had neither style nor distinction. He looked like a star just drawn from a "barnstorming" company. The poverty of his dress was accentuated by his very bad acting. He was indescribably awkward. His walk was that of a peasant. His gestures lacked both direction and purpose. His poses were invariably undignified.

The writer of these lines would like to rehearse some of his conversations with Mr. Conried, but unfortunately that shrewd showman imposed upon him the pledge of confidence. But there is no betrayal of good faith in the statement that the impresario's first labors with the great tenor were directed to impressing upon him the importance of costume and deportment on the stage.

In his early seasons here Mr. Caruso sometimes made astonishing excursions into the realm of the picturesque in dress, but in the course of time he acquired a clearer view of the proprieties. But despite his improvement he was never able to achieve delicacy or subtlety in garb. Headgear seemed always to be a puzzle to him and some of his hats were indeed fearfully and wonderfully made. Of course, his Buster Brown wig and white kid gloves in "Faust" will go down in history, but the caps of "La Gioconda" and "Cavalleria Rusticana" should not be forgotten. However, when he sang "Cielo e mar" in "Gioconda" one cared not a whit what he wore. His delivery of that aria was the high water mark of his vocal art. It was one of the supreme pieces of singing of our time.

Mr. Conried never succeeded in eliminating all of the crudeness from Mr. Caruso's action. He dearly loved to play the clown and unfortunately many persons in his audiences encouraged him in doing it. His undignified antics when before the curtain often obliterated the whole effect of some of his loftiest vocal achievements. Nor could he easily assume on the stage the urbanity of the courtier or the nobility of a knightly character. His Raoul in "Les Huguenots" was distinctly bourgeois.

His Chevalier des Grieux never ceased to suggest the son of a merchant prince.

Much more could be written about the career of Mr. Caruso, about his personality, about his art, about his courage in facing the opposition of his compatriots to his incursion into French classic and modern operas; and about his voice. But future historians of opera will not be confronted with the insuperable obstacles which meet them when they wish to speak of Rubini and Mario. What sounds these singers made can be divined only by reading the pages of Chorley or some other contemporaneous commentator.

The phonographic record will reproduce the beautiful song of Caruso as long as human beings desire to hear it. The historian will know precisely what were the merits and what the faults of his vocal style. The teacher of singing will be able to present some of his famous arias as examples to his pupils and to point out in their delivery what should be imitated and what should not.

For Mr. Caruso's art was far from faultless, and in its last years it had more vices than in its earlier seasons. But there has never been a faultless singer.

Even Plancon, one of the greatest masters of vocal technique that ever trod the stage, had some faults. In his last years Mr. Caruso sacrificed some of the early beauty of his delivery to vociferous and ex-clamatory effects, incessantly demanded by that small body of Italians which governs the expression of public opinion at the opera. Mr. Caruso should not be incontinently dropped from the pages of operatic annals because he has been removed from the scene. His was one of the great voices of vocal history, his art had genuinely great qualities, his sincerity and devotion were beautiful, the man was singularly lovable, and his untimely death was lamentable.

12

Geraldine Farrar

April 16, 1922

NEXT SATURDAY AFTERNOON, WHEN MISS GERAL-
dine Farrar has finished her performance of Zaza
she will cease to be a member of the Metropolitan
Opera House company. It ought to be understood
by opera-goers that Miss Farrar is not leaving the
Metropolitan temporarily. She is leaving it for good.
It might be added that her departure is regarded
with great satisfaction in certain high quarters.

With the causes leading to her retirement from
the company the present moment need not be concerned. The story has been told, and no matter
how often it is repeated each opera-goer will place
his own construction upon it according to his inclinations. It is no longer a matter of importance.
The only fact worth considering is that the American prima donna, who in sixteen years of service
in the Metropolitan built up for herself a large following and a high artistic reputation, will not again

be heard in that lyric theater, and that no other American singer is in sight to take her place.

At this time, then, it may be interesting to review a little of the history of Miss Farrar's achievements in this city. It will not be necessary to tell the whole story, to make a catalogue of all her rôles and all her appearances. Her early days here should prove to be interesting, for without doubt most of us have forgotten much that she did then.

Miss Farrar made her début at the Metropolitan Opera House under the management of Heinrich Conried on November 26, 1906, at the age of 24, singing Juliette in Gounod's opera "Romeo et Juliette." Her début was a subject for much animated discussion. She came at a time when the public acquaintance with the highest type of singing was far greater than it is now, when taste was much more fastidious and knowledge much more general. In these days Miss Farrar's Juliette, as it was sung in 1906, would be regarded as a marvel of beautiful vocal art. We have not had all these years of educational opera for nothing.

But in 1906 it was deemed inadequate, and there

was much talk about the difference between succeeding as Juliette in Berlin and here. Some of
Miss Farrar's stage business was condemned as
being too realistic and it earned for her the undying
hostility of some opera-goers. But it is safe to say
that if a new Juliette were to emerge to-morrow
and repeat that business there would be no more
than a gentle flutter of amusement. The bedroom
drama had not swept the veils of reticence from
the stage when Miss Farrar's chamber scene startled
the venerable guardians of the public morals in
1906.

On December 7 Miss Farrar sang her first Marguerite, not her of Gounod, but the heroine of
Boito's "Mefistofele." The devil on that occasion
was a perfect gentleman, M. Plancon, and Rous-
seliere, Mr. Conried's very expensive tenor, was
the Faust. The production was costly and hopelessly unprofitable. Mr. Conried banished it from
his stage until he could secure a more impressive
fiend.

On February 6, 1907, Miss Farrar gave one of
the most artistic impersonations she ever disclosed
to this public, an impersonation of which few pres-

ent-day opera-goers have even heard. She sang Elizabeth in "Tannhaeuser" with Mme. Fremstad as Venus, Mr. Burrian as the erring minstrel and Mr. Van Rooy as Wolfram. No better performance of a Wagner drama has been given on the Metropolitan stage since Jean de Reszke retired.

Miss Farrar's Elizabeth was not only one of her best achievements but it was one of the most beautiful and touching impersonations of that character ever given by any artist on any stage. The present reviewer is almost ready to express the opinion that it was the finest creation of Miss Farrar's entire career. Certainly she never surpassed it. And yet this exquisite embodiment of Wagner's ideal woman was permitted to pass into disuse and almost out of the memory of the living.

On February 11, 1907, the first performance of "Madama Butterfly" at the Metropolitan took place. The cast embraced Miss Farrar as Cio-Cio-San, Mr. Caruso as Pinkerton and Mr. Scotti as Sharpless. Others have since been heard as the little Japanese bride, but the rôle became indissolubly associated in the public mind with Miss Farrar.

Her first Mimi in "La Boheme" was sung on March 15 of the same year. This rôle, which seemed so well suited to her powers, did not continue long in her active list, and when she sang one act of it in the present season at the performance in aid of the Caruso fund, she had not been heard in it for eleven years. On November 20, 1907, she sang again her Marguerite in Bioto's "Mefistofele," but this time with Mr. Chaliapin, who made his début here.

Miss Farrar's share in the Mozart festivals at Salzburg had been famous in Europe, but she was not heard in a Mozart opera here till February 12, 1908, when she sang Zerlina in "Don Giovanni." On February 28 she essayed the rôle of Violetta in "La Traviata," but with no success. On March 6 she sang the title rôle of Ambroise Thomas's "Mignon," but this opera never kept a strong hold on the public fancy. On December 3, 1908, Mr. Conried put on what was regarded as a star cast of "Carmen." The title rôle was sung by Miss Maria Gay, Don Jose by Mr. Caruso, Escamillo by the eminent baritone, Jean Note, who died only a few days ago, and Miss Farrar was the Micaela. Probably very few can remember her in that part.

"Le Nozze di Figaro" was brought forward on January 13, 1909, with Mme. Eames as the Countess, Mme. Sembrich as Susanna and Miss Farrar as Cherubino. This impersonation of Miss Farrar's has disappeared from the stage, together with the opera. However, the soprano is not physically suited to the part now and if the opera were revived some one else would be cast for the page. Falstaff sang "Quand ero paggio di Duca del Norfolk ero sottile, sottile, sottile." Pages in general should be "sottile."

Miss Farrar's first Manon was given on February 3, 1909. She has sung the part often since that, but has never had a monopoly of it. At the New Theatre (now Century) she sang Charlotte in Massenet's "Werther" on November 16, 1909. Her first appearance as Tosca took place on November 22 in the same year. She was not regarded as a successful impersonator of the Roman singer, but in the course of time she built up an excellent version of her own, one in which careful treatment of the music was made to signify more than physical activity.

It was on December 28, 1910, that the American soprano revealed to this public one of the most beautiful portraits in her gallery, namely, the Goose Girl in Humperdinck's "Koenigskinder." Those who have admired Miss Farrar's art will cherish their recollections of that assumption. Perhaps less memorable by reason of the elusive character of the opera was her impressionistic delineation of the wife of Blue Beard, Ariane in Dukas's "Ariane et Barbe Bleu."

These are some of the contributions of Miss Farrar's earlier years in the Metropolitan Opera House. But while it is not necessary to prolong the catalogue, it would be a pity to omit mention of her Louise, especially in Charpentier's fantastic sequel to the first opera, his "Julien." No one who takes the soprano at all seriously is likely to forget her realistic art in the last act of that work.

Her Lodoletta was not interesting to the public, but even Mr. Caruso could not make the opera interesting. That is one of the failures of Miss

Farrar's career. She was admirable in "La Reine Fiamette," but here again the opera itself was quite hopeless. In the immediately recent seasons Miss Farrar has continued to impersonate characters sufficiently well known to the public. She sang Carmen for the first time on November 19, 1914, with Mr. Caruso as Don Jose, Mme. Alda Micaela, Mr. Amato Escamillo and Mr. Rothier Zuniga. Mr. Toscanini conducted.

The morning's record here after that performance contained this sentence: "It may be said without hesitation that she added to her repertory a character in which she will long be admired by the public." And again: "Above all, it was beautifully sung. Miss Farrar has never sung anything else better and hardly anything else as well."

And yet Carmen is to-day not regarded as the American soprano's representative part. Probably Metropolitan patrons will remember her longest as Cio-Cio-San in "Madama Butterfly," a rôle in which she has been without a rival; and as Tosca, into which last Monday evening she put all the resources of her art and all the emotion in her heart.

13

Victor Maurel, Greatest of Singing Actors

October 28, 1923

THE FIRST PERFORMANCE OF VERDI'S "AIDA" IN THIS city took place in the Academy of Music on November 26, 1873. The cast was this: Aida, Mme. Octavia Torriani; Amneris, Miss Annie Louise Cary; Radames, Italo Campanini; Amonasro, Victor Maurel; Ramfis, Nannetti; the King, Scolara. All of these with the exception of the last named were choice and master spirits of that age. They were stars of the first magnitude.

A half century has passed since that memorable production and the world of music learns that Maurel has just closed his splendid artistic career. The writer of these lines did not hear the first performance of "Aida" in New York. In the days of Maurel's triumph at the Metropolitan old men with lips moist with traditions declared that even in 1873 when he was young and bursting with vigor the celebrated baritone did not have a great voice.

It was undoubtedly true. Maurel did not belong to the army of resonant organ pipes. He sang chiefly from the mouth upward. Perhaps there was never a time when he melted hearts. He was no handkerchief singer. He never came upon the stage silently invoking his audience: "If ye have tears prepare to shed them now." His art was intellectual, reflective, analytical, subtle, even hypnotically masterful at times. But it was the art of a mind ceaselessly active, inquiring, unsatisfied.

It is therefore not strange that his most note-worthy successes were in rôles demanding analysis. It is true that he suggested to Leoncavallo the pro-logue to "Pagliacci." But assuredly not for the sake of the high note at the end which endears the num-ber to Leoncavallo's countrymen. For Maurel the prologue was a genuine prologue, designed to direct the minds of the auditors to the fact that a tragedy among clowns is just as tragic as one among tra-gedians.

Maurel's fame seems likely to be most closely identified with his Iago. This is a singular outcome of his career, for his most striking achievement was his Falstaff. It is quite true that his Iago made all others seem small and limp of purpose. His Iago was a devil incarnate, but a cool, purposeful, relentless and supremely brainy devil. Maurel himself had a remarkably powerful superiority complex. His ego swam out of him at every performance and pervaded the house. Without doubt he was somewhat vain, a little pompous and not a little self-glorified. But what traits to serve as the foundations of the character of Iago!

Otello's chosen friend was filled with contempt for the sensitive and yielding Moor. He revelled in his own superiority. He played with his victim, tortured him, bound him on the rack. And withal how fiendishly subtle he was. And it was subtlety that characterized every scene of Maurel's magnificent impersonation. By means as delicate and fragile as the handkerchief of the tragedy Maurel swayed Otello. Yes, there was a brutal burst of passionate triumph when he set his foot on the fallen hero and cried "Ecco il leone." But that was not the climax of the impersonation.

It was the fortune of this writer to be present at

the first performance of Verdi's "Otello" in the Lyceum Theater, London, in 1889. The original cast (with one exception) had been brought over from La Scala, together with the chorus and orchestra and Faccio, the conductor. The late John Reid, who was then managing editor of the London edition of *The New York Herald*, had no one on his staff who was acquainted with the opera and he asked the writer of this department to come to his aid.

It was a great night for certainly one listener, who had never before heard Tamagno (the original Otello) or Maurel. Tamagno possessed what Maurel described as "la voix unique du monde." His thrilling delivery of Otello's farewell to the pomp, the pride, the circumstance of war gained great applause; but not the greatest of the evening. That was awarded to Maurel's recitation of Cassio's dream, whispered sotto voce into the ear of the writhing Otello. This delivery was one of the most consummate pieces of vocal finesse this writer ever heard. That London audience literally broke into cheers at the end of it.

Maurel's operatic Iago could be paired only with

Edwin Booth's dramatic impersonation, just as Tamagno's Otello found no peer on the theatrical stage except that of Salvini. And this same Maurel found one of the supreme artistic joys of his career in the impersonation of Don Giovanni. Here again one felt that subtle intellectual power was the moving force of the character. Renaud published more gorgeously the romantic quality of Don Juan. He was the great lover. Maurel was merely a new incarnation of Mephistopheles. He was the arch tempter.

It must have been Verdi's unerring insight into the requirements of the rôle of Falstaff that impelled him to invite Maurel to undertake the impersonation. An actor with brains who secondarily was a singer was what he desired and he knew that the great barytone could meet the demands. Theatergoers who found themselves dumbfounded before the disguise and transformation of the elder Sothern in "The Crushed Tragedian" were no more amazed than operagoers who beheld the waddling man mountain of Maurel's Falstaff uttering the incomparable complacency and fatuous folly of the fat knight in a recitative new to the artist and setting forth a pictorial action wholly foreign to anything he had exhibited before. It was all an astounding piece of theatrical virtuosity performed with the perfect poise of the ever confident Maurel.

The career of this unique artist ought to be instructive to every student of lyric art. When Maurel sang the heavens did not open and the chanting of the heavenly choir descend upon a waiting earth. The lyric stage has known scores of barytones who could produce more beautiful tones than Maurel. He was thousands of miles removed from Battistini. But his singing was sufficient to meet the demands of a masterly interpretative art. Maurel was perhaps the highest embodiment of the "singing actor" created by the futile yearning of Wagner for some one who could deliver both his melodies and his messages.

It has been intimated that he accomplished some of his operatic triumphs by the use of pure vocal art, as in the case of the narrative of Cassio's dream. This does not, however, mean that the barytone aroused his audience by the sheer beauty of his tone as some tenors have done, for example, in the "Cielo e mar" in "La Gioconda." It means that as Edouard Clement ravished the ear with the infinite variety and significance of his nuances in the "Rêve" in "Manon," so Maurel enchanted auditors by the subtlety of his inflections, the shimmering variety of vocal color and the far reaching eloquence of his interpretation in the "Otello" narrative.

So he has gone to his rest and one more of the great commanding figures of the lyric stage is departed. Lilli Lehmann, sitting in her seclusion over yonder in the Gruenewald, will sadly shake her head. Maurel was one of her heroes. She knew him well. She knew his art. She was one of his comrades in the brave days of Maurice Grau's all star casts. Jean de Reszke in the quiet of his studio in the Rue de la Faisanderie will ruminate on the bygone days when he and his brother Edouard together with Maurel were the big three of opera.

Mme. Marcella Sembrich, dwelling now in the sunny line of Central Park West, will linger amid bright memories of her glorious days when she sang Zerlina to Maurel's Don Giovanni at the

Metropolitan, or the Queen in "Les Huguenots" when he was the De Nevers. Antonio Scotti will remember that when he sang Falstaff after the veteran had retired Maurel went to his dressing room to congratulate him on the excellence of his performance.

So one by one the ancients fade away. The younger operagoers never knew them. The older patrons of the house have learned to interest themselves in younger singers. This is as it should be. We must all live in the present. Doubtless Malibran and Pauline Garcia and Lablanche and Rubini and the other historic stars of opera were great personages and their art died with them. But for us there remain Galli-Curci and Easton and Jeritza and Gigli and Danise and Whitehill; and in a few days the doors of the opera house will be thrown open and we shall all hasten to our accustomed places to listen to the voices of the living.

Barytones and tenors and sopranos and contraltos may come and go, but opera goes on apparently forever. And this is for encouragement. Art after all does not lie in the hollow of any one man's hand.

Walk around the corridors of the Metropolitan on an opera night and listen keenly for conversational lament over the absence of the great Caruso. Not a word. He is no longer there. New voices intone his old melodies and new listeners are thrilled by them.

14

The Necessity for Good Acting in Opera

January 10, 1925

A LETTER HAS REACHED THE WRITER OF THIS DE-
partment demanding and commanding a more extended answer than the chronicler could give in a
short private epistle. Furthermore, since the cor-
respondent has touched upon a topic often discussed
among operagoers, it seems a good opportunity to
chatter about it once again in this place. Here is
the letter:

MUSICAL EDITOR OF THE SUN—*Sir:* In order to settle a
dispute will you kindly advise me if a real music lover is
interested in the acting of the stars at an opera to the extent of the singing, and is it essential for the opera star to
be a proficient actor as well as a singer? In other words,
does the success of the opera star rest with the acting as
well as the singing?

ROSE BESNER.

This inquiry cannot be categorically answered.
Real music lovers, for instance, will differ in their

attitudes toward the relative values of acting and singing in opera. A student of voice will probably give almost no attention to the acting, but sit up waiting to ascertain whether the singer carries the head tone down or strives to pull the medium up.

However, reading between the lines, we suspect that in Miss Besner's opinion a real music lover listens to the music and relegates the acting to a secondary position. Well, let us begin at the beginning. What is an opera? In the infancy of the form it was christened "drama per musica," which means a drama through or by music. This certainly can be better expressed in our language by the expression musical drama or play. An opera is a form of the poetic drama in which lyric utterance takes the place of spoken lines.

In any play no matter whether it be sung or spoken there are different kinds of rôles, some serious and essentially lyric and some belonging to the line of character parts. Therefore the question whether the success of the opera impersonator rests upon acting and singing equally must depend on the nature of the rôles he assumes. A tenor with a good voice and technic and with something like style can walk through such marionette rôles as Faust or Vasco da Gama without acting any more than is implied in an occasional gesture and walking on and off the stage.

These are purely singing rôles. But suppose the same tenor is required next week to impersonate Canio in "Pagliacci" and that he walks on the stage just as he did in Faust and standing comfortably on his two feet addresses his laments to the gallery without acting. What will happen to that gentleman? He will surely achieve a brilliant failure.

Let us glance at one or two other tenor parts, since it is conceded by most experienced operagoers that tenors are usually bad actors. Meyerbeer wrote two of the most celebrated heroic tenor rôles, Raoul in "Les Huguenots" and John of Leyden in "Le Prophète." It is possible to make a pleasing success in the former part by merely looking handsome and singing the music well. But what about the latter?

If the tenor is unable to add to his singing some physical portrayal of the emotions by which the misguided young man is torn, or at any rate to indicate them by facial expression, he cannot by mere singing reach the full stature of the rôle. Now suppose we take the case of the Wagnerian tenor. Lohengrin is frequently sung almost well by tenors who send us home, not with the feeling that we have been listening to a mystic messenger from the enchanted realm of the Holy Grail, but to a soldier of fortune who makes a business of taking up ladies' quarrels. What is wrong with this tenor? Simply that he cannot look or carry himself like a knight of Monsalvat.

The young Siegfried must be not only a singer but at least a handsome young man. Given a certain amount of vivacity of movement and good looks, the Siegfried is good if he can sing all the music, which is his chief duty. But what about Tristan in the third act? There singing becomes unquestionably secondary and the impersonator must be a tragic actor of real power.

Let us drop the tenor and turn to the bass. Mr. Chaliapin is not a singer of the first rank. His vocal technic is defective and his treatment of musical phrases brutally unmusical. He can deliver recitative passages with marvelous effect; but at least half of the secret of this delivery lies in his subtly skillful employment of means which are theatrical, not musical. His Boris Godunov is an imposing and poignant piece of acting, in which there are some fleeting moments of tolerable singing.

Think of such barytone rôles as Tonio, Chim Fenn, Scarpia, Figaro and Amonasro. What would become of the "stars" in these parts if their impersonations consisted wholly of the delivery of the music correctly and lyrically? However—and now we come to the core of the matter—the chief business of an opera singer is to sing. The drama is created to be published in musical utterance. Therefore the actor, instead of reading the lines, sings them.

What made Edwin Booth's delivery of Hamlet's soliloquy thrilling? Not what operagoers call acting, by which this writer has always found they meant action, but by his delivery of the lines. Now in opera, when the composer reaches an emotional situation he seizes the opportunity to let music have its sway, for music can assuredly either express or arouse emotions. We need not stop to ponder that matter. It must suffice at this instant to say that since music can excite our emotions the composers of opera endeavor to make it do so in scenes charged with the feelings of the personages on the stage. At such moments the singer enacts his rôle by singing it just as a great actor in a similar position would by reading his lines.

But the art of acting in so far as it can be practiced under the difficult limitations placed upon it by the measured movement of music cannot be dissociated from the art of the operatic impersonator. If the singer takes no thought of character portrayal, but is content to attire himself in the costume of some period and stand like a statue while he delivers the lyric passages created for him by the composer he is ignoring that very composer's purpose, which was by the combination of his music with costume, make-up and action to produce a dramatic illusion.

The opera has not the slightest pretext for existence except as a form of the poetic drama. Otherwise it is worse than a marionette show so far as art is concerned. It becomes a toy for intellectual babes. The fact that this is what the majority of operagoers endeavor to make of it does not constitute an excuse for persons who desire to respect music as an art. Such people can have nothing in common with those to whom the opera exists for the purpose of providing them with an hour's diversion.

Therefore the singer who takes his profession seriously will strive always to build up a semblance of character. Even such operatic dolls as Violetta and Gilda have been transformed into presumable people by great artists who have discovered how to infuse the breath of life into the music and to surround the song with movement, pose, facial expression and costume which would tend to heighten its expression. The art of the opera singer is an art of the theater, and while its most important element is singing, the rest is essential.

15

The Art of Jean de Reszke

April 16, 1925

IT WILL BE IMPOSSIBLE TO CONVEY TO THE YOUNGER generation of music lovers any conception of the art of Jean de Reszke. There exist even old opera-goers who cannot discern any difference between the excellent Romeo of Mr. Gigli and that of Mr. de Reszke. Style is something not always appreciated. The younger opera-lover has gained his ideas of what constitutes a tenor from a series of Italian singers, most of whom were distinguished by great power of voice and a liberal use of it. Mr. de Reszke's voice was sufficiently powerful for the most exacting heroic rôles in the operatic repertory. It was also suited to the most lyric parts.

But it was not one of the great voices of history as Mr. Caruso's was. A lady once said to the writer, "Has Jean de Reszke a wonderful voice?" The writer answered, "No, he has a good voice, but it is by no means extraordinary." "Then," said the lady, "what makes him such a wonderful singer?" This kind of discussion might be paralleled by asking, "Has Heifetz a $25,000 Strad?" "No, he has not." "Then what makes him such a wonderful violinist?"

Mr. de Reszke's voice was by no means incomparable, but his art was. There is nothing known to the younger operagoer to which it can be likened. A recital of the rôles in which he excelled may give some faint hint of his greatness, but even that will not be completely illumining. He was the greatest Romeo that ever walked upon the stage. He was the greatest Tristan since Niemann and he sang the music of the part better than anyone probably since Schnorr von Carolsfeld.

He was great as Faust, great as Siegfried. He was matchless as Lohengrin. He was the ideal Walther von Stelzing. He was the finest Chevalier des Grieux, the unequaled Raoul in "Les Huguenots" and John of Leyden in "Le Prophète." No one except Italo Campanini rivaled him as Don Jose and perhaps only Caruso as Radames. As Vasco da Gama he has had no rival.

He sang fluently in French, Italian and German. He spoke these languages well. His mind was one of aristocratic cast. He viewed art from the standpoint of a man of exquisite refinement. The Germans did not like him. They called him a "carpet knight." But I am confident that his Tristan was closer to Wagner's ideal than that of any German singer after Schnorr except possibly Heinrich Vogl, whom the Germans regarded as a mediocre Tristan.

Mr. de Reszke's vocal technic was the greatest I have ever known in a man with the one exception of Plançon. Sembrich, Melba and the lamented Lillian Nordica may be listed as women who possessed similar command of the vocal mechanism. But his art was something far beyond technic. His searching analysis of every phrase he had to sing was based first upon a demand for the innermost significance of the text. Having satisfied himself as to this he proceeded to construct a vocal delivery which would combine precisely the right degree of volume, the most illuminating color and the vitalizing dynamic curve.

I learned more about singing from Jean de

Reszke than from any other artist. I cannot claim to have been a pupil, but nevertheless I received many hours of instruction from him in the privacy of his apartment in the Gilsey House. I am glad to make acknowledgment of my debt. But I am still more grateful for the years of affectionate intimacy with this artist of exquisitely fine fiber and lofty idealism. It is possible that from time to time I may indulge in reminiscences of him, but one must be cautious, for, after all, we live in the present, and the lyric stage of to-day offers us much material for consideration.

Mr. de Reszke made his last appearance at the Metropolitan Opera House on April 29, 1901. The occasion was one of those varied performances with which seasons were often concluded in those days. The only complete work presented was a one act play presented by Sarah Bernhardt and Constant Coquelin, then under the management of Maurice Grau, the opera impresario. The second act of "Tristan und Isolde" was given, with Mme. Nordica as Isolde, Mme. Schumann-Heink as Brangaene, Jean de Reszke as Tristan, Edouard de

Reszke as King Mark and Mr. Bertram as Kurvenal. Mme. Schumann-Heink is the only member of that cast now living.

The greatest Isolde the Metropolitan ever knew was Lilli Lehmann. When I visited her some years ago there was on the wall a large photograph of herself as the Irish princess and on the other side of a window a large photograph of Jean de Reszke. I asked her if she remembered a certain matinée when the audience seemed to be breathless and the representation one long thrill.

"I remember it well," she replied; "it was the ideal 'Tristan' performance of my life."

She had sung with all the Tristans from Niemann down. And that was her answer to her countrymen who spoke of her best Tristan as a carpet knight. Mr. de Reszke never sang Tannhaeuser or Siegmund. The tessitura of the rôles was too low for him. His low scale was without baritonal quality, which goes to show that his judgment was right when he reached the conclusion that nature did not intend him for a Don Giovanni.

In recent years he had grown fat. When he was

singing here his figure was full, but muscular and symmetrical. He was amazingly strong, and he was strikingly handsome in such parts as Raoul and Vasco. He was in his day the same kind of a popular idol that Mr. Caruso was.

16

With Flaunting of Banners

February 20, 1926

It is a singular coincidence perhaps that the début of Miss Marion Talley at the Metropolitan Opera House took place so soon after Lincoln's Birthday. Many persons doubtless will recall some words of that immortal American in regard to the public. Nothing would have given any healthy American greater pleasure than to see a youthful countrywoman obtaining a more splendid artistic triumph than any of the loudly heralded foreign stars who have invaded our country with considerable flaunting of banners.

But in the case of the young woman from Kansas City the banners were waved before her appearance much too vigorously and the agitation of them afterward was only a continuation of that vigor. No other débutante in the history of opera in this city had been heralded as such a wonder. No singer could live up to such réclame. There was much chatter about Adelina Patti, who was no more than

340

a name to most of the chatterers, and who never got a whole column after any of her New York appearances.

When Patti at the age of 16 made her début, the newspapers carried no front page stories and the event was not flashed over the land by the telegraph wires. Nevertheless in the brief critical accounts of that début was the statement that one of those rare stars that sometimes cross the lyric firmament had arisen. Mme. Patti lived to enjoy a long and glorious career. Her own art was her advertisement.

It is much too soon to tell what kind of a career lies before Miss Talley. No one can predict the future artistic development of a youthful singer. It will, of course, depend on the young lady herself and on the attitude of her nearest friends and advisers. That she has a voice of operatic caliber is indisputable. It is not an extraordinary voice, except to those who never heard a great vocal organ, but one quite equal to the demands of the florid rôles. It has metal though not gold and it has sufficient range and volume.

If the young woman and her advisers are willing

to recognize the fact that she has just begun her career and has not yet established a right to be enrolled in the list of the world's great artists she may rise to enviable heights. If she or her advisers are under the delusion that what dexterous management and twentieth century methods of publicity caused to take place on Wednesday evening have made further effort unnecessary, they are going to have a painful awakening.

Failure to do a thing as well as one knows how is one of the inevitable results of nervousness. Doing things the wrong way because one has learned to do them that way is not caused by any condition which prevails but for the moment. The medium of Miss Talley's voice in Gilda was consistently hollow, pallid in tint and tremulous. It lacked what the French call "point d'appui." It had too much spread tone. Because of its want of solidity and stable location it lacked the firm and vital quality necessary for expression.

The upper range of the voice differed entirely from the quality of the medium. Above F the tones became pinched and therefore shrill and piercing. It is not improbable that the search after extreme brilliancy in the upper register and the consequent pinching of the tones were what developed the bad placing in the medium.

Of course the difference in quality between the middle and upper voice produced the effect of two registers with a break between them. A properly placed voice has no registers. That tenet is at least as old as Giovanni Lamperti, and the theory is maintained to-day by most of the great authorities. But whether there are registers or not, they should not be publicly exposed. All singers admit that.

The full range of Miss Talley's voice may not have been made known in "Rigoletto." The rôle of Gilda is not a florid one, and the débutante was wisely advised not to try to turn it into one. The trill at the close of "Caro nome" was not perfect, but that means little. The exit up the stairs and through the dark doorway might easily have caused the inexperienced girl some anxiety and marred the trill. Judging from the one or two passages of florid music Miss Talley has facility in it, just as other florid singers have. But her Lucia will afford better opportunity for learning what her "colorature" equipment is. The cadenza at the end of the mad scene has long been the delight of sopranos who excel in the ornaments of song.

The staccati which Miss Talley sang on Wednesday were disagreeable to the ear because of the excessive pinching. The young lady's attack was not always ideal. Neither was Caruso's. Like him she sometimes reached a tone by a "scoop" starting a little interval below. Attack means little to the casual operagoer, but to the singer it means much, since without a good one the production of a round full firm tone is uncertain. But this is enough of voice study. The reason for discussing it is simply that you cannot play on a good instrument if your technique is bad.

The present writer discerned very little evidence of musical talent in Miss Talley's singing. Her delivery of "Caro nome," for example, did not convince the writer that she perceived Verdi's design in beginning the germinal phrase of the melody with two slurred notes and following them with four detached ones. Musically talented singers grasp the expressional purpose of such devices and convey them to the audience. Miss Talley sang the phrases as if they were mere successions of notes.

The employment of color is one of the best of the singer's means of expression. Great artists like Calvé have an astonishing range of tone tints, but less gifted ones should at least know the use of the bright voice and the somber. Neither of these was at Miss Talley's command because of her defective tone production.

To sum up, this young singer should be serving her apprenticeship to the great art of song instead of undertaking principal rôles in such a conspicuous institution as the Metropolitan. It is not essential to prosperity in the profession of singing to start at the top. It is true that beginning in a minor position at the Metropolitan would make it difficult, if not impossible, to advance to prima donna parts. But one might learn one's business in Italy and arrive at the Metropolitan when adequately developed.

It is not easy to determine why the young lady was accorded the privilege of entering at the cabin port instead of through the hawse hole, as the sailors have it. And it is still more difficult to form an opinion as to the reason for the sudden reversal of the proclaimed policy of the house. However, the entire matter will be settled in the end by the jury, namely, the public—the opera-going public of New York, not Kansas City. If opera-goers like Miss Talley it will make no difference whether her singing is good or bad. About this more will be known when she sings before audiences which have not been excited by passionate publicity.

17

Mme. Jeritza Sings Carmen

January 14, 1928

MME. JERITZA SANG CARMEN FOR THE FIRST TIME here last night at the Metropolitan Opera House. It was not her first appearance in the rôle, as she has exposed the wicked gypsy many times in Vienna and elsewhere in Europe. There was a large audience last evening and plenty of applause, many recalls and flowers thrown upon the stage in such profusion as to suggest that a new generation of Jerryflappers had grown up.

The applause was not wholly for the prima donna and she shared the flowers with the others. But, of course, the town always sits up when a new interpreter of Carmen steps forward and concentrates its consideration on the novel version of the Spanish Lilith.

At such a time every writer of musical comment is expected to emit a long essay on the character of Carmen and its interpretation. But two things should be kept in mind, first that the Carmen of Meilhac and Halevy is an operatic distortion of the heroine of Merimée's tale, and second, that an actress is compelled to make her own version of a part. She cannot be anyone but herself. In early days the traditional Carmen of this town was Minnie Hauk's but that subsequently gave way to the creation of Emma Calvé.

But the last Carmen of Calvé was not the first. She began with a consistent and entrancing impersonation compelling in its combination of action with eloquently delivered music, but success was more than the lady could endure, and before her first season had ended she abandoned her finesse and indulged in all kinds of catchpenny devices to astonish the unthinking. In spite of this she left behind her the memory of a Carmen sunk with unsurpassable command of vocal color. Her utterance of the one word "l'amour" in the closing phrase of the toreador number stamped her Carmen as the sister of Cleopatra, Delilah and all the other supreme wantons of legend and history. These closing murmurs of "l'amour" have been cut out in all recent performances of the opera and were last evening.

The omission signifies nothing to the general public, though it might not be difficult to establish the theory that in the utterance of this one phrase any singer must condense her entire revelation of the character of a gypsy. But to-day it seems to be the custom to regard Carmen not as a singing but an acting part. If the prima donna introduces enough action and inserts into her scenes some stage business not done by her predecessors, she has given a new reading.

Mme. Jeritza was very busy. She made a vigorous attempt at a Spanish dance; she sprawled on tables and chairs, put her feet in men's laps, jumped on tables and off again and smoked cigarettes even while singing—a new and valuable addition to vocal technique. But with all her energy she did not seem to get far beneath the surface of the rôle. There was an abundance of ice in her tones and when she was catty she was completely convincing. But she never breathed passion. Her Carmen played with love.

It was her game, and she enjoyed it except when her moves were not met with yielding response. Then she was a perfectly good vixen. Her vocal color had some variety, but it was not at any time dark or tragic. Nor was there any verisimilitude in her seductions. They had pose and persistence, but little of that quality which Elinor Glyn has cleverly denominated "It." The French language did not seem favorable to her and she sang often in a hollow and strident style. But she gave vivacity to her impersonation and kept the eye occupied. The audience apparently liked her.

Mr. Johnson's Don Jose is not unknown. It has fervor and grace and in the final scenes the note of despair. He sang last night with excellent style and with a delightful command of French. Mr. Tibbett was a good Escamillo though for him the French was not unobstructive and his toreador song lacked brilliance. Miss Fleischer was a thoroughly respectable Micaela, though perhaps not quite as shrinking among what Mulvany would have called a "brutal and licentious soldiery" as might have been wished. And she did sing to the gallery rather than to the other people on the stage. The minor parts were creditably done, but particular mention of their singing must be reserved for another time.

18

From Baritone to Tenor

February 11, 1928

LET NO YOUNG SINGER BE TEMPTED TO CHANGE THE
stature of his voice. The feat of Louis Graveure
may persuade some with low voices that they can
become masters of high tones, but to what end?
One of the greatest living singers is Battistini. Unfortunately, he has never been induced to cross the
Atlantic, of which he has a profound fear. Battistini
is a baritone and for many years has enjoyed fame
as a consummate artist of the school of bel canto,
which does not mean scales and trills, but simply
beautiful singing.

His tone production is apparently effortless and
every tone in his scale seems to be formed in the
same place. His cantilena is as smooth as velvet and
his style the perfection of artistic taste and intelligence. Why should such a man desire to become a
tenor? He probably has not yet thought of such a
thing, but Mr. Graveure's transformation may sug-

351

gest the desirability of the move to others. If a man is an opera singer there can be but one object in changing one's voice from baritone to tenor, and that is to obtain the larger salary which a great tenor commands.

But suppose that having been a fairly good baritone one becomes a fairly bad tenor, what then? A great baritone undoubtedly gets more salary than a bad tenor, for in the end the latter finds himself singing minor rôles and pocketing a very small pay check. There are without doubt some singers who would rather be genuine artists than mere money grubbers, but they are not held in high esteem in this happy land. When Mr. Coppicus emitted his statement the other day that Miss Talley had earned nearly $350,000 in concert since her opera debut, he was endeavoring to prove that the young woman had attained the topmost pinnacle of artistic glory.

When he added that he had advised her to retire for two years and devote herself to study in order to remove from her singing the faults pointed out by critics in various parts of the country, he must have been pretty sure that she would not do it.

The fact that Marion Talley is a singer whose fortune was made by news stories before she ever opened her mouth should not be forgotten. Other young singers now before this public and possessing quite as good voices, much better vocal skill and more interpretative talent than Miss Talley, are slowly making their way by their own merits in spite of the unspeakable injustice done to them by the exaltation of the young soprano from Kansas City. Most of these young artists will be happier if they fix their minds on their art and not on Miss Talley's earnings. And perhaps they will be content to sing with the voices presented to them by nature and not try to manufacture new ones for themselves.

Much befuddled history has been disseminated by the writers of the publicity matter attending Mr. Graveure's leap into the regions above the clef. We have been told how Jean de Reszke began his career as a baritone and then raised his voice to a tenor. The truth is that M. de Reszke made his début in 1874 as Alfonso in "La Favorita" and afterward sang Don Giovanni, Almaviva, De Nevers and Valentin. As late as 1876 he sang Figaro in "Il Barbiere." None of these are low parts. Don Giovanni can be sung by either a baritone or a tenor, although it was written for the former.

Critical comment while he was singing these rôles frequently pointed out that his voice was not a true baritone, but had the timbre of a tenore robusto. That undoubtedly was the case, and when he realized it, he went into retirement for a time and emerged in Madrid in 1879 singing the title rôle in Meyerbeer's "Robert le Diable." He soon found his feet firmly planted in Paris, singing as Massenet's own choice the leading part in "Le Cid," and afterward Romeo in Gounod's opera when it was introduced into the repertory of the Grand Opera in 1888. The familiar books of reference do not contain any mention of a baritone career by Tamagno.

The significant fact is that De Reszke did not force his voice up on to the tenor region, but that it belonged there and in the beginning was improperly cultivated with a view to making the middle and lower tones heavy and baritonal. It is a pity that singers are not better acquainted with the methods of the masters of the Italian bel canto. They never sought to compel a voice to extend in any direction, but allowed it to go where it tended to go.

The pitch of a voice is determined by the thickness of the vocal cords. Those of men are wider and thicker than those of women. Men's are about seven-twelfths of an inch long and women's about five-twelfths. Therefore the man's voice is about an octave lower than woman's. There are three types of voice—high, low and middle—and the majority belong to the middle class. There are, of course, exceptional voices like Malibran's, which was a contralto with much of the soprano added, and Agujari's, whom Mozart heard. He made known that she sang in his presence passages which he wrote down and which extended from D below the clef to C in altissimo—three octaves, less one note.

But these were not forced up voices. In the early seventeenth century when perfection of emission, purity and beauty of tone and elegance of style were regarded as the highest accomplishments of singers, the teachers began by exercising voices on six tones in the middle of the clef—F to D. When extension studies were introduced, the student was made to touch one tone below and one or two above, but without force or any attempt at prolongation. It did not require long practice to demonstrate in which direction the voice was inclined to grow.

There have been some striking illustrations in our time of the evil wrought by endeavors to raise voices out of their natural places. We have witnessed the premature destruction of some excellent contralto organs through their owners' assaults on high soprano rôles, made simply because new celebrity and larger salaries were sought. Forcing the voice in any manner is ruinous. Singers may well shun rôles with a high tessitura, that is a preponderance of phrases in the uppermost part of the scale. If these could be sung in mezza voce they might do no harm, but composers usually write them over a full and powerful orchestration so that they have to be sung forte.

To sing in full voice is not necessarily injurious, but too many singers fail to recognize the difference between doing this and driving the tones a little beyond their natural strength. Conductors can do much toward helping singers by keeping the orchestra down, but it must be admitted that the obvious intentions of composers often have to be violated in order to attain this end.

The Town Hall held an eager audience last Sunday afternoon. There were singers and teachers and managers and critics all wondering what they were about to hear, and when they had heard it, asking one another how it had been done. That is Mr. Graveure's own private affair. If he desires to go into the business of teaching obscure baritones how to take a chance at bettering their fortunes by becoming tenors, he will probably be very busy. Some years ago a gentleman who had a fondness for knowing all things said to the writer:

"A tenor is a manufactured voice."

"Then," answered the hard-hearted scribe, "you would better start a tenor factory; they are paying big money for them now."

The gentleman went away and digested the reply. Months afterward he broke out again with this declaration:

"The tenor is a freak voice; it is unnatural. That's why they make such a fuss about them."

Unfortunately, neither of this wise man's assertions was correct. The tenor voice is neither a manufacture or a freak. It is a gift. If a man's vocal cords are made for tenor sounds, he will produce them. He can even be a soprano if he makes the decision early enough, but if he waits too long he will have to be a tenor, a baritone or a bass. If he is none of these, he may perhaps become a vaudeville singer and carol about love and the joys of life in the melancholy wailings which so enrapture the lovers of the latest song hits.

Mr. Graveure may now enjoy a career as a tenor. When he becomes tired of impersonating Rodolfo and Faust, he may perhaps discover to his delight that his voice has unexplored subterranean possibilities and he may grow his beard again and come out as a basso profundo. It has been done. But why should it? Basses are not rare or unduly expensive.

19
Lilli Lehmann

December 8, 1928

IN THE GRUENEWALD, JUST OUTSIDE OF BERLIN, there dwells a stately old lady who in this present year passed her eightieth birthday. She is still a power in the world of music, in which she was once a queen, clothed in the majesty of a magnificent personality and the splendor of an incomparable art. Her name is Lilli Lehmann and she belongs to us as much as she does to Germany, for some of her most glorious deeds were done in the Metropolitan Opera House.

When Dr. Leopold Damrosch passed away, Edmund C. Stanton, newly appointed director of the opera, accompanied by young Walter Damrosch, assistant conductor, went to Europe to engage artists for the next season. Among them were Mme. Lehmann and the greatest Hans Sachs, Emil Fischer. The season opened on Monday, November 23, 1885, with "Lohengrin," and on Wednesday evening, November 25, "Carmen" was given with the spoken dialogue instead of the recitatives. Mme. Lehmann made her debut in the name part, and astonished operagoers by presenting a Carmen of heroic mold, sinister and tragic, but with none of the subtle sensuality associated with the character in the minds of a public brought up with the Minnie Hauk tradition.

Mme. Lehmann in that season sang several other rôles with which her fame is not associated, including Marguerite in "Faust" and Bertha in "Le Prophéte." But her peculiar grandeur of style and imposing personality were first revealed to this public on November 30, when she sang Bruennhilde in "Die Walkuere." It became clear that she was possessed of that rare combination of traits and equipment which made it possible for her to delineate the divinity in womanhood and womanhood in divinity, the mingling of the unapproachable goddess and the melting pitying human being which no one else has ever portrayed on our stage as she did. Her "Todesverkuendigung" scene remains unrivaled. It was the perfection of awe-inspiring solemnity and underlying sympathy.

On Wednesday, December 1, 1886, "Tristan und Isolde" was sung at the Metropolitan Opera House for the first time in this country. The cast was Mme. Lehmann as Isolde; Brangaene, Marianne Brandt; Tristan, Albert Niemann; King Mark, Emil Fischer; Kurvenal, Adolf Robinson; Melot, Rudolf von Milde; Shepherd, Otto Kemlitz; helmsman, Emil Saenger; a sailor, Max Alvary; conductor, Anton Seidl. It was in this work that Lilli Lehmann's full artistic stature was disclosed.

She sang Bruennhilde in "Siegfried" on November 9, 1887, when the drama was performed for the first time in this country, and Max Alvary as the young Volsung made himself the idol of every matinée girl in the city. She sang the "Goetterdaemmerung" Bruennhilde for the first time on any stage when the final drama of the tetralogy was produced at the Metropolitan on January 25, 1888. The unforgettable Siegfried of that revelation was Niemann. The famous soprano finished her engagement when German opera was discontinued in the spring of 1889. The following season Abbey,

Schoeffel & Grau took possession of the house and restored opera in Italian and French.

These managers presented to the public the casts of famous stars which made the Metropolitan famous all over the world, and in the season of 1891 and 1892 Mme. Lehmann was a member of the company, singing rôles not in German, but in other languages. She was heard as Aida, Valentine in "Les Huguenots" and Donna Anna in "Don Giovanni," with the great Maurel in the name part. On February 5, 1892, she sang Filina in "Mignon," with Marie van Zandt in the title rôle, Valero as Wilhelm Meister and Scalschi as Frederick.

On November 27, 1895, Jean de Reszke sang for the first time in German, creating a new Tristan, conquering by vocal eloquence of the highest type. On January 12, 1897, Mme. Lehmann reappeared in a song recital in Carnegie Hall after an absence of four years. In the following spring Walter Damrosch gave a season of opera in German at the Metropolitan after the Grau series had closed. Mme. Lehmann sang the "Walkuere" Bruennhilde, with Fischer as Wotan, on March 8, arousing extraordinary public enthusiasm.

As Jean de Reszke had much influence with Mr. Grau the result was inevitable, and Mme. Lehmann was engaged for the next season with the Grau forces. She sang Donna Anna, Breunnhilde, Isolde, Fricka and Valentine among other parts. The greatest performance of "Tristan und Isolde" ever given in the Metropolitan, possibly the greatest ever given anywhere, was that of the Saturday matinée January 7, 1899. The cast—Lehmann as Isolde, Marie Brema as Brangaene, Jean de Reszke as Tristan, Anton van Rooy as Kurvenal, Edouard de Reszke as King Mark, Lempriere Pringle (one of the first bassos of the company) as Melot; conductor, Franz Schalk. Years later, sitting in Mme. Lehmann's drawing room in the Gruenewald, I asked her if she recalled that particular performance. "Yes," she said, "it was the ideal 'Tristan' of my life."

This majestic artist made her final appearance in opera here on March 22, 1899, in "Tannhaeuser." The complete cast read: Elizabeth, Emma Eames; Venus, Lilli Lehmann; Tannhaeuser, Ernest van Dyck; Wolfram, Anton van Rooy; Landgrave

Hermann, Pol Plancon; every singer one of world-wide fame. Mancinelli conducted.

Mme. Lehmann returned to this country in the season of 1901-02 for a concert tour and made her final appearance in a recital at Carnegie Hall on January 2, 1902. Though she did not visit America again, she was not unknown to opera stages in Europe. About twenty years ago in Berlin I said to her: "You will go for your vacation to Tyrol, as usual?" "Yes," she replied, "but first I go for three performances at Ischl." "What will you sing?" I asked. She smiled a demure smile and answered, "Violetta." At 60 she could still entrance an audience with her delivery of the music of Verdi. I, who had heard her sing Donna Anna and Filina, knew well that for her florid music was a beautiful art of which she was past mistress.

But she was of the heroic mold. When she sang "Je suis Titania," you felt like saying, "Yes, your majesty." Her Violetta was far larger than the frame in which the opera set it. But Mme. Lehmann's vocal art was founded on the old bel canto, and she sang the old-fashioned music with noble suavity and aristocratic elegance of finish. How-

ever, she was more convincing dramatically in the
tragic rôles. Her Donna Anna in "Don Giovanni"
was supremely authoritative because she could deliver with irresistible power a dramatic recitative
such as "Don Ottavio, son morta" and with flawless
technique and style the florid air following it.

Nevertheless, her untrammeled spirit craved the
freedom of the Wagnerian manner. When the curtain rose on the second act of "Die Walkuere" and
disclosed her as the young goddess, her radiant face
and splendid figure, both alive with an elemental
beauty, sent a thrill through the house which was
intensified fourfold when her clarion tones rang
out in the "Hojo-to-ho." Nor can one ever forget
the impression almost of awe with which an audience received her imposing delivery of Bruennhilde's immolation or the threnody of Isolde.

Mme. Lehmann's voice was a full-toned dramatic soprano, immense in volume and resonance,
and of voluptuous quality. The range was actually
three octaves, though, of course, her dramatic repertory compelled her to sing within the two-octave
scale from C to C. But she could always reach the

high F and frequently did so in practice. Her vocal studies began at an early age and when she was only a girl she obtained valuable experience singing soubrette and colorature parts in light operas. Her attack was not flawless in some of her tragic rôles where she sacrificed it often to declamatory effects. But her tone production was that of a consummate singer.

What seems to me most important to record was the impressive grandeur of her greatest operatic impersonations. This grandeur was inherent in the woman; she could not rid herself of it when she sang such parts as Filina. But in Bruennhilde and Isolde it fit her like a royal robe. She sang Sieglinde once, and that once we beheld the true Volsung, daughter of a god, swept into a passion of love. And her Fricka was indubitably the queen of Walhalla. In moments of tragic fury her voice pealed like a trumpet and her action was that of a Boadicea. Scenes that can never leave my memory are those of Isolde's rage in the first act and the all-conquering wrath of her personification of violated justice when she hurled aside the retainers of Gunther, and, seizing the haft of Hagen's spear, pealed forth her "Helle Wehr; heilige Waffe."

When "Goetterdaemmerung" was produced at the Metropolitan I wrote "the performance concluded at so late an hour that little can be said about it at present. It must be stated briefly that the evening was one of veritable triumph for Fraulein Lehmann, whose superb acting and singing as Bruennhilde have never been surpassed on the operatic stage in this country." That was a large assertion; but the writer has not yet found cause to retract it.

20

Minnie Hauk

February 9, 1929

THE DEATH OF MINNIE HAUK AT TRIEBSCHEN EARLY
in the week removed from the list of living, though
retired, opera singers the prima donna who spread
through this then innocent village the first excitement about the long-enduring opera "Carmen."
Mme. Hauk was not a one-part singer; she was a
good Selika, for example. But no doubt gray-haired
patrons of the lyric drama will remember her only
as an interpreter of Merimee's gypsy as arranged
by Meilhac and Halevy, librettists, and Georges
Bizet, composer.

Mme. Hauk passed away at her villa on the
promontory of Triebschen, near Lucerne. Her
house there was next door to the one occupied by
Wagner in 1865 and six years thereafter. In that
villa he busied himself with the score of "Die
Meistersinger." Inmates of his home for a time were
Cosima von Buelow and her children. Hans von

Buelow arrived somewhat later and began there his piano arrangement of the score, completing the first act. Hans Richter was a visitor while copying the orchestral score of the same act.

Catulle Mendes, accompanied by two friends, also visited the master. They were greatly astonished to find themselves received in the town of Lucerne with royal honors. People bowed to the earth and the landlord kissed the hand of Mendes. They subsequently learned that these good folk thought that Mendes was King Ludwig of Bavaria and that the lady was Adelina Patti, bound on her way to study Wagnerian rôles at the foot of the throne of genius. When Mendes tried to set the landlord right that estimable man replied: "Your Majesty's incognito shall be respected."

King Ludwig did visit Wagner at Triebschen. So did Judith Gautier, who wrote a charming account of her experience. Liszt went, too, and there played on the piano the new creation, "Die Meistersinger," exclaiming over the last act: "Such things only Wagner could have written." And there, too, Mendes saw Wagner clad in satins with pearl buttons and surrounded by other evidences of his love for sybaritic luxuries. Eheu fugaces! A rich American afterward owned the house and would not allow any one to see the interior of the cradle of the greatest lyric comedy.

One does not connect Minnie Hauk with Norma, Juliet and Aida, least of all with Amina in "La Sonnambula." Yet it was in the last named that she made her début on October 13, 1866, in Brooklyn, now part of New York, the city of her birth. There was no vigorous publicity campaigning before the début, but a Brooklyn critic predicted a brilliant future for the young singer, who continued to study her art right here under Achille Errani. En passant she sang Juliet in the American first performance of Gounod's opera. She began her European career at Covent Garden in 1867, at the age of 15.

It was at the Theater de la Monnaie in Brussels that she made her first appearance as Carmen two years after the Parisian production of the work at the Opera Comique in 1875. It was given there with the spoken dialogue, which had to be replaced by recitative when it was introduced at the

Grand Opera. Recitatives were used when it was given in Vienna in the fall of 1875. Mme. Hauk's instantaneous success as the gypsy was not long in reaching the knowledge of Col. James Henry Mapleson, the eminent British impresario, who controlled opera at the Academy of Music in this city, and he engaged her.

The work was produced at the Academy on October 23, 1878, Italo Campanini being the Don Jose and Giuseppe del Puente the Escamillo. Minnie Hauk's Carmen was regarded as the standard until December 20, 1893, when Abbey & Grau opened their season at the Metropolitan with the opera. The principals were Emma Calvé as Carmen, Emma Eames as Micaela, Jean de Reszke as Don Jose and Jean Lassalle as Escamillo. This writer has said in his introduction to the Dodd, Mead & Co. edition of the libretto, "Mme. Calvé's bold, picturesque and capricious impersonation of the gypsy became the idol of the American imagination and thereby much harm was wrought, for whereas the gifted performer began the season with a consistent and well-executed characterization, she speedily permitted success to turn her head and lead her to abandon genuine dramatic art for catchpenny devices directed at the unthinking. The result has been that operagoers have found correct impersonations of Carmen uninteresting."

This conclusion, of course, is drawn from the last Calvé. The first was incomparably superior.

Minnie Hauk had a highly serviceable voice, a mezzo-soprano, rich and powerful. There is no soprano in the present company of the Metropolitan who could hope to be accepted as Amina, Juliet, Norma, Aida and Carmen. Singers of Amina and Juliet are in the Galli-Curci class. Imagine her as Carmen, if you can. This recorder heard the adorable Adelina Patti try the rôle at the Metropolitan many years ago. His comment was that Carmen may have been a cat, but Patti made her a kitten. Minnie Hauk made her an undulating seductive creature of impulse. She created a sensuous and even voluptuous atmosphere by legitimate acting and singing. She had no need for eccentricities of stage business. The writer would like to say more about her impersonation, but many years have elapsed since he witnessed it and he was very, very young and inexperienced then. But he can add that her Selika had something of the lure of Carmen and was excellently sung.

Mme. Hauk returned to New York in the period of the German opera seasons at the Metropolitan on February 10, 1891, after an absence of six years. Her voice had become hard and rather harsh, and the German text of "Die Afrikanerin" did not help matters. But she achieved a considerable success with her old rôle of Selika. In the cast with her were Miss Broch as Inez, Andreas Dippel as Vasco da Gama, Theodore Reichmann as Nelusko, Emil Fischer as Don Pedro and Conrad Behrens as the Grand Inquisitor. Walter Damrosch conducted. On February 20 Mme. Hauk sang Carmen with all her former penetration of the true character of the part, but with something less of the airy buoyancy and physical elasticity which had made her so irresistible in the brave days of Mapleson.

We noted at the time that the voice, never one of the great organs of operatic history, had lost some of its timbre and some of its flexibility. "It responds rather slowly," we wrote, "to the singer's demands upon it and the tardiness is rendered more notable by the undulatory character of Bizet's Spanish rhythms." But there could be no question of the dramatic correctness and eloquence of the impersonation. What was said about the voice probably would not be said now. Present day operagoers would regard Minnie Hauk as the possessor of an exceptionally fine voice. In those days music lovers were fewer and far harder to satisfy.

The last record this writer has of Mme. Hauk's singing in New York is that of her appearance at what was called an American concert given under the direction of C. Mortimer Wiske in the Brooklyn Academy of Music on February 24, 1891. She sang Elsa's dream and Stephen Foster's "Old Folks at Home," both so as to evoke expressions of regret from the commentator. I wish, however, to repeat that we expected much more of singers in those days than we do now, and Mme. Hauk was long past the meridian of her career. When she sang Carmen at the Academy of Music in 1878 she was 26 years of age and had all the magnetic power of youth.

But she already had ten years of hard operatic labor behind her and thirteen more were added before she had those last appearances in New York.

Five years later she retired from the stage. She had sung Carmen 500 times and in four languages— English, French, German and Italian. Her repertory numbered 100 rôles. There is no room for doubt that her Carmen was the best legitimate and correct impersonation of the part, but it was surpassed by Calvé's in that marvelous skill in vocal color which the erratic Emma possessed.

The Opera and the Singer

December 28, 1929

THE WHOLE PROBLEM OF OPERATIC PRODUCTION IS
puzzling and for the most part depressing. It may
be accepted as almost an axiom that the finer the
art the less hope of popular success. This is true of
all kinds of art. If fineness be its salient characteristic, the populace will have none of it. One may
pause to wonder what became of all the blazing
black and white prints of pictures by Gustave Doré.
The pictures themselves, painted on canvases anywhere from eight to ten feet long and with plenti-
ful use of the palette knife, used to attract crowds
when they were put on exhibition in rented stores
much as prize cows or museum curiosities might
be. But where are they now? Who of the younger
generation knows anything about Doré? And who
of that same generation is concerned about art, any-
how? It is not so long ago that the young patrons
were discussing the Mona Lisa of Leonardo. But

it was not the picture as a picture that they were talking about; it was the smile that would not come off.

So, too, when the men and women who make the life of this metropolis go to the opera, it is seldom the opera of which they speak. It is the opera singer. In at least twenty years this chronicler of musical doing has not received a single letter from an irate reader rebuking him for what he said about a musical composition or a composer. He has received hundreds from raging persons who apparently would gladly have seen him meet with a violent death because he disapproved of the performance of some unimportant singer or player whose doings pleased the objecting reader.

A commentator on music can open a campaign to-morrow against the public rating of Bach or Beethoven without so much as causing a ripple on the musical life of New York. If this writer were to begin to-day a series of articles to the effect that the ninth symphony was not a leading creation and that the Beethoven piano sonatas were absurdly overrated, there might be one lonely letter from some pianist who found it possible to evoke praise for his readings of Opus 111 and Opus 57, but not from anyone else. An "attack" on the music of the so-called modernists will perhaps lure one of the brotherhood into expostulation, but not any concertgoer.

But dare to say that this or that fiddler played out of tune or that singer made little but loud noises and the storm of indignation breaks with irresistible fury. The admirers of these singers and players do not care a whit what they do to the music given them to present. They may tear it to tatters and throw it on the stage and trample on it in the violence of their methods. It is all right because they do it and any critic who presumes to say anything to the contrary should be led immediately to the stake.

With the feelings of these incensed adorers of performing musicians this chronicler has deep sympathy. If he had his own way it would undoubtedly be the way which Ernest Newman has of late been yearning to follow, the way lying far from the madding crowd of puny celebrities amid the gentle fields of scholarly research. This writer would dearly love to retire into solemn meditation and to study of the great periods of musical thought and their relations to general movements of the human mind. He would be utterly happy if he might sit in his den and probe the fundamental principles of musical art and seek to arrive at a conclusion as to their permanence or impermanence.

But these matters are not news and have no place in the columns of a daily newspaper. On the other hand, when an elongated soprano wakes up in the middle of her somnambulistic promenade through the rôle of Valentine in "The Huguenots" and, like Pitts Sanborn's magnificent Helma Seymour, discovers that she is singing the fourth act like a true "falcon," that has to be treated as of more importance than the fact that one Meyerbeer created a period and a style or that there might be an interesting comparison made between courtly operas of various schools, say for a beginning, "Les Huguenots" and "Euryanthe."

But there you are again. No one cares about that. Did the tenor sing the high C in the sextet? What kind of a part has the prima donna in the new opera? Is it really true that Elizabeth Rethberg drives her own car from away up in Delafield Avenue down to the Metropolitan and back every time she sings? These and other such, dear friends, are the questions which must be answered. As for the impresario who has to dig in the dust heap of antiquity for discarded scores possibly useful, let him go dig. If he produces thirty-two failures in the next ten years shall we not still have "Cavalleria" and "Pagliacci" and celebrated opera singers?

An Adieu to Galli-Curci

February 8, 1930

WHEN MME. GALLI-CURCI MADE HER FIRST APPEAR-
ance in this city she was already a celebrity because
she had made so many false starts. She left the
Metropolitan a few days ago, declaring that opera
no longer had any charms for her since it was an
outworn form of musical art. Maybe she is right;
but it would be interesting to see how exhausted
the public appetite would be if some one came
along with a score like "Aida" or "La Bohême" in
his pocket.

The truth is that the opera is always going to
the dogs, but the dogs never get it. Some new master appears and then opera takes a fresh hold on the
world. A hundred little fellows spring up with
clever imitations of the new model and a good time
is had by all till the warmed-over meals of the imi-
tators cease to stimulate the public, and then opera
starts for the kennels again. But it never arrives.

Mme. Galli-Curci had a brilliant American career of sixteen years as a prima donna. She had a voice of extraordinary quality, mellow and rich, though of light texture, and she sang with great facility. The so-called coloratura voice (soprano leggiero) is not as a rule varied in tint, or suited to the expression of the more tragic passions. But it can be used with bewitching effect in the communication of archness, playfulness, gayety, whimsicality, petulance, capriciousness. Mme. Galli-Curci's Rosina in "Il Barbiere di Siviglia" was not a pretty example of scherzando singing. It was a well-made impersonation, and by it the lady will perhaps be best remembered by operagoers. For two or three seasons it had been evident that Mme. Galli-Curci's fragile voice was yielding to the strain of arduous service. She sang very often in her first years on the stage, doubtless because there was a lively public demand, not to be lightly put aside. Singers must make hay while the tonal sun shines and there are few who have the courage to refuse the temptations of the present in the hope of making a long career. If the singer can establish a sufficiently brilliant reputation in the beginning she can live on it for some years after the qualities that made it have become obscured or have even disappeared.

It will be much easier for Mme. Galli-Curci to sing in concerts with a piano accompaniment than in tone-devouring opera houses behind a sonorous orchestra. But since the youthful white hope of opera retired to a chicken farm (not so far away that she had to give up opera matinées) and Mme. Galli-Curci has passed out of the picture, one begins to tremble for the future of "Lucia di Lammermoor," as well as that of "Il Barbiere di Siviglia."

The latter at any rate is essential to the current repertoire. Rossini's gay and melodious masterpiece is needed to help out the comedy department of opera, which is none too rich. Good Rosinas are not to be found on every corner. We hope the benign Signor who ponders the horoscope of art in Thirty-ninth street will find some bewitching prima donna to sing the rôle which Mme. Galli-Curci made so pleasing and which the white hope wisely left untouched.

Meanwhile it may not be impertinent to offer a suggestion. American composers are in the air again and one hears once more discussions of subjects. About these nothing demands immediate attention, except the passing note that the composers of some other countries have not found it fatal to draw their subjects from other lands than their own. Let us hope that the Indian and the Spaniard may not be maltreated in the future. And still more fervently let us hope that some American composer may think it worth his while to study the delightful art of opera buffa.

If there is at this moment any American composer walking about who is capable of writing anything within hailing distance of "Don Pasquale," "Il Segreto di Susanna" or "L'Amore Medico," let him without further ado "go to it." We do not require any more "Cavallerias" or "Pagliaccis." Let us have cakes and ale and ginger hot in the mouth.

23

A Singer in the Great Tradition

February 8, 1930

IT MUST BE CONFESSED WITHIN THE PRIVACY OF *The Sun's* columns that the season of opera, now moving gravely toward its twilight, has not been one of intolerable glory. But it has not been without its interesting incidents. One of these was the sudden outbreak of protests from operagoers against what they regarded as inadequate recognition of the merits of Rosa Ponselle. Now that this famous prima donna has retired from the company for the season, it may not be amiss to inquire how any opera-goer could form the opinion that either the patrons of the Metropolitan or the scurvy knaves who report the doings in the great temple of art have failed to discern in Miss Ponselle a singer possessed of a noble voice, a throbbing temperament and a power to establish a magnetic current between herself and her audience.

This writer is under no obligation to defend the

aforesaid scurvy knaves, but since he is here expressing in privacy a very personal opinion he may venture to assert that the scribes have perceived far more of Miss Ponselle's excellence than the all-seeing public. When this lady made her début at the Metropolitan as Leonora in "La Forza del Destino" on November 15, 1918, this writer said: "If Miss Ponselle never sang in opera before last night, she must have been born with a ready-made routine. However that may be, she is the possessor of one of the most voluptuous dramatic soprano voices that present-day operagoers have heard. Some day doubtless Miss Ponselle will learn how to sing, and then she will be an artist.

"At this moment she is almost naïve in method. But she has the precious gift of voice and she has real temperament, not the kind that drives people into acrobatic excursions all over the stage and to wild shrieks of vocal anguish, but the kind that makes itself felt in the eloquent quality of tones and the accentuation of melody. Her début was very interesting and we hope an incident of the evening having permanent importance."

The following season Miss Ponselle slipped

slowly backward. When she sang with Caruso in the memorable revival of "La Juive" we said: "Miss Ponselle did not fulfill the promise of last season. Her voice sounded much more constrained and less noble in tone, while her action was primitive indeed." These statements evoked some hostile correspondence, as usual, and much of it equally, as usual, was what might have been expected from gangsters, not from persons interested in one of the fine arts. But en passant it has been demonstrated that good music does something to the savage breast certainly not soothing.

Rosa Ponselle continued her descent for a considerable period. She had everything but a sound and resourceful vocal technic and consequently her singing deteriorated. Thousands of operagoers supposed that something had happened to the great voice. Miss Ponselle one day awoke to a realization of her own condition, and from that time her ascent was steady from the valley into which she had descended toward the clouds of glory which she now trails.

We have read about the voice doctors who repaired the damage to the vocal organ and who restored Miss Ponselle to her pristine state. We have signally failed at any time to discover anything approaching loss of voice in this singer. She simply did not know how to get her tones out or how to join them together in long, fluent phrases. Without doubt some one helped her. A singer has to be helped because she cannot hear herself accurately. But once upon a time a teacher of singing said to this scribe: "There are no good teachers—only good pupils."

Like all sweeping assertions this is probably an overstatement. But Rosa Ponselle's attainment of the level on which she carved out her Julia in "La Vestale" and her Norma is due first and last to Rosa Ponselle. If she had not had the good sense to see her own deficiencies and to set about improving her art, she would have sunk into comparative insignificance in spite of the exceptional voice which nature bestowed upon her. As it is now, she is without doubt the foremost dramatic soprano of the Italian opera. She does not sing German operas, and very wisely. Her artistic bent, her mind and her feeling do not run in their channels. That is, so far as we can judge from observing her from our age-long aerie at the left end of a certain orchestra row.

Nor does this watcher of the stars believe that Miss Ponselle's Norma has yet reached its limit. The artist will surely confess to herself that she has not penetrated the secret of the classic recitative which, when superficially sung, seems to be a heavy deterrent to the progress of an opera. Recitatives are almost uniformly sung badly at the Metropolitan. Miss Ponselle's best achievement in this misunderstood department of the older lyric drama was not in Norma but in her Donna Anna.

The writer, continuing this private confession, will admit that it is almost a waste of time to discuss such matters as recitatives and style. Recitative is the basis of style. But who cares? As long as Miss Ponselle can sing her arias with all the opulence of that gorgeous voice she need not concern herself with the matters which the artists of Pasta's day took so seriously. She has departed for this season. We shall have opportunities to study the art of others.

24

The Rarity of Singing Talent

December 13, 1930

MARCHING DOWN THE SUNLIT PATH OF LONG MUSI-
cal years, the writer has many, many times wished
that something might be done to prevent the study
of music by young persons who have no faintest
chance of success. The wish was never more fervent
than it is now when thousands and thousands are
crowding the conservatories. None of them studies
music for sheer love of it or with the desire to become an accomplished amateur. They are all going
to be professionals—and that at a time when the
openings for profesisonal musicians are fewer than
they have ever been before and are likely to become
even fewer than they are now.

Thousands of young men and women who have
a real love for music are studying under the lamentable delusion that the love is talent. This is
little short of tragic, for it means that bitter disappointment and lifelong disillusionment are going to

390

be the fate of a countless company of hopeful aspirants. Much good might be accomplished if these
young persons could clarify their conceptions of
success.

There are two kinds of success possible for them.
Most of them are keeping continually before their
minds the first kind, which means making money.
The minority cherishes the thought of the second
kind, which consists in becoming a genuinely great
artist. It is not impossible to have both kinds. In fact,
the greatest artists before the public all earn good
incomes. But to become a genuinely great artist requires far more than a love, even a passionate love,
for music.

This is a love often unrequited. The passionate
lover too frequently fails to understand the adored
one and finds himself rejected. It needs creative
imagination to win the heart of music, and an appalling percentage of music students have no imagination at all. They acquire technical facility on
their instruments and a good grasp of their theoret-
ical work; but the printed page of a composition
remains a foreign language, which they cannot
translate to an audience.

There is much talk about talent and genius. Neither one has ever been quite clearly defined. But doubtless most of us will agree that genius is a super-something. The possessor of it is a superman. We need not concern ourselves with him at the moment. We may confine ourselves to the girl or boy of talent.

At the risk of being tiresome the writer must revert to a subject he has discussed many times. The best illustration of the student of music who goes boldly forward to certain failure is the singer. It is taken for granted by millions of fairly intelligent people that a good singing voice makes a singer. It can be conclusively proved that it does not. The public knows nothing about singing. It rarely even knows when a singer is singing out of tune, which is the first and most unpardonable of all vocal offenses. It has no knowledge of style. It knows nothing of technique. Ninety per cent of the persons in any audience have no idea whether the songs are correctly interpreted or not; they do not understand the language in which they are sung. This is doubly true at the opera where more than half of the audience either does not know the story of the opera or has only a vague and partly incorrect version of it in mind. As for the significance of the dialogue those are indeed few who catch it.

It is no wonder then that the immense army of music lovers believes that beauty of voice, and that alone, is needed to make a singer a public favorite. Yet the fallacy of the public's own creed can be proved out of the public's own mouth at any concert or opera performance.

If a singer sings out of tune, some will hear it. They do not know that it is singing out of tune that disturbs them. They invariably say: "What is the matter with her voice?" The writer has heard this hundreds of times.

If the singer makes numerous bad attacks, phrases disjointedly, breathes laboriously, lacks a smooth legato, pushes holes through the register bridges or does not know how to produce the upper tones of the scales (as the vast majority of them do not) the auditor says precisely the same thing—"What is the matter with her voice?"

Therefore the singer who believes that voice and voice alone without a sound technique behind it can guarantee success is facing a very unpleasant disillusionment. Some "get away with it" for a time, while the natural voice is fresh and vibrant, but the time is very short. But to the "average" concertgoer it is all voice.

"What is the matter with her voice?" she says to the critic.

"Nothing; it's a beautiful voice, but she does not know how to sing," answers the critic.

And to the inquirer that is a meaningless answer.

What is talent for singing? What first is talent for the violin or the piano? We should say that the fundamental element in talent for either was an imagination which creates in the mind an ideal of beautiful violin or piano tone. The ultimate aim of all technique is beautiful tone. It makes no difference to the sensitive music lover how fast a pianist plays or how many notes a violinist can grasp in a feat of double stopping if the sounds produced be disagreeable to the ear. A talent for singing begins with the same idea, beautiful vocal tone.

Unfortunately, nature bestows upon hundreds of

young persons voices capable of producing beautiful tones but without endowing these same persons
with musical constitutions. In the world of music
there is no one more hopelessly dull and stupid than
the singer who can make pretty vocal sounds and
do nothing beyond that. Singing is at this disadvantage, that the singer cannot hear himself exactly as
others hear him. Think of the poor tonemaker, who
has to rely wholly on his tone making for his
slender living, staggering along the steep highway
of song without a coach. Some one has to teach him
how to use every one of his pretty tones, because he
would never by any chance discover the way for
himself, and second because he will never, no,
never, know precisely how he sounds to the world.

But when this tonemaker is brought to a suspicion that all is not right with her, there is always
the helpful army of relatives and friends to fill the
ear with false encouragement. Time and time again
one goes to a song recital and finds a hall packed
with friends and relatives who are distinctly not
concertgoers, are totally unfamiliar with the conditions surrounding the musical world, ignorant of
singing, strangers to the songs on the program, but

filled to the eyes with a brave determination to "put her over." They make a magnificent demonstration, work themselves up into a fine state of emotional excitement, go home thrilled by the spectacle of a triumph, and a week later are wondering why the musical world is not clamoring for Jane or Marguerite to come and get the engagements.

The chances are that the news has gone forth that Jane or Marguerite emits a series of beautiful tones without any imagination behind them and that after you have heard them for a quarter of an hour there is no reason why you should ever, ever hear them again.

When the case is that of a pianist or a violinist it is none the less the same. The foundation of the technic and its ultimate object are still the creation of a beautiful tone and the preservation of it through any and all difficulties of passage work. Now books teem with stories of the immense labor of great men and how genius works harder than mere talent. Shelley said that God had given men arms long enough to reach the stars, if they would only stretch them out. But how does it happen that there is only one Hofmann, one Paderewski, one

Heifetz, one Zimbalist? How does it happen that among the thousands of little boys studying violin in this country there is only one Menuhin, only one Ricci?

It is a monstrous error and injustice to all these students to say that they are not striving with all their might to be Paderewskis or Kreislers. Don't make any mistake about them; they work. What is missing? Just talent; that is all. They love music and they would like to spend their lives performing it. Without doubt almost all of them could learn to play well enough to bring an artistic joy into their own lives and a pleasure into the lives of their friends. But when it comes to offering their wares in the market place, it is a very different matter. The world is not interested in them personally, only in the goods offered for sale. If these are not of the highest kind, the callous world goes on about its business and the would-be vendor is left unnoticed.

These girls and boys have worked hard. Indolence or inattention is not the cause of failure. The real cause is the absence of a real talent for music. The comparatively early acquisition of a glib facility in producing the tones of an instrument does not signify the presence of a talent. The tones must have something behind them and that something is the intellectual conception of tone quality and the relation of tones in a melody—the meaning of melos. The secondary and musical meaning of the Greek word "melos" is song—a good thing to remember.

One would suppose that a singer would have less difficulty than other musical performers in ascertaining just what the relation of tones is, because the singer has text to guide him. But over and over again the chronicler hears singers delivering songs without apparently the slightest conception of the meaning of the words or the composer's plan in setting them. But this will never end. Papa and Mamma and Aunt Mary and the school teacher and the minister and the city librarian's wife (who plays the organ in the Second Church) have all said that Ethel has a voice and therefore she was selected by a Divine Providence to be a singer and must go to Paris to "have her voice trained."

25

Miss Ponselle and Violetta

January 24, 1931

MISS PONSELLE'S ASSUMPTION OF THE RÔLE OF VIO-
letta in Verdi's "La Traviata" seems to have been a
cause of dissensions and tirades. The root of all the
evils in this case is apparently a misunderstanding
of the opera itself. This has probably arisen from a
confusion of mind created by contemplation of the
list of famous singers who have impersonated the
Italian opera reproduction of Marguerite Gauthier.
There is a persistent belief that Violetta is a "colorature" part because it has been sung by Melba, Sembrich, Galli-Curci and others of their class. But no
one has yet asserted that Mimi and Juliette are
coloratura parts, though these singers have sung
them.

Again it is declared that it is a coloratura part
because there are cadenzas and a passage of florid
recitative in the first act. The duration of Violetta's
floridity is less than five minutes. Juliette sings a

florid cadenza at the end of the waltz, but she is never called a colorature person. Leonora in "Il Trovatore" sings "D'amor sull' ali rosee," which has a cadenza of much brilliancy ranging from D below the clef to the high B flat. We have never heard any one class Leonora as a colorature rôle. The part is almost always sung by a dramatic soprano.

We may also invite attention to Leonora's "Di tale amor" (the cabaletta following the andante "Tacea la notte" in Act I) which is quite as scintillating and florid as Violetta's "Sempre libera." Leonora is not called a colorature part because colorature sopranos do not sing it. The Metropolitan Leonoras of greatest achievement were Lillian Nordica and Lilli Lehmann.

Both of these women sang Isolde and the Bruennhildes. Nordica was also one of the great Kundry representatives. They were adequately trained in the old Italian school and roulades and trills offered no difficulties for them. It may be added here that both sang Violetta beautifully. Lehmann sang Filine in "Mignon" and Nordica sang Marguerite in "Faust." But both were classed as dramatic sopranos.

Calvé sang Marguerite in "Faust" and became a colorature soprano of the first rank when she sang Ophelie in Ambroise Thomas' "Hamlet." Her mad scene was a combination of dramatic interpretation with florid singing such as the operatic stage has rarely known. Her Santuzza—which, despite the fame of her Carmen, was her supreme rôle—was powerfully dramatic and somber in voice. No one ever thought of classing Calvé as a colorature singer, probably because she did not sing the other mad scene, that of Lucia.

Miss Ponselle has sung admirably, except in one passage, Elvira in Verdi's "Ernani." The part has been sung at the Metropolitan by Mme. Sembrich. It has one air, "Ernani involami," containing a florid passage demanding all the technical resource of a colorature singer, but we have never heard Elvira called a colorature part. The confusion caused by the versatility of the thoroughly trained singers of the older generation will not be easily dispelled, but the fact remains that Violetta and Gilda are essentially lyric rôles and Leonora, with all her fiorituri, is dramatic.

It has been acutely observed by W. E. Haslam

in his sound little book, "Style in Singing," that
"one may have style, and one may have a style. The
former is general; the latter individual." Miss Ponselle has a highly individual method and one which
exercises a potent spell in the theater. But such a
sharply defined personal manner is not unlikely to
erect obstacles in the path of a singer striving to
enrich her repertory. Miss Ponselle manifestly
aimed at a reconstruction of the obvious style of
Verdi's music in "La Traviata." Instead of adapt-
ing her own style to the music, she sought to adapt
the music to her way. She made a gallant effort to
do something that could not be done without destroying the musical nature of the work.

The melodic character of the entire rôle of Violetta is lyric. For the matter of that, so is the melodic
character of the music of Alfredo and Germont.
From end to end the opera is a long drawn cantabile. Legato singing must be the foundation of its
interpretation. Verdi composed that kind of music
for the work and the singer cannot elude its demands without courting failure. Sobbing, panting,
breaking phrases with emotional gasps and indulg-
ing in much gesticulation will not save the day. The
singer who can bring the right "metallo di voce" to

the rôle and can sing the music with perfection of legato will triumph without much movement or facial expression. It was not for nothing that "Dite alla giovine," "Addio del passato" and "Parigi O Cara" were almost invariably sung by sopranos sitting down. And all of them, the two solos and the duet, are indisputably of the cantabile type, to be sung with the finished legato of the old school.

What is the right metal of the voice? We have been told by Legouve that there are three kinds— gold, silver and brass. The first is the most brilliant, the second the most charming and the last the most powerful. The last then is not concerned with such rôles as Violetta. Either of the other two will meet the requirements of the score. Given a voice of silver or of gold and a command of the long, sweeping curves of the old-fashioned cantabile airs, backed by feeling and by good taste, a soprano may hope for success in the rôle of Violetta, even if she has to simplify the florid passages which the composer placed in the first scene to express his heroine's forced gayety.

It is highly improbable that any singer in these days takes much account of the history of opera.

Otherwise one might be led to suppose that the records of the success of Mme. Piccolomini as Violetta had served to mislead some as to the possibilities of the part. She is said to have "made a hit" as Voiletta when the opera was produced in Turin in 1855. She had later in life a career in this country. But before that, when she sang in London, we find the discerning Chorley writing thus:

"Her best appearance was in 'La Traviata.' The music of the first act pleased, perhaps because it is almost the solitary act of gay music from the composer's pen, and her affrontery of behavior passed for being dramatically true to the character, and not, as it afterwards proved, her habitual manner of accosting her public. In the repulsive death act, too, she had one or two good moments of serious emotion, though this was driven at times to the verge of caricature, as when every clause in her last song was interrupted by the cough which belongs to the character.

"But the essential homeliness of her reading of the part, which could only be redeemed by a certain born refinement indicated in the frail heroine, was to be seen when Mme. Bosio undertook it at the rival opera house, and when by the superior delicacy of her treatment of it as an actress she effaced the forwardness of her predecessor. To compare the two as singers would be ridiculous. 'La Traviata' showed all Mme. Piccolomini's paltry resources. She never improved her singing, but she exaggerated the gayeties and gravities of attitude and gesture in every subsequent attempt."

Much instruction is to be drawn from this piece of enlightened criticism. The refined and delicate Violetta was pronounced superior to the attempt at "dramatizing" the part by exaggerations in song and action. In justice to history the record must be completed with an admission that the general public of that day was openly shocked, though perhaps secretly thrilled, by the wickedness of the opera. Chorley shook his head. He had never noticed that the opera house was a temple for the cultivation of purity and righteousness. What he did note and write down in clear English was that when the British public became acquainted with Mme. Bosio's version of Violetta, it felt rather shamefaced over its applause of Piccolomini's extravagances.

There is an almost limitless variety of detail in

the study of style. But there is one thing which cannot be denied or overlooked. Every composer has his own style, and no matter how many "periods" he passes through, he carries his individuality with him. Nevertheless, he produces operas which present to our minds astonishing and often baffling superficial departures. Verdi is one of the masters who exhibit such differences brilliantly. And yet even a moderate amount of study of his styles will satisfy the music lover that under all of them rests the same foundation, the native Italian faith in the compelling eloquence of the lyric line. No student of opera scores is astonished when he finds Verdi employing in "Aida" for the expression of the despair of Amneris precisely the same melodic and rhythmic formula that he had used for Leonora in "Il Trovatore."

The long lyric line sustains the whole drama of the Nile, from "Celeste Aida" all the way to the matchless and poignant "O terra, addio," which brings down the final curtain. "Otello," liberal as it is in declamatory phrases, nevertheless rests firmly on the Italian love for melodic utterance, and "Falstaff," the incomparable scherzo of the master who never grew old, sings with a lyric song of joyous youth.

The public has been officially informed that Miss Ponselle had an "ovation," the like of which has not been known since the now fabulous day of Caruso. Mr. Gatti gravely exhibited a portrait of Marie Duplessis, the original of Dumas' heroine, and lo! she was a full-bosomed lady, not unlike Miss Ponselle. There have been very fat Violettas. Miss Ponselle is not fat. She did not miss her target at the first performance because she was too fat or too thin. Indeed, she did not miss it at all, if all she sought was applause. The people who dwell in the secret places behind the scenes, so the official statement said, gave her another "ovation," which must be handed down in opera house history.

Only a few days ago Walter Lippmann in commenting on the slow disintegration of "yellow journalism" told his hearers that nothing and no one could be a sensation every day. Miss Ponselle was indisputably a sensation at her first appearance as Violetta. But it is the conviction of this music lover that the public excitement was aroused, just as it was in London by Piccolomini more than seventy years ago, by the application to the rôle of methods directly in opposition to those clearly designed by the composer. That kind of sensation is not new. Conductors are especially fond of it and it is not unknown to pianists. Singers have experimented with it many times, but only to learn in the end that immortal works of art are certain to outlive vulnerable interpreters.

Miss Ponselle is no seeker after sensationalism. She has not now to prove herself a sincere artist. She has made a mistake about the possibilities of Verdi's Violetta. The public which, like the Athenians, incessantly clamors for some new thing, has made a sensation of it—with a little sympathetic help from the powers that reign near Seventh avenue and Thirty-ninth street.

26
Pons and Patti

February 7, 1931

ADELINA PATTI HAS BECOME A LEGEND. SHE SEEMS
to be regarded as one who lived in a far-off age of
fable. Yet she died no longer ago than September
27, 1919. The occasion of this reflection was the
death of Andrew Dam, who used to be one of the
great men of the hotel business in this town. He
passed from the scene last Sunday at the age of 83,
and it was justly recorded of him that he had been a
patron of opera. It was also set down that he was
one of the group which sponsored the first appearance of Mme. Patti in this country.

The operatic introduction of Patti in this country was her début on any stage as an opera singer. It
took place on November 24, 1859, at the old Academy of Music down in Fourteenth street, when she
was 16 years of age. The rôle which she assumed
was that of Lucia in Donizetti's familiar work. At
that time Andrew Dam was 11 years old. We find

it too hard to believe he lent Maurice Strakosch any money toward financing that memorable season.

If Robert Dunlap, "smooth Ed" Lauterbach and Henry Dazian could communicate with us, they might tell how they welcomed Andrew Dam once more into the company of supporters of Henry E. Abbey, who in the autumn of 1883 opened the doors of the Metropolitan Opera House with a performance of "Faust." Adelina Patti was not in the company. She was singing side by side with Etelka Gerster in Col. James Henry Mapleson's company at the Academy of Music. She had been out of this country for years after her début, but returned for concerts in 1881. A little later she was entangled in an unfortunate operatic enterprise downtown, but finally she became the mainstay of Mapleson's last seasons at the Academy.

It was not until after Mr. Abbey's failure at the Metropolitan that she came under his management. Her last operatic appearances in New York were made in 1893, when she came for one of her numerous farewells and sang in a one-act opera called "Gabrielle," which had been written for her. Nevertheless, there is an army of gay young bucks ready to flood the town with information about Patti and her art whenever her name is mentioned. None the less she has become a legend and her easily accessible history is buried under an imposing structure of fable.

Much authoritative information has been disseminated as to how Mme. Patti sang. The present writer has been sternly rebuked by one gentleman who said that Miss Pons had Patti's lyric line. Perhaps that is true; we should be the last to contend to the contrary, being somewhat uncertain what Patti's lyric line was. Others have told us just how the famous diva's voice sounded, though unfortunately they could not reproduce the sounds and the phonograph was not then working the wonders of to-day. Still others have endeavored by ingenious comparisons of the voices of Gerster, Melba and Sembrich to bring us to a proper realization of the magnificence of the new Patti.

Now all this is utterly futile. You cannot tell anyone how a musical tone sounded. He has to hear it if he is to know; and the younger generation, which was not born nearly forty years ago when the gay young bucks referred to above were saturating themselves with knowledge of Patti, can hear Miss Pons, but not the voice of the dead past. Miss Pons will have to sing as if Melba and Patti and all the rest never lived and the flaming youth of to-day (when it takes time off from its innocent sports long enough to go to the opera) will have to pronounce its own verdict on the charming prima donna just as if there had never been any other.

The elder James Gordon Bennett is credited with laying down a good newspaper rule: "First get your news; then make a domned fuss about it." The experiment of making the fuss first and putting the goods on show afterward, only to have the article declared below the promise, has been tried at the Metropolitan with fatal results. In the case of Miss Pons it was adjudged the part of wisdom to follow the advice of Mr. Bennett. But the fair young soprano has not been benefited by the plan because everything possible has been done through stentorian ballyhoo to place her in an untenable position. She is not to blame for this. Probably no one else in the whole world is more astonished than this unknown singer from a small-town theater in Eu-

rope at the riot raised over her in this naïve metropolis. The opera-going public will have itself to thank
when it awakens to a realization of the fact that she
no longer enraptures it.

After the début of this young lady *The Sun* said:
"The demonstrations made by the disinterested auditors of Saturday afternoon were doubtless evoked
by the astonishment and delight of an assembly
which found on the Metropolitan stage a new singer
who could actually sing." It is no news that in the
kingdom of the blind a one-eyed man is king. Miss
Pons is not the only real singer in the Metropolitan
company, of course; there are others. But there is
an astonishing preponderance of bad singing, worn
voices, false intonation and general vocal slovenli-
ness. The Wagner list suffers most. About that let
there for a moment be silence.

When in such conditions we are made acquainted
with a youthful voice fresh and unspoiled, and a
delivery in which fluency and smoothness usually
preserve medolic lines, we naturally rejoice. And
when the owner of the voice belongs to the imperishable breed of florid singers, the select circle of
"divas" whose utterances are decorated with all the

graces of the most ornate vocal art we bow in worship; for the dramatic soprano may strut and sob and stagger and die of aromatic pain under her manzanilla tree, but the prima donna, trailing her celestial garments of colorature and crowned with her glittering diadem of high tones, reigns immortal on the throne of public adulation.

To New York operagoers, who had for several seasons listened with fading pleasure to a diva grown weary with long well doing, the advent of Miss Pons assumed an importance not entirely justified, and now the young woman is suffering the sudden cooling of the warmth which glowed around her début. After her Lucia one heard only of her merits; after her Rosina one heard plaintive catalogues of her defects.

The unconsidered references to famous singers of the past, most of whom have not been heard by those making the references, should be taken with large grains of salt. And furthermore, when the reference is made by one who has heard the famous singer, his knowledge of the art of song should be carefully examined. There was a thunder of history

when Miss Ponselle sang Violetta and those who
stood firmly for the observance of the style of
Verdi's music were severely chided for failing to
recognize the superior claims of Miss Ponselle's passionate acting.

The answer is simple. Verdi declared that the
ideal singer of his Violetta was Adelina Patti. The
great soprano displayed in all her impersonations
about as much passion as one of the ladies on the
frieze of the Parthenon. Comedy she had indeed;
her Rosina was enchanting. Only the beloved Sembrich ever rivaled her in that rôle. But when Mme.
Patti sang Aida, which she ventured once or twice,
the tortured slave of the Nile became a perfect lady. And once upon a time—such a lamentable time—she sang Carmen, right in the Metropolitan Opera House. This writer said of that
impersonation that Carmen was a cat, but Patti
made her a kitten.

She was the ideal Violetta of Verdi because she
attended strictly to her business of singing the
music into which the immortal master had trans-
lated the soul of the courtesan glorified by love. All
the successful singers of the part have reached their

ends by pure singing, not by pantomimic demonstrations, gasps or coughs.

Reverting to Rosina, the question may be asked, what made Patti irresistible in the part? Two things: first the elegance, the élan and swallowlike grace and swiftness of her delivery of the music; and second, the captivating daintiness and charm of her comedy. As the distinguished baritone Ffrangcon-Davies once said to this writer, "Patti was a witch." There was never any doubt in the mind; when Patti sang Rosina, she was simply adorable. And Rossini's gay and volatile music seemed to be the natural and spontaneous utterance of her own spirit.

We do not wish to make too ponderous a theme of Miss Pons; but here is a charming and (in the beginning, at any rate) modest young woman whose promise has been treated as the full fruition of a rich talent. The truth is that she has much, very much, to learn. "Ars longa; vita brevis." Artists are made, not born. The singer may be born with the voice of a decade, but she has to learn how to use it, and after that to find the way to penetrate the meanings of masterpieces and publish them to auditors.

Violin prodigies like Ricci and Menuhin are born with a special gift for the violin, but they have to learn how to play upon the instrument and afterward to interpret great compositions. Little boys do not come into the world with some magic power which enables them to grasp the form and content of the Beethoven concerto. They have to toil up the long slopes of Parnassus before they reach the top. Year by year the relation of the various parts of such a work to the whole is made clearer and clearer by study till one day the infant phenomenon, grown to the stature of a young master, sends out the strains of the master-work into the crowded auditorium with the voice of authority.

Miss Pons has precious gifts. Some day she may be a great singer. She is not one yet. Applause is hurled at her in masses, but how long will that last if she stands still? The public is indifferent to all things save its own pleasure. It is fatally ready to shout: "La reine est mort; vive la reine."

27

The Art of Melba

February 28, 1931

WHEN THE NEWS OF NELLIE MELBA'S DEATH WAS
published Monday morning some authorities could
find no way to speak of her except to compare her
with Adelina Patti. But as they had already done
the same thing with Marion Talley and Lily Pons,
the comparison had little value. Nor did anyone
first establish the premise that Mme. Patti was the
standard by which all other singers were to be
judged. Doubtless when some of the obituary writers went back to the 1893 files of their own papers
they were amazed to find that Mme. Melba's début
was treated in from a third to two-thirds of a column. Marion Talley received six times as much
space and Miss Pons from three to four times as
much. The art of ballyhoo had not been fully developed in the gay nineties. Nevertheless Mme.
Melba enjoyed a long and famous career.

Old operagoers can remember her in the zenith

of her glory. Her latest appearances in New York were not to the advantage of her reputation. Mme. Melba made her stage début at the Theatre de la Monnaie, Brussels, October 12, 1887, as Gilda in "Rigoletto." Dubious statements have been made about her age. It was said at the time of her first appearance to be 26. Agnes Murphy wrote a biography which bears out this assertion by giving the year of her birth as 1861. Thus she must have been 32 when she came to the Metropolitan. Whatever the number of years, the voice was in the plenitude of its glory and it was quickly accepted as one of the great voices of operatic history.

The quality of musical tone cannot be adequately described. No words can convey to a music lover who did not hear Melba any idea of the sounds with which she ravished all ears. Maurel used to say of the voice of Tamango, "C'est la voix unique du monde." One could equally as well have said of Melba's: "It is the unique voice of the world." This writer never heard any other just like it. Its beauty, its power, its clarion quality differed from the fluty notes of Patti. It was not a better voice, but a different one. It has been called silvery, but what does that signify? There is one quality which it had and which may be comprehended even by those who did not hear her; it had splendor. The tones glowed with a starlike brilliance. They flamed with a white flame. And they possessed a remarkable force which the famous singer always used with continence. She gave the impression of singing well within her limits.

In Handel's time the composer adapted his rôles to the voices in his company. Doubtless some of the success of the amazing Faustina and Cuzzoni was due to this. Melba, however, had to take her operas as she found them, and achieve her fame by singing them in her own way. Her voice was of the full range needed for the colorature and light lyric rôles of the modern repertoire. It extended from B flat below the clef to the high F. The scale was beautifully equalized throughout and there was not the slightest change in the quality from bottom to top. All the tones were forward; there was never even a suspicion of throatiness. The full, flowing and facile emission of the tones has never been surpassed, if matched, by any other singer of our time,

The intonation was preëminent in its correctness; the singer was rarely in the smallest measure off pitch.

The Melba attack was little short of marvelous. The term attack is not a good one. Melba indeed had no attack; she opened her mouth and a tone was in existence. It began without ictus, when she wished it to, and without betrayal of breathing. It simply was there. When she wished to make a bold attack, as in the trio of the last scene of "Faust," she made it with the clear silvery stroke of a bell. Her trill was ravishing. On the evening of her début at the Metropolitan she sang in the cadenza of the mad scene a prodigiously long crescendo trill which was not merely astonishing, but also beautiful. Her staccati were as firm, as well placed, and as musical as if they had been played on a piano. Her cantilena was flawless in smoothness and purity. She phrased with elegance and sound musicianship as well as with consideration for the import of the text. In short, her technic was such as to bring out completely the whole beauty of her voice and to enhance her delivery with all the graces of vocal art.

She was not a singer of what is called "dramatic"

manner, though not devoid of sentiment or the ability to express a gentle pathos. But her interpretative power was superficial. She conquered rather by the sensuous spell of the voice, by the brilliancy and fluency of her ornamentation and the symmetrical lines of her delivery than by the awakening of feeling in her hearers. Her limitations did not prevent her from undertaking a wide variety of rôles. Immediately after her first Lucia she sang Nedda, Semiramide, Juliette, Gilda. Comment at the time was that she was deficient in sentiment in the last named part. But it must be borne in mind that much more was expected of singers then than now, and that Mme. Melba surprised her hearers in later rôles.

In her second season she sang Micaela, Marguerite, Elaine in Bemberg's opera of that name, and the Queen in "Les Huguenots." It may mean nothing to contemporaneous operagoers, but the cast of that production of Meyerbeer's masterpiece is historical—Nordica as Valentine, Scalchi as the Page, Melba as the Queen, Jean de Reszke as Raoul, Edouard de Reszke as Marcel, Plançon as St. Bris and Maurel as de Nevers. There was without doubt never before or since such a star cast. Present-day operagoers may get a hint of its caliber from the statement that every member of the roster could be ranked with Caruso.

Mme. Melba did not sing Violetta in "Traviata" till December 22, 1896, when she astonished her public by the degree of pathos she developed in the second act. It was, however, all in the singing; the action throughout the opera was unequal to the musical exposition. It was on December 30 of the same year that she made her lamentable attempt at a dramatic Wagnerian rôle. She sang Bruennhilde in "Siegfried" on the evening when Jean de Reszke impersonated the young Volsung for the first time on any stage. What prompted Mme. Melba to undertake the Bruennhilde has never been known. She herself was at one time credited with having charged Mr. de Reszke with persuading her to make the experiment, but the story was generally disbelieved. Those who knew Jean de Reszke intimately pronounced it incredible. The prima donna did not sing the part a second time.

Her first "Aida" was accomplished on January

24, 1898, and, although she was not then or at any other time able to create any illusion in the rôle, her beautiful singing of the music enabled her to retain the part in her repertory for some years. What is more strange is that she first sang Rosina in "Il Barbiere di Siviglia" on January 28, of the same year. The opera, now a familiar one, had not been given at the Metropolitan since 1890 when the Rosina was Adelina Patti. Mme. Melba's impersonation found favor. To be sure she was not the scintillating, coquettish, enchanting Rosina fashioned with bewitching spontaneity by Patti, but she was sufficiently vivacious to sustain interest and despite hoarseness in the opening measure of "Una voce poco fa" she had a vocal triumph. In the lesson scene she was warmly applauded for her delivery of Massenet's "Sevillana." For an encore she seated herself at the piano and to her own accompaniment sang Tosti's "Mattinata," which became inseparably associated with her lesson scene from that time.

Since this is not a biographical sketch, it is unnecessary to follow Mme. Melba through her various opera and concert seasons. But it should not be forgotten that the Metropolitan was not the sole New York stage of her triumphs. In 1907 she sang Lucia, Gilda, Mimi and Violetta with Oscar Hammerstein's company at the Manhattan Opera House. This writer then noted a little deterioration in the voice. It had acquired a slightly acidulous quality. The soprano was 46 years of age and the alteration of the voice was not a matter for wonder.

Those who heard this celebrated singer in her latest appearances here can have formed no true conception of her greatness. That she was not an artist of constructive imagination is undeniable. That she was a mere "diva" of the older type, who walked on and off the stage and enchained audiences by sheer outpour of tones, is equally undeniable. Melba had much more than that to give her public, though beyond question the incomparable voice stood before all else. But this singer was a good musician as well as a complete mistress of the technique of singing.

Good musicians are not as numerous on the opera stage as some music lovers believe, for the reason that young persons with voices refuse to go through the labor essential to the mastery of musical theory and practice. All they desire is to learn how to make pleasing sounds with their voices and then let patient coaches take care of the rest. Neither voice teachers nor coaches can turn out Melbas. They are self-made. They appear only at intervals. One of the remarkable features of the record of the Metropolitan is that the roster of its company once contained at the same time the names of Sembrich and Melba.

The present writer had not the honor of Mme. Melba's acquaintance, but from those who knew her well he heard many stories of her amiability, of her generosity, of her genuine kindness to beginners struggling to get their feet on the first rungs of the ladder she had climbed.

28

Singers of Florid Songs

February 20, 1932

Vocal art is looking up. The columns of the public prints have lately contained accounts of laudable achievements in the realm of song. Place aux dames; most of the glory has belonged to women. Lily Pons, Goeta Ljungberg, Lotte Lehmann, Conchita Supervia—these are recent additions to the roster. And there are such established leaders as Rosa Ponselle, Lucrezia Bori, Elizabeth Rethberg and Sigrid Onegin. These are artists of worth and they have been the causes of considerable comment and discussion.

When this writing is printed Miss Pons will have sung Lakmé, which is the rôle in which she made her first success. There have been many Lakmés even in this town. Adelina Patti assumed the rôle once at the Metropolitan on April 2, 1890. The famous "diva" sang out of tune and without much spirit till she reached the bell song, and even in that

427

her staccati were not impeccable. However, her audience applauded until she added to the score her inevitable "Home, Sweet Home."

Marie Van Zandt, the original Lakmé, was also heard at the Metropolitan and others were Maria Barrientos, Marcella Sembrich and Amelita Galli-Curci. Every performance of the work serves to demonstrate that the song of the pariah is not all that is necessary to triumph as the Indian maiden. But this is wandering from the main theme. The recent recital of Conchita Supervia moved the writer's esteemed colleague Pitts Sanborn to indite a learned and pithy article on the subject of colorature. Some one had called Miss Conchita a colorature (Italian, "coloratura"), which moved Mr. Sanborn to judicial wrath. He indignantly declared that one might as well call her a staccato.

Which is indisputable, since colorature is not a singer, but a thing sung. This writer wishes he knew when this word began to be commonly used. Of course Rossini could not have lent his sanction to the custom. In these days a colorature singer is held to be a soprano with a high voice and a command of agility. Colorature signifies music filled

with runs, trills, staccati and all the familiar ornaments used by celebrated opera composers in "mad
scenes." What did Handel or Mozart know about
colorature singers? What did the opera composers
of the latter part of the seventeenth century know
about them?

Nothing, of course. If any of these writers had
known that colorature was a specialty they would
have reserved it for their specialists instead of giving it to everyone in the cast. But to-day, for some
inscrutable reason, not dissociated, we think, with
the advent of the Wagnerian era, singers are not
supposed to cultivate the delivery of florid music
unless they have high and light voices.

One wonders what Sofia Scalchi would have
thought about it. She was a contralto with an aston-
ishingly uneven scale exhibiting no less than three
sharply differentiated qualities in its range, but who
could sing florid music with a rapidity and brilliancy rarely equaled. When she and Adelina Patti
sang the duet "Giorno d'orrore" in "Semiramide"
there was a display of elegance in floridity such as
the stage does not know now. What does Mme.

Schumann-Heink think about it? Many young music lovers are sure that the celebrated singer impressed herself upon this public first as an interpreter of Erda and Waltraute. The fact is that it was at a Sunday night concert at the Metropolitan that she first made the town sit up and it was by her delivery of the brindisi from "Lucrezia Borgia." Her cadenza, which included a two-octave leap, evoked thunders of applause.

Some music lovers asserted with confidence that Conchita Supervia was not a colorature singer. The assertion was based on the mezzo-soprano range of her voice and on her ability to sing music which belonged entirely to the lyric class. But note here a popular inconsistency. Violetta in "La Traviata" is denominated a colorature rôle despite the fact that it contains only one florid air and after the first act is wholly lyric. In almost one breath some music lovers tell us that it is a colorature rôle and that Rosa Ponselle is not a colorature singer but a dramatic soprano. On the other hand, no one ever classes Leonora in "Il Trovatore" as a colorature part, though it contains the florid air "Di tale amor che dirsi," which has a brilliant cadenza.

All confusions in these matters could be abolished by the simple process of dropping from musical terminology the expression "colorature singer." No one speaks of Almaviva in "Il Barbiere di Siviglia" as a colorature singer and yet he is called upon to sing difficult florid music in the first act. Even Gounod's Mephistopheles has his roulade in the opening scene of the opera. And when you travel back to the Rossinian period you find that in many operas every singer was required to be a master of colorature. Rossini's "Semiramide" is a shining example of this species and his "Italian in Algiers" is equally florid. One recalls with sorrow the struggles of the Metropolitan company with the latter work. Because they had all learned to regard colorature as the exclusive field of the high soprano they were completely floored by Rossini's decorative music.

In the so-called "golden age of song," which means the Handelian era, florid music was in the ascendant. The principal voices in opera were high voices. The typical distribution was such as that of Handel's "Teseo," two sopranos, two contraltos and two tenors. But it was not astonishing to opera-goers in those days to hear an opera in which there was not a single masculine tone, though some of the singers were men. The male soprano and contralto were the stars of the stage. Hence the delivery of florid music was less difficult than it was in the time of Rossini.

It is conceded that low voices cannot execute florid passages as glibly as high ones. Tosi, writing in 1723, said volubility was better suited to tenor and soprano than to contralto or bass. But it never occurred to Rossini to eliminate colorature from all his parts except the high soprano. The limitations of florid singing, however, began to be marked in his period. Neither Bellini nor Donizetti habitually strewed the flowers of song all over their pages as he did. And the young Verdi, following in their footsteps, was similarly sparing in his use of colorature. Rossini as well as Verdi found colorature unsuited to his purpose in some of his works. Finally, as the desire for dramatic verity became stronger than the singer's ambition to display his skill as a virtuoso, the opera dispensed with most of its florid charms. But it remains incontestable that singers who are entirely without command of agilita make modern operas heavy and dull and the classics impossible.

It may be admitted that Miss Supervia's delivery of the "Cenerentola" air was not flawless either in technique or in taste, but it was, nevertheless, virtuoso singing of a very high order and possessed an individual charm. We have abundant information that the world-famous singers of Handel's day and the glorious galaxy of stars that shone in the Théâtre des Italiens, Paris, in the early years of the last century were none of them perfect and that those who had the most technical imperfections brought the world to their feet by the spell of personality, dramatic temperament or intellectual authority.

We are not badly off for interesting singers at this moment. True, this is not an age of vocal giants. There are a few phonograph records which would enlighten young music lovers. Unfortunately there are none worth while of Patti or of the generation of the de Reszkes. But there are some excellent records of Battistini and one of the writer's associates lately heard some made by Lilli Lehmann at the age of sixty-five which gave him a great impression of her voice and style.

But the contemporaneous opera stage cannot become dull and unprofitable when one can hear such delightful florid singing as that of Miss Pons and Miss Supervia, such charming lyric art as that of Ljungberg, Rethberg and Mueller and such dramatic delivery as we receive from Miss Ponselle or Mme. Onegin.

There have been some dissenting voices in the past as to the general level of florid singing. None of the old masters or writers appears to have questioned the necessity of the study of florid song, but Mancini, who wrote near the end of the eighteenth century, said that lightness (or nimbleness) of voice "is a particular gift of nature and if she refuses it, one cannot acquire it in any way." Bernard Bacilly, a famous French master, writing in 1668, asserted that every air was more beautiful and pleasing when executed with the proper ornaments. Tosi, who published his delightful observations on the florid song in 1723, accepted the employment of all the graces as a matter of course, but did implore his pupils to be moderate in the use of passages and divisions instead of overloading every air with them according to the custom of the time.

Perhaps a word about more recent opinions would be of more value. Lilli Lehmann, the greatest Isolde the stage has yet known, was also an admirable Violetta in "La Traviata," and even sang Filina in "Mignon" at the Metropolitan. She attributed her artistic success largely to her training in the Italian florid song. Lillian Nordica, who also sang both Isolde and Violetta, as well as the Bruennhildes and Marguerite, Leonora in "Trovatore" and Valentine in "Les Huguenots," held the same view. When Jean de Reszke sang the narrative of Siegfried in the third act of "Goetterdaemmerung" his repetition of the bird's music from "Siegfried" was the perfection of florid ease and grace. So it seems that colorature is a necessity, not an ornament.

29

Antonio Scotti

January 14, 1933

AFTER THIRTY-THREE YEARS AT THE METROPOLI-
tan Opera House, Antonio Scotti will retire with
the performance of "L'Oracolo," at a special matinée on Friday. The distinguished baritone will take
his leave not only of the local theater, but of the
operatic stage. It is fitting therefore that some record of important incidents of his career should be
made. Mr. Scotti has for some time enjoyed the
doubtful honor of being called a veteran, but it
cannot be said that he lagged superfluous on the
stage. Wisely he abandoned rôles making demands
which his voice could no longer meet and retained
those in which his great ability as an actor served
to sustain public interest. In selecting the portrait
of the sinister Chinese as the last he is to draw for
us, he has followed that policy. Of Scotti the famous
singer we took leave some seasons back. We now
bid farewell to Scotti the illustrious impersonator
of operatic characters.

436

This admired and beloved artist was born in
Naples in 1866 and made his début at Malta November 1, 1889. It was ten years later that he
reached Covent Garden, London, where he sang
Don Giovanni with success. Thence he came to the
Metropolitan, making his New York début on December 27, 1899, in the Mozart rôle just named.
Lillian Nordica as Donna Anna, Marcella Sembrich as Zerlina and Edouard de Reszke as Le-
porello were other famous singers in the cast.
Comment was made on Mr. Scotti's début in these
words:

"He is a good-looking man, graceful and dignified in bearing, and elegant in manner. His voice is
fresh, mellow, well schooled and well managed.
It has plenty of volume, but was not at any time
last night forced. Possibly the quality of the voice
is not of the richest, but it was a pleasure to hear
such a fresh, unworn organ, used with so much
freedom. Furthermore, in his treatment of the recitative Signor Scotti showed understanding and at
times finesse. He sang the 'champagne song,' as it
is sometimes called, with fine dash and vigor and
won two hearty recalls. The details of his work as
Don Giovanni will bear further discussion, but it

may be said now that his conception of the part was according to the traditions and was well generally carried out."

In his first season the singer gave the public a knowledge of the versatility which added luster to his career. He sang Amonasro, Dr. Malatesta in "Don Pasquale," Tonio, De Nevers, Nelusko, Escamillo and Valentin in "Faust." It may seem astonishing to find in the old reports that his greatest "hit" in that season was with the rôle of the Madagascar savage in Meyerbeer's opera. But without doubt the impersonation of Tonio deserved deeper consideration, since it was authoritatively pronounced one of the best pieces of acting ever seen on the Metropolitan stage. In "Les Huguenots," Mr. Scotti brought to De Nevers his artistic taste in make-up and costume. A handsomer picture than his could hardly be imagined. His Dr. Malatesta made known to New York the baritone's delightfully buoyant and elegant comedy.

All the rôles mentioned have dropped from the catalogue of Mr. Scotti's recent seasonal duties. It was in the second winter of his activities that he was seen and heard in one of the parts by which the younger generations of operagoers know him. Puccini's "Tosca" was sung for the first time in this country at Metropolitan Opera House on February 4, 1901. The title rôle was assumed by Milka Ternina, the best Tosca the local stage has revealed. Cremonini was the Cavaradossi, Gilibert the Sacristan, Dufriche the Angelotti, Jacques Bars the Spoletta and Scotti the Scarpia. There has never been any other Scarpia. Many have essayed the character, but Scotti's portrait of the scheming police chief has remained the unapproachable model.

"La Boheme" reached the Metropolitan the season of 1900-01. It had previously been sung by a traveling Italian company in a colorless manner. With the history of the opera we are not now concerned. Mr. Scotti's first Marcello was sung on December 16, 1904. The Mimi was Melba, Bella Alten was Musetta, Caruso the Rodolfo and Journet the Colline. Mr. Scotti's happy impersonation of the irresponsible painter remained in his repertory even after its original physical elasticity and effervescence of spirit had vanished.

Three years later he added to his repertory a rôle in which the lovable nature of the man could exhibit itself freely and exercise its conquering charm on a responsive public. Puccini's "Madama Butterfly" had its first American performance at the Metropolitan on February 11, 1907. Geraldine Farrar was the Cio-Cio-San, Louise Homer the Suzuki, Caruso the Pinkerton and Scotti the Sharpless. Without injustice to others it may be said that his impersonation possessed qualities which were missed when he was not in the cast.

Mr. Scotti achieved no greater triumph in the course of his artistic life than his portrayal of Shakespeare's fat knight. Verdi's "Falstaff" was not new to the Metropolitan, for it had been given with Victor Maurel, the original Falstaff, coached by Verdi himself. That famous artist was in the audience on March 20, 1909, when Mr. Scotti appeared as the ludicrous lover of the comedy, and was one of the first to felicitate him on his brilliant success. Emmy Destinn, Frances Alda and Giuseppe Campanari were in the cast and Toscanini conducted. Many operagoers of to-day have enjoyed the unctuous humor of Mr. Scotti's Falstaff.

"L'Oracolo," the short opera in which the eminent baritone will make his final appearance, was given at the Metropolitan for the first time in the United States on February 4, 1915. Lucrezia Bori, Didur and Sophie Braslau were in the cast and the young Chinese victim of Chim Fen was sung by Luca Botta, a pleasing tenor who died before his time. Mr. Scotti's Chinaman will surely remain in the memories of present-day operagoers as a remarkably powerful piece of acting.

The baritone was heard in numerous other rôles in his years at the Metropolitan, but most of them are not to be regarded as milestones along his path. This is not because he failed. It is significant that no distinct failure of Mr. Scotti comes to the mind. The parts which did not add to his reputation did not subtract anything from it. The music lover feels that the defect was in the rôle itself and not in the singer. The impersonations which have been selected for special mention are those by which this genuine artist will be remembered by those who have had the good fortune to live in his period.

In some of his creations he was not at first correctly judged. This was because other singers had not been heard in the rôles. When a considerable number of them had been, it was apparent that Mr. Scotti had realized the intentions of the composer more successfully than the others. After the first performance of "Tosca" the present writer's report read:

"Mr. Scotti's Scarpia is a brilliantly vigorous and aggressive impersonation. His voice is admirably suited to the music and he sings his measures with a full appreciation of the brutality of the nature of the creature he represents."

If that Scarpia had been revealed to us twenty years later, we should probably have written a greater number of lines about it.

The retrospective glance at the career of this celebrated artist impresses one thing deeply on the mind. Mr. Scotti has never been guilty of bad taste. He has succeeded in comedy rôles of various types without ever descending to buffoonery, and in serious parts without extravagance or bombast. There have been opportunities for sensationalism, but he has shunned them. He has gone his way steadily, a dignified and well-poised gentleman. We do not recall any exciting news stories of the doings of Scotti. He has not aired his views of times and

singers and the public attitude toward art. He has
remained within his field. He has been an opera
singer and nothing else. He has contented himself
with the faithful and adequate performance of his
duties on the stage, with the significant result that,
while others have come and gone, he has remained
a member of the Metropolitan company for thirty-
three years. Furthermore, during that prolonged
period he has enjoyed the favor of operagoers.
There have been times when people said: "Oh,
Scotti's voice is worn out." But these people were
in a minority, and the great army of opera patrons
continued to delight in the eminent baritone's resourceful art.

Of his versatility we have already spoken, but
let us not close this insufficient survey of his remarkable career without one more comment on
that. All opera singers are required to impersonate
characters of widely different types, ranging from
tragedy to low comedy. Most of them acquire a
routine; and indeed, operatic acting must inevitably
fall into routine much of the time, because of the
inexorable necessity of performing each action at
the place prepared for it in the music. But it will

probably be conceded that Mr. Scotti has been eminently successful in fulfilling the demands of operatic routine and in many signal instances of going far beyond it. Those whose memories go back to his Tonio and Iago will undoubtedly be ready to declare that an operatic impersonator who could meet all the calls of such rôles with Scotti's psychologic insight and technical ability was an actor, a true man of the theater.

As such, his name will be recorded in the pages of opera history. It is likely that something will be added. The opinions of Scotti's colleagues, his public and the news writers who have carefully weighed his achievements will be that he was a true gentleman of the theater.

30

The Singers of the Golden Age

January 21, 1933

IN A RECENT ARTICLE IN THE PICTORIAL REVIEW, Lawrence Tibbett expressed the opinion that those who lamented the passing of what he called "the golden age of singing" were merely suffering from the loss of their own enthusiasms. They were bowed in sorrow because no one could make such biscuits as mother made. Now the only historical "golden age of song" was that of the Handelian period. However, certain troubled minds have lately assumed that the brilliant seasons at the Metropolitan Opera House when the company included a dozen genuinely great singers was called the golden age. No one who lived in it called it that, nor has any authoritative historian of that time applied to it such an imposing title.

That matters little. The assertion has been made that there were more good singers then and that the ideals of singing and the average of achievements were higher. On the other hand, the writer of an article published last year intimated that in all probability the singers of thirty-five seasons ago were overrated by the critics who heard them, and that they were not in the least respect any better than those of to-day.

It is now twenty-four years since the last remnants of the scattered and worn fragments of the famous company which made the Metropolitan celebrated throughout the world disappeared from its stage. Antonio Scotti was one of the latest recruits in that company and he is now retiring for reasons which have been sufficiently published. Mr. Tibbett's acquaintance with the performances of the so-called "golden age" at the Metropolitan must have been acquired in the perambulator or from conversation with elderly persons preserving enthusiasms when there was no longer ground for them. The young writer of the other article was not born when Grau's parades of stars in "Les Huguenots" took place.

Lillian Nordica as Valentine, Sembrich or Melba as the Queen (sometimes it was one, sometimes the other), Mantelli as Urbain, Jean de Reszke as

Raoul, Edouard de Reszke as Marcel, Scotti as de Nevers and Plancon as St. Bris were the glorified seven. Their names mean nothing to the present generation, which has heard only Mr. Scotti in his declining years and regards him as a perfect exemplar of the singing of that period. Those old artists were just another set of Lauri-Volpis, Pinzas, Maria Muellers, Rethbergs and Lily Ponses. Why, every one has heard Schumann-Heink. That was one of the goddesses of the divine era, and she is not to be compared with Branzell.

The plain facts are that most of those who are telling us about the singers of the gay nineties were babes or non-existent when they were singing. And instead of being overrated those artists were distinctly underrated. They were censured time and time again for faults which are ignored in most of the singers of to-day. They were expected to sustain all the time the standards which they had raised and were mercilessly rebuked when they fell below them. No young historian need be in error about this. The files of the daily newspapers of that time have not gone out of existence.

Probably every music lover has heard of Adelina Patti. The present writer remembers well the temper of criticism in regard to her. It is said that she was one of the greatest singers that ever lived. This does not mean and it never was asserted that Patti had emotional communication or that she possessed anything but an extraordinary voice, an almost flawless technique and a witchery of gay and infectious spirit in such rôles as Rosina. Her Violetta in "La Traviata" was faultlessly sung, but was not very moving.

Now within a few years this writer has read a mass of critical comment on a third-rate soprano who toured the country in concert, and the plain truth must be told that never in her career did Adelina Patti receive such newspaper laudation as that soprano had. Patti was lamentably underrated according to the methods of contemporaneous criticism. A little browsing through the pages of Henry Edward Krehbiel's "Chapters of Opera" should satisfy any reader that the eminent critic of the *Tribune* in the "golden age of singing" was not given to intemperance in commendation, but rather to restraint and careful analysis.

The gay nineties were not the day of ballyhoo. It was reserved for the era of Marion Talley, whose advent at the Metropolitan was the basis of the most absurd, extravagant and even mendacious publicity. Nothing of that kind was known in the days when Sembrich, Melba, Calvé, the de Reszkes, Lasalle, Maurel and their companions were enjoying reputations which will go down in the annals of music beside the records of Grisi, Malibran, Mario, Rubini and Lablache. There are singers in the Metropolitan company at this hour who would have stood well in the brilliant assembly of 1894, but they are receiving emotional laudation which they would not have received in those days.

The début of Mme. Melba was reported in a leading morning paper in an article less than half a column in length. The amount of space devoted to the soprano was about one-eighth of a column. It required from two to four columns to tell about Marion Talley. The nature of the comment on Melba was just that which has lately been made on the début of Lily Pons. For years Melba was regarded as the foremost Juliette. When she sang it for the first time here the *Times* spoke of the beautiful quality of her voice and her phrasing, especially in the balcony scene. "Throughout the remainder of the evening," continued the comment, "her singing was in every way worthy of an artist of the first rank. It must be remembered that this praise is evoked by her singing considered as singing pure and simple. There was much to be desired in respect of warmth and sentiment, and Mme. Melba made little attempt to give dramatic significance to her action."

Jean de Reszke was the best Romeo and the best Faust the present writer has heard in a long experience. The comments made by this reporter on M. de Reszke's appearances in these rôles in his early seasons here seem positively ludicrous when read to-day. They were so restrained that they assuredly may be said to have underrated the impersonations lamentably. It was not till he sang Tristan in 1895 that adequate criticism was bestowed upon him by this writer.

Acknowledgment was then made that he had achieved the greatest triumph of his career and that he sang Wagner's music as it had never been sung before. When he sang it in Germany he was censured for making the music so smooth and polished. So was Lilli Lehmann when she first sang Bruennhilde there. The Germans no longer cherish their false ideals of Wagner. One has only to note the style adopted by Mr. Melchior, or the vocal line and color of the Brangaene of Mme. Olszewska to realize that to-day Wagner has to be sung beautifully. Jean de Reszke first sang Siegfried in "Goetterdaemmerung" on January 24, 1899. This writer found his early scenes deficient in weight, but noted that the second act was better. The death scene was deeply impressive. The recorder concluded that later performances would surely develop the impersonation, and this proved to be the case. In the end this came to be one of M. de Reszke's most moving characterizations. He sang the heroic pages with broad dignity of style and depth of feeling. And he put all the forest birds to shame by singing their music in the narrative "aus meinem jungen Tagen" better than any of them ever had. We scribes all yearned to hear Melba sing the forest bird, but, of course, no opera house could afford such a luxury.

Finally, how many of those who believe that the so-called "golden age" was one of fable and that its

artists were overrated can quote names of the many
singers who were not glorified? Do the dissatisfied
music lovers know what happened to the Ravogli
sisters, regarded in London as stars, to Libia Drog,
to Susanne Adams (with a marvelously beautiful
voice), to Susan Strong, Frances Saville, Imbart de
la Tour, Ceppi and a score of others? There was
Cremonini, who sang in the first Tosca. We held
him distinctly second rate, but if he were to walk
upon our stage to-day, we should laud him enthu-
siastically. Who remembers the charming Bessie
Abbot? She was cruelly underrated. She was an
excellent artist, but had the misfortune to live in the
"golden age," when she was outshone.

On the other hand, it remains the unshaken conviction of this reporter that there is no such Isolde
or Bruennhilde as Lilli Lehmann on the stage to-
day. That Lillian Nordica, Marie Brema, Olive
Fremstad, Marcella Sembrich and a dozen others
have not been replaced. The important fact upon
which the older recorders of musical activities insist is that in the "golden age" there were more
singers possessed of adequate technical equipment
than there are now, that there was a larger number

of exceptional voices and that there was a more general comprehension of style. Audiences in those days would not have tolerated the amazing variety and conflict of styles which mar some otherwise commendable performances in this time.

The old operagoer must often wonder why so many singers embark upon operatic careers before their voices have been securely placed and their knowledge of technique equal to the tremendous demands of the modern lyric theater. Why do we so frequently hear singers not over 35 years of age with voices marred by bad holes and verging on tremolo in so many tones? There were bad singers in the "golden age," too. But they had no permanent place in principal rôles on the stage of the Metropolitan. Many singers traveled through life advertising that they had sung at the Metropolitan, when the truth was that most of them had sung there two or three times and some only once. Mr. Grau brought over one tenor who made his début on a Friday night and was on a steamer bound back to Europe the next afternoon.

The foremost singers now at the Metropolitan are daily receiving far more extended laudations and frequently much more emotional ones than the great singers of the "golden age" received. The stars of Mr. Grau's company had to be at their best in order to get praise and when they were not at their best there was no mincing of matters. Viewed from the standpoint taken by newspapers to-day most of them were underrated.

Maurice Renaud and Operatic Acting

October 21, 1933

THE DEATH OF MAURICE RENAUD ON TUESDAY
brought forth the inevitable crop of blunders. He
was described as one of the famous singers of the
Metropolitan Opera House in the golden age of
Grau. He was best remembered as Don Giovanni.
He had a great voice. There is no need to continue
the catalog. M. Renaud was one of the admirable
company assembled by Oscar Hammerstein at the
Manhattan Opera House in 1907. The famous
French barytone has been engaged by Maurice
Grau for the Metropolitan, but when Grau's health
broke down, Conried, who became impresario, can-
celed the Renaud contract.

The French artist is remembered by older opera-
goers as Don Giovanni, Mefistofele in Berlioz's
"Damnation of Faust," Athanael in "Thais," Boni-
face in "Le Jongleur de Notre Dame" and Scarpia
in "Tosca." He was the handsomest Don Giovanni

ever seen in this town. He had a consummate skill in make-up and most artistic taste in costume. He made Don Giovanni wholly plausible not only with picturesque appearance, but also by means of grace and significance of action.

His Athanael has never been rivaled. No one else succeeded in creating the same impression of intensity or conveying to an audience a realization of the man's panic-stricken state of soul at finding himself completely under the sway of a fleshly passion. Does any old *Sun* reader recall his singing of the "Legend of the Sage Bush" in "Le Jongleur de Notre Dame"? Its finish of style and its tenderness of expression have lingered in this writer's memory among the more precious experiences of opera.

Noteworthy also was his revelation of the secret thought of Mefistofele in the Berlioz work. It was made plain that this devil regarded his own business of tempting men with something like contempt because the men were not worthy of the trouble he took. Such pitiful specimens should have been left to go to ruin by themselves. They were beneath the genius of an arch fiend.

There was nothing in the text to communicate this thought. Renaud did it with his eyes. And so one comes to a question: Do operagoers adequately gauge the value of a masterly operatic impersonation? Sometimes when attending a distinguished performance this observer has suspected that too many of the auditors were aware only of the vocal sounds emitted with so much vigor by singers proud of their big voices. Renaud had a voice of moderate power.

M. Renaud is reported to have said that he studied his rôles as characterizations and endeavored to fit every movement and gesture into the music so that everything should have a meaning. Now this is by no means an easy thing to do. The operatic impersonator is bound by the musical tempo. He simply cannot do things ad libitum. He must do them in time to the music or at least in such time as the music permits. He cannot retard the movement of a scene nor hasten it. He has to follow the beat of the conductor.

Nevertheless the operatic stage has been glorified by some remarkable acting. That same old Manhattan Opera House Company gathered in Europe by Oscar Hammerstein contained some of the best operatic actors ever seen here. Hector Dufranne, Huberdeau, Dalmores, Gilibert, Bressler-Gianoli, Mary Garden—all these knew the art of operatic acting and created character portraits which have never been excelled. The Metropolitan Opera House disclosed to this public the art of Maurel, who was one of the greatest operatic actors ever known. Scotti, who recently retired, was an actor of the highest skill.

Among women, without doubt Calvé must be accorded a place in the first rank. She had that singular insight which enabled her to compose characters convincingly. Olive Fremstad possessed histrionic ability of a high order, and if one cares to go back still further along the line of celebrities one can recall Marianne Brandt and Lilli Lehmann.

But must we always delve into the past for examples? Surely not. There are operatic impersonators among contemporaneous artists who challenge comparison with the illustrious stars of the earlier eras. Lawrence Tibbett's Emperor Jones will go down in operatic history as one of the striking achievements of the stage. Edward Johnson as Pelleas, Leon Rothier as the elder des Grieux, and Lucrezia Bori as the Duchess of Towers furnish pictures of lasting worth. Those who frequent the opera will easily recall others. There is complaint among the younger set, who naturally know nothing about the stars of forty years ago, that old writers busy themselves too much with fond recollection. But a score of years hence they will be doing the same thing themselves. There can be no harm in remembering the good old days provided one does not for that reason fail to take note of the very good new ones.

There is much rejoicing over the exhibitions of real interpretative power on the operatic stage. But, on the other hand, there is perhaps a little too much laudation of mere ability to sing loudly or brilliantly. Voice is not all that is needed to make a great opera artist. The fact is that many have left imperishable records who had not extraordinary voices, but who did possess brains and imagination.

32
Marcella Sembrich

January 19, 1935

THE PASSING OF MARCELLA SEMBRICH OCCURRED
just too late to be the subject of last Saturday's
comment in this place. But it is still time to assert
that this famous soprano was not only one of the
greatest singers of her period, but of all lyric history. There was something indescribable, elusive,
intangible in her art, as there is in all supreme art,
but that her singing wove an irresistible spell and
probed the hearts of her hearers is beyond question.
The secret was partly in the peculiar quality of the
voice itself, a quality which might have suggested
Sidney Lanier's thought about the fragrance of a
certain fluted note, "as if somehow a rose might be
a throat."

Technicalities cannot explain the magic of singing like hers. It is true that she was an extraordinary musician. She played violin and piano excellently and without doubt her inborn sense of tone

went far toward creating almost unconsciously the right tint for every note she delivered. But there was also an unfailing instinct for expression which caused her to place her tonal tints with unerring fitness. There have been more astonishing singers than Sembrich, but none who made hearers more completely subject to the spell of an art incomparable and authoritative, yet invariably gentle and winning.

In its best days her voice extended from C below the treble clef to F above it. It was wholly devoid of the metallic quality so often found in brilliant colorature voices. Its natural fluidity and transparency made it perfectly capable of the bird-like flights of florid rôles, though it seemed sometimes as if it exercised more magic when heard in purely lyric music embodying tender pathos. A voice indeed which was quite as much at home in the scenes of Mimi in "La Boheme" as in the bravura of the Queen of the Night in Mozart's "Magic Flute."

But it is necessary to keep ever in mind that the voice alone could not have made Sembrich one of the immortals of song. Her most important equipment was her profoundly musical nature. She once said in an interview that the inspiration of her life had been music. This was indisputably the case and perhaps in a degree greater than she herself realized. She had sufficient talent for violin and piano to have made a creditable career with either, but when she discovered that she had in her throat a better instrument, one that was a part of herself, she found her true artistic field.

Mme. Sembrich's operatic repertoire was remarkable for its scope and variety. It must be remembered that her voice forbade any attempt at heroic rôles. From light and joyous comedy through sentiment to the loftiest lyric poetry she swept a marvelous gamut. Elsa and Eva were her only Wagnerian rôles. Her greatest part was surely Violetta in "La Traviata." Her singing of "Ah fors e lui," "Dite lala giovine" and "Addio del passato" was never equaled by any other prima donna in depth of expression or perfection of phrase and tonal coloring. She sang Rosina in "Il Barbiere" supremely; only Patti rivaled her in that rôle, but her musicianship made her singing superior even to that of the famous Adelina.

In Mozart this same musicianship enabled her to sing Zerlina, Susanna and Astrafiammante incomparably. Within the memory of this generation there was no other Mozart singer like her. Her Gilda in "Rigoletto," her Marguerite de Navarre in "Les Huguenots" and her Manon all had individuality in their perfection of style and their unerring conception. In the gay humor of "Don Pasquale," "La Fille du Regiment" and Nicolai's "Merry Wives of Windsor" she was bewitching. She had forty operas in her list, some heard very seldom. But it is incontestable that she sang all her rôles well, though naturally some were more congenial than others.

She sang Mimi at the Metropolitan for the first time December 19, 1902; Nedda in "Pagliacci," with Caruso, December 9, 1903; Adina in "L'Elisir d'Amore" in the revival of January 24, 1904. In the brilliant production of "Die Fledermaus," at the Conried benefit of February 16, 1905, she sang Rosalinde. "Lakme" was revived for her on December 24, 1906, but this was one of her least successful undertakings. She took a formal public leave of the operatic stage on February 6, 1909, appearing in acts from "Don Pasquale" and "Traviata" and the lesson scene of "Il Barbiere."

Her song recitals continued till early in 1917. She had given the first on March 14, 1900. These recitals became leading features of the local seasons of music. In certain respects they were literally unique and it was not long until the music-loving public recognized this. The first time an audience rose to its feet to show its admiration for an artist coming on the stage for a recital was at one of Sembrich's.

Mme. Sembrich was the greatest lieder singer among women ever heard in New York. This can be said with recollections of Lehmann, Gerhardt, Culp and others clearly in mind. Mme. Sembrich did not attempt heroic numbers, which Lehmann could sing magnificently. Hers was a more intimate art and rose to its supreme heights in songs of subtle character. Her singing of the "Brautlieder" of Schumann cannot be described. It was heart searching in its complete publication of the emotions of the lyrics. At the time of her retirement the writer said:

"The depth of expression attained by her in her wonderful song recitals is due to a combination of perfect tone with musical intelligence." These words are lamentably feeble. Her own are better. She said once to Mrs. Henderson, "When I do an opera part or sing a song I do not just sing it; I am it." She possessed in rare degree the power of identifying herself with what she was delivering. Her imagination was vivid and unceasingly active. It vitalized everything she did in music.

Certain songs beside those already named were peculiarly suited to her temperament. Schumann's "Auftraege" has never been sung by anyone else as she sang it. The serenade of Strauss was positively a revelation from her lips. The song was introduced here by Mme. Sembrich with Isidore Luckstone, her first accompanist. It seems hopeless to expect another rendering of Brahms's "Wie Melodien" such as she gave, and the same master's "Mainacht" was peculiarly her own. No one sings Lowe's "Glockenthuermer's Tochterlein" now, but no one could make the effect with it that Sembrich made. Another of her most famous achievements was "Immer leiser wird mein Schlummer," into which she poured a wealth of emotion. Her "Sand-mann" was the perfection of winning archness and humor, and the deftness of the vocal touch was matched in her delivery of Bach's "Patron, was macht der Wind?"

Her mastery of languages enabled her to sing with fluency in French, Italian, German, Russian and English. Her folksong recital, which was in a way epoch making, revealed the fact that she was not helpless in some more remote tongues. The singer, who drew the vocal line of Violetta with such perfection, who vitalized every phrase of Lucia and who bubbled over with the comedy of Rosina, was the same artist who drew the vocal lines of scores of songs as no one else has drawn them. Whatever the power was that guided her, dramatic instinct, pure musical genius or a deep and subtle womanhood, which it is not for a mere commentator to estimate, she was an artist unique and supreme.

Frank La Forge, her accompanist for years, told the writer that her preparation for a song recital was long and laborious and some songs were sung a hundred times in study. The arrangement of each program was made with meticulous care to the end that there might be an artistic progression from start to finish. Francis Rogers uttered a lament a few days ago that the classic traditions of the old Italian operas were likely to die with Mme. Sembrich. Of the younger singers only Miss Bori appears to possess any knowledge of them. But Sembrich's phrasing, tempi, nuance and general style were authoritative in such works as "Traviata," "Nozze di Figaro," "Don Pasquale" and others in which she was famous. There are some phonographic records, but by no means as many as desirable.

At a time when there is constant distortion of the old music and misguided endeavors to impart novelty to it by singing it as it was not meant to be sung, it is a pity that there is no edition of Sembrich's celebrated airs made by her own hand. It may be possible that some of her pupils will hand down the traditions, but this is and always has been an uncertain method of preserving them.

A word may and indeed should be said about the woman. Mme. Sembrich was blessed with a happy nature. In all the trials of her later years she remained gentle, patient, cheerful and unfailing in loving attitude toward all her friends. A German newspaper several years ago called her "the internationally beloved" Mme. Sembrich. So indeed she was. She was beloved by thousands of music lovers who had no intimate acquaintance with her and by associates in the opera who might have felt envy or jealousy toward one less winning in her own personality. She lived her last years quietly among her pupils, her close friends and her mementos of a beautiful past. She had the daily companionship and self-effacing devotion of her daughter-in-law, Mme. Juliette Stengel. Perhaps the writer may be forgiven for quoting the last lines of the poem he read at the banquet in celebration of her farewell to the operatic stage:

> "So take our salutation, we who stay
> To face the dawning of a darker day.
> Queen of the Night, queen of the singer's art,
> Queen of the stage, queen of the public heart,
> Hail and farewell. Your name is writ above;
> Supreme in song; still more, supreme in love."

33
Mme. Flagstad

March 22, 1935

As THE SEASON AT THE METROPOLITAN OPERA HOUSE
draws toward its close the public approval of Mme.
Flagstad becomes even more demonstrative. Naturally music lovers are not sure that they will hear
her again next winter, for the plans of the new
manager, Herbert Witherspoon, must as yet be incomplete. But whether Mme. Flagstad remains with
the company or not, her advent has been something
to go down in operatic history and to suggest some
valuable reflections. It has been asserted frequently
that no more singers comparable to the company
which gave the Metropolitan its world-wide reputation could be found.

This assertion has persisted in spite of the presence on the stage of Miss Bori, a vocal artist of the
finest type; Miss Ponselle, Mr. Schipa, and the
others who have often been glorified in these columns. But it is certain that singers with such a good

foundation as Mme. Flagstad's are seldom discovered. She has voice, technic, temperament and imagination. It is true that she does not clothe herself in thunder and lightning, but it is equally true that she plumbs depths of emotion with a moving eloquence which makes her mistress of every audience.

What every student of vocal art ought to observe and never forget is that Mme. Flagstad accomplishes her aims in interpretation by pure singing. There are no evasions of the demands of the music. She does not alter rhythms, introduce questionable tone qualities or indulge in any of the other tricks which some singers use when trying to make effects beyond their reach by sheer singing. Holding up Mme. Flagstad as an example of respect for vocal art does not mean that she is alone in her excellence. In her second song recital, given a week ago, Mme. Lehmann demonstrated in the same manner the power of perfectly musical singing to convey the message of every song.

It is to be hoped that the young aspirants for vocal honors will profit by the lessons which these distinguished artists are giving. Singing is just like other branches of musical art; the prime requirement is a finished technic. With that one can interpret freely and fully, provided one has the imagination needed for a living re-creation of the composer's thought as recorded on the printed page. Imagination, however, is what too many singers lack. They have voice, but they do not know what to do with it. And they cannot be taught. No coach can supply the place of imagination. But with that and technic the singer can triumph.

The public response to the offerings of Mme. Flagstad indicates that the power of good singing is just as great as ever. But let us not neglect to consider the importance of this artist's action. At Sunday night concerts one often sees opera singers having a hard time resisting the impulse to make gestures. But the typical operatic gesticulation means very little. The singers rush about the stage and wave their arms, but what they do seems much too often to bear no relation to what they are saying. Mme. Flagstad has been reticent in movements about the stage and in gesticulation. She has emphasized the value of repose. When she does something it means something.

Let us suppose that next season we shall witness operatic performances in which all the singers in the cast sing the music with good tone, accurate intonation and all the essential subtleties of expression, and that they all act, not individually without regard for the others in the scene, but harmoniously with movements, poses and gestures planned to convey to the audience the thought and feeling of the work. Let us add that they do not sing in half a dozen different styles, but in only one —that of the score.

Is it not likely that a performance of this kind would prove very interesting to the audience? There is a tendency to lay just a little too much stress on the singing. That indeed claims the first and ruling place, but much of its effect can be nullified by bad action incoherent and meaningless, and by the clash of conflicting styles. There is a great field here for the conductor and stage manager. But it is not going to be easy to impose on opera such imperative direction as that governing a moving picture.

Nevertheless this is one of the things that opera sorely needs. And it need not in any way hamper the individuality of any singer. The famous stars of the screen are handled by directors clothed with authority, but the final results appear to be the fullest and most convincing revelation of the personality of the actor.

34
Other Days, Other Carmens

January 11, 1936

WHEN WALI DAD, REPOSING MEDITATIVELY IN THE
house on the city wall, sagely remarked "Lalun
is Lalun, and when you have said that, you have
come only to the beginnings of knowledge," he
was assuredly not thinking of Carmen, for the excellent reason that he never had heard of her. But
all the ladies who belong to the oldest profession
in the world seem to have certain traits in common,
chief of which is an insuperable objection to the
peace of the community. They do not ponder the
matter. They are like Mary Garden, as portrayed
in the highly individual prose of the matchless
Huneker, "She never analyzed her will-to-raise-
merry-hell." Schopenhauerian considerations do not
enter into their scheme of life.

Now because Rosa Ponselle has paraded the
Metropolitan Opera House stage with her hands
firmly placed on her swaying hips (according to

the description by Merimée of Carmen's first appearance) much talk has been expended. Is this the real Carmen or not? And how does it compare with the famous Carmens of other days? Well, there have been Carmens and Carmens. For example, there was Lilli Lehmann's, revealed in her first season at the Metropolitan. According to the immortal Lilli, Carmen was the most regal of all courtesans, the grande dame of perdition, built on noble lines and dwelling perennially in the realms of magnificence. And she sang in the heroic style. It was overwhelming, but it was not Bizet. Bruenhilde turned gypsy and finding her "highest hero of worlds" in a champion bull fighter; that was Lehmann, the superb.

Once upon a time there was a vastly different Carmen on the Metropolitan stage, Adelina Patti. Rosina had eloped from Don Basilio's domicile with a corporal in Almaviva's regiment and was playing gypsy on top of a heaven-kissing hill. We were impelled to declare that everyone knew that Carmen was a cat, but Mme. Patti's Carmen was a kitten. Patti was a capricious queen of song. She even sang Aida when she ought to have been busy with

Amina or Semiramide. Nevertheless it is not of Patti that men speak when they strive to recall the golden age of song at the Metropolitan. They always murmur the magic name of Calvé.

What no one seems to remember is that Emma Calvé made her American debut on November 29, 1893, as Santuzza in "Cavalleria Rusticana." The present writer's report, published the following day, said: "Mme. Calvé is a dramatic soprano of the first rank. It is long since New York operagoers have had the pleasure of seeing and hearing an artist of such splendid emotional force. Her voice is not a great one, but it is sufficient in power and range for her work and it is of good quality. It is in her ability to delineate character and to express feeling that she is notable. Her acting is uncommonly fine for the operatic stage. In bearing, gesture and facial expression she is at all times eloquent and powerfully influential, and she knows how to put emotional meaning into her singing, never hesitating to sacrifice mere sensuous beauty of tone to true dramatic significance. Her success was immediate, pronounced and thoroughly deserved."

She first appeared as Carmen on December 20. "Her Carmen is a creature of unbridled passion, graceful with a sensuous, suggestive grace, and careless of all consequences." She showed the same theatrical skill as she had already revealed in her Santuzza. "In the second act her impersonation approached the boundaries of the hazardous." Her dance aroused memories of the then profoundly condemned Midway Plaisance. Her associates in that performance were Jean de Reszke as Don Jose, Lassalle as Escamillo and Emma Eames as Micaela. The season ended on February 24 with the fourteenth performance of "Carmen."

There were derogatory comments on Miss Ponselle's dance. It had been carefully prepared under the guidance of competent authority. It was correct. That was not the subject of comment. It was not good dance, good posing or good acting. Mme. Calvé's was not good dance either. And when people were shocked by it they were living in the age of innocence. The gay '90s were conspicuously naïve. They are now derisively called Victorian, which means that their scheme of virtues was made according to the principles enunciated by the Widow of Windsor. But in these degenerate days the domestic dignity and purity of the present royal family have failed to produce a Georgian era of impeccable manners and perfect morals. We have what the Victorians could not have conceived, the rule of the racket, the high speed mania and the cocktail hour. Calvé's dance would not strike us as wicked. We would say it was an awkward evasion of the candor which we worship.

Calvé's Carmen went to artistic pieces long before the season ended. The prima donna could not stand her enormous success. She became extravagant, whimsical, erratic, irresponsible. She did anything that occurred to her to accomplish a passing sensation. But in the beginning her Carmen was a striking characterization and had most of the merits which marked her Santuzza. What is too often forgotten is that Mme. Calvé did most of her acting with her voice. She was past mistress of vocal coloring. She knew how to utilize every shade from the most somber to the brightest tone. And she used them for purposes of dramatic delineation. Her Ophelia in "Hamlet" was one of her most noteworthy achievements and in this part she proved that she was a consummate singer of florid music. Her "mad scene" was of the first rank.

She was also an excellent Marguerite in "Faust." But we are speaking of Carmens. Minnie Hauk was the first in this country. A capable singer, not of the first rank, but of competence, she was also a good actress and she had in a considerable degree the sensuous suggestiveness essential to a good impersonation of the gypsy. She was in good company. Italo Campanini's Don Jose has never been surpassed in dramatic fire and communication. Del Puente was the only Toreador who ever measured quite up to all the requirements of the music. He had just the right voice for it, sufficient in range and sonority and yet rich in that indescribable champagne quality which is so valuable in creating vitality in the rôle. Del Puente was a capital Figaro in "Il Barbiere." He gave us the champagne there, too.

In the days of Maurice Grau Zelie de Lussan was for a time the Carmen and by no means a bad one. She would probably be welcomed with acclamations in these uncertain times, but then she was subjected to fatal comparison with the only Carmen an unfeeling public would accept. But in the long line of Carmens there have been many who need not be named. We are not trying to publish a complete catalogue. Without effort of memory, however, Trebelli, deep-voiced contralto of the first season of the Metropolitan; Mary Garden, a Carmen sui generis; Bressler-Gianoli, one of the best; Geraldine Farrar, charming; Bruna Castagna, who made an unexpected impression at the Hippodrome, and Maria Jeritza—but there let us draw the veil.

There was a Carmen once who inspired men to rapturous utterance. This historian, alas, never heard her. She was Georgette Leblanc, famous actress of the French stage, wife of Maurice Maeterlinck, who created a Melisande as far removed from her Carmen as Simla from Skagway. Fierens-Gevaert wrote of her with a pen filled with the flame of passion. She wore a long robe covered with spangles. Her splendid body was not hidden by this "indiscreet drapery." Her arms and shoulders were bare. "Alma, gypsy, daughter of the East, princess of the harem, Byzantine empress, or Moorish dancer? All this is suggested by this fantastic and seductive costume." More: "In a tavern where

gypsy women meet soldiers she evokes the appari-
tion of a woman of Mantegna or Botticelli, de-
graded, vile, who gives the idea of a shameless creature that has not lost entirely the gracefulness of
her original rank."

Still more: "Miss Leblanc makes light of her
voice. She maltreats it, threshes it, subjects it to
inhuman inflections. Her singing is not musical,
her interpretation lacks the naivete necessary to
true dramatic power. Nevertheless she is one of the
most emotional impersonators of our period.
Thanks to her, Antioch and Alexandria, corrupt
and adorable cities, live again for an hour."

Well, up to the present writing nothing like that
has happened to us and it does not look as if it
were going to. So let us rest in peace and be grateful that Bizet's immortal work cannot be killed by
bad usage. It has survived a deal of mishandling
and will doubtless live to be made a convenience
for singers now in their cradles, but coming in the
fullness (or emptiness) of time, like other singers,
to the point at which something has to be done to
keep the illustrious name on the page of history.

35
Ernestine Schumann-Heink

November 21, 1936

I<small>T IS DIFFICULT FOR THOSE WHO HAVE JUST READ OF</small>
the death of Ernestine Schumann-Heink to realize
that she finished her engagements as a regular member of the Metropolitan Opera House Company as
far back as 1904. She sang there afterward, but only
occasionally as a guest artist. She even sang at the
Manhattan Opera House as a guest under Hammerstein. Her one rôle there was that in which she
made her operatic début at the age of 17, Azucena
in "Il Trovatore." She sang in German and the rest
of the cast in Italian. The experiment was not repeated. Azucena towered above Leonora, Manrico
and Di Luna. Such a tremendous tragic figure was
better suited to the Clytemnestra of Strauss' "Elek-
tra," in which she did not sing here.

Tremendous is probably the most convenient
word for the operatic creations of Schumann-
Heink except, of course, those which were in

lighter vein. Ortrud, in which she made her American début in Chicago in 1898, became in her hands a portentous and sinister character with all the power and concentrated significance of a typical personage in Greek drama. She embodied dire fate in deadly accents. As Erda she was again tremendous even in the one short scene of "Rheingold." When she last appeared in the rôle at the Metropolitan her voice was hard and worn with the usage of years, but the magisterial authority of her reading of the vocal lines and the profundity of the feeling she put into them were things for all young singers to remember as perhaps unattainable by most of them, but none the less eagerly to be sought.

She came to the Metropolitan in 1899 and she had not been there long when the present writer said in one of his weekly articles: "People are talking just now more about Mme. Schumann-Heink and her singing of the brindisi from 'Lucrezia Borgia' than they are about 'Der Ring der Nibelungen.' " Whereby hung a tale. The great contralto had been on the stage twenty years when she came here, but was still a young woman. She was only 17 when she went to the Court Theater at Dresden and boldly applied for a job as contralto. They gave her an audition and she sang "Oh, My Son" from "The Prophet" and that same brindisi. She was engaged on the spot and made her début in October, 1878, as Azucena. For eight years after that she was at the Stadt Theater, Hamburg. In 1896 she sang Erda, Waltraute and one of the Norns at Bayreuth and soon began to be heard outside of Germany. The astute Maurice Grau engaged her for the Wagner cycle at Covent Garden in the spring of 1898 and the next season she arrived here.

Her début at the Metropolitan took place on January 9, 1899, as Ortrud in "Lohengrin." Her associates were Lillian Nordica as Elsa, Jean de Reszke as Lohengrin, David Bigpham as Telramund, Edouard de Reszke as the King and Adolf Muhlmann as the Herald. Franz Schalk conducted. The dramatic content of "Lohengrin" was superbly revealed by this ensemble. It was at the Sunday night concert of January 22 that Mme. Schumann-Heink astonished the public with her bravura. She had sung as her program number her long-time favorite air from Max Bruch's "Odysseus." None who ever heard her sing it can forget the intensified tragedy of her great cry, "Ilium. Ilium." The record of the following day said:

"Her encore number, however, electrified the audience. It was the threadbare brindisi from 'Lucrezia Borgia,' but she put such brilliant life into it and sang it with such a wealth of voice, such astonishing range, such agility and such infectious spirit that she made the music sound like a revelation. It is quite safe to say that no music lover of the present generation ever heard it sung so admirably."

In a weekly article of later date the writer said: "She has a really majestic voice, and her command of it is well-nigh perfect, as her flawless execution of the two-octave jump at the end of the brindisi proves. In its upper register the voice is a trifle hard because some of the music she sings is a little too high for her, but how admirably she overcomes the difficulties of such passages only a trained singer can wholly appreciate. In passages which lie within the natural range of her voice—one as large as Alboni's—her emission is smooth, sonorous and productive of unfailing beauty of tone. Her phrasing is almost invariably the perfection of art and her enunciation of the text shows a perfect command of vocalization. These features of her method enable her to sing such a thing as the brindisi with all the beauty of color ever imparted to it by an Italian singer, while her keen intelligence, her glowing temperament, her subtle humor and her winsome personality enable her to fill the hollow melody with a wealth of vitality which it certainly has not known since the prime of Alboni."

Marietta Alboni was living in retirement in Paris when Schumann-Heink made her New York début. Chorley recorded her vocal equipment thus: "Hers was a deep, rich contralto of two octaves from G to G, as sweet as honey, but not intensely expressive, and with that tremulous quality which reminds fanciful speculators of the quiver in the air of the calm, blazing summer's sun. I recollect no low Italian voice so luscious." The brindisi was one of two or three airs into which Alboni put dramatic life, but generally she was given to monotone. The inference to be drawn from Chorley's finely drawn comment is that Schumann-Heink had a little more range than Alboni and was an immeasurably more dramatic singer.

Wagner's "Der Ring der Nibelungen" was given

its customary annual airing at the Metropolitan in the early days of 1932. "Das Rheingold" was sung on the afternoon of February 26, and Mme. Schumann-Heink delivered the solemn warning of Erda with an aging voice, but with the authenticity of style and the dramatic significance which she learned in 1878 at Bayreuth. On March 11 "Siegfried" was reached and the great contralto again impersonated Erda. For the sake of the record it may be noted that Gota Ljungberg, sang Bruennhilde; Editha Fleischer, the Forest Bird; Lauritz Melchior, Siegfried; Michael Bohnen, the Wanderer, and Hans Clemens, Mime. Artur Bodanzky conducted. This was Mme. Schumann-Heink's last appearance on the operatic stage in New York.

She was last seen here in the floodlight of public glory at the fourth of a series of concerts in aid of unemployed musicians at the Metropolitan Opera House April 26, 1932. Walter Damrosch conducted. *The Sun's* reviewer said: "If anyone ever labored under the delusion that either of these celebrities was lagging superfluous on the stage he had only to note the behavior of the audience. It applauded and cheered and even rose to its feet when the white-haired contralto made her way to the front to sing her first solo."

It was an all-Wagner program and Mme. Schumann-Heink was heard in two excerpts, the Erda warning from "Rheingold" and the Waltraute appeal from "Goetterdaemmerung." The reviewer commented: "One listens with reverence to this veteran and bows before the authority of her interpretations. She was recalled many times, and there could be no question of the affection and admiration of her hearers."

Probably nothing more to the point has been said than the words of this reviewer's domestic guardian: "She was the most beloved of all singers." Others have been regarded with esteem and affection, but the whole nation loved Schumann-Heink. Everyone felt the power of the big-hearted womanhood that radiated from her on the stage and off. The soldiers and sailors called her Mother Schumann. She had the mind and the temperament maternal and could take the whole world in her embrace.

It is impossible to convey to the younger generation of music lovers any realization of the effects

wrought on the lyric stage by the singers of Schumann-Heink's operatic period. Much ill-founded
reference is made to the existence in those days of
great star casts without any support of dramatic
background in choral and orchestral forces, well-
knit ensemble, scenic attire. Stage management in
the days of Maurice Grau was not imaginative, but
was in fact usually routine, and often preventive,
that the chorus was wholly inadequate or the orchestra under Mancinelli, Seidl and Damrosch in-
competent is not correct.

As for the star casts, they usually created their
own dramatic background. "Lohengrin" has never
been sung here as it was when Jean de Reszke impersonated the swan knight. "Tristan und Isolde"
demonstrates to-day at every performance the
power of true artists to create its atmosphere. Consider what it meant to us of those old days to hear
the sublime measures of "Die Walkuere" delivered
by Lilli Lehmann, Ernst van Dyck, Anton van
Rooy, and their contemporaries. One would suppose that all who heard Schumann-Heink in her
final appearances at the Metropolitan would understand that a "Siegfried" in which her impersona-

tion was matched by the others would be something revealing the full dramatic meaning of the score.

And a thoughtful listener would surely recognize the commanding power of an authentic style. Schumann-Heink was no slave to tradition, but her Wagner was that of Bayreuth in the days not long after the death of the master and when the force of his teachings had not been diminished by the remarkable discoveries of Cosima and Siegfried. And the famous contralto's own methods and manners indubitably stamped themselves upon all her art and made of it a medium for the projection of one of the most vital personalities the stage has known in our time.

Since she is gone let us be grateful that there are still great Wagnerian artists. But did any of the present generation of opera-goers ever hear Schumann-Heink as Fides in "The Prophet"? Well, when she sang "Ach, mein Sohn," she voiced the yearnings of all the mothers of the world, and rose to the peak of interpretative power that has seldom been equaled. Mother Schumann? Yes, and yes, and again yes.

36
Flagstad and Other Great Isoldes

January 2, 1937

THERE HAS BEEN A FLOOD OF ANNIVERSARIES, golden jubilees, centenaries of deaths and other cheering affairs, but one of some importance to the history of music in this town has been overlooked. For New York "Tristan und Isolde" is 50 years old. It had its first performance in America at the Metropolitan Opera House on December 1, 1886. The principals were Lilli Lehmann as Isolde, Marianne Brandt as Brangaene, Albert Niemann as Tristan, Adolf Robinson, Kurvenal, and Emil Fischer, King Mark. Max Alvary, soon afterward a matinee idol as the young Siegfried, sang the music of the unseen sailor. Anton Seidl conducted. It was a great performance and in dramatic intensity has not yet been surpassed. The music of the drama has been better done. Mme. Lehmann and Emil Fischer did most of the singing in the first New York "Tristan."

A professional brother of the younger generation asked this patriarch a few days ago how Mme.
Flagstad compared with the Isoldes of the elder
days. The question set this writer's memory to action. Who were the great Metropolitan Isoldes and
how would Mme. Flagstad compare with them?
Mme. Lehmann, of course, was the first and in certain respects the greatest. If Isolde was a woman of
heroic figure, of majestic mien and gesture, of
imposing plenitude and splendor of voice, of passion intense and incessant, of tempestuous outbursts
of tragic utterance verging on violence, then Lilli
Lehmann was the ideal impersonator of Wagner's
Irish princess.

Lehmann's Isolde was paired with her "Goetterdæmmerung" Bruennhilde, which has not been
remotely suggested by any successor—a vessel of
divine wrath, a minister of avenging justice, a goddess of prophetic vision, proclaiming herself in
song conceived and delivered in a grand tragic
style comparable only to the creations of Aeschylus
and Euripides. In those days there were some men
who secretly believed that no one of their fellows
would ever have dared to whisper of love to such

a tremendous being as Lehmann's Isolde. In the "Goetterdæmmerung" scene of the oath on the spear she became positively appalling. In Isolde's liebestod she was crushing. She was associated with Albert Niemann, who came to us an old man with remnants of a voice, who sang in shattered and brittle phrases, but who poured into the last act of "Tristan," as he did in the death of Siegfried, the vials of all agonies. He was heart-rending. And there were Brandt, not a perfect singer, but authoritative in interpretation; Robinson, who sang like an Italian baritone, and Fischer, whose Mark was filled with the humanity that made his Hans Sachs immortal. Seidl waved a magic wand over the whole performance.

Mme. Flagstad in very little resembles the Isolde of Lehmann. She stands closest to the second of the Metropolitan's great Isoldes, Lillian Nordica. German opera had been banished from the house, but the de Reszke brothers ardently desired to sing Wagner and in the original tongue. One of their dreams was realized on the night of November 27, 1895, when Jean for the first time sang Tristan and

Edouard King Mark. Nordica was the Isolde, Brema Bangaene, Kaschmann Kurvenal and Seidl conductor. Nordica had sung everything from Marguerite, Filine, and Violetta to Aida and Valentine, but this observer declared the morning after that Tristan performance that she had amazed all who knew her and had set herself beside the greatest dramatic sopranos of her time. Nordica was not tempestuously temperamental and she had not a grand tragic voice. Her vocal tone was one of the most limpid, floating kind, exquisitely poised and possessing a singular bird-like quality, yet always giving the impression of largeness.

But the woman was all brains. She sang Isolde so intelligently, so opulently in respect of gradation, subtlety of tint and significant treatment of text, that she left the hearer convinced that this was the real Irish princess of the drama; not a rampant passion in woman's garb, but a sensitive, responsive, and rational being, quite capable of giving herself for love, though hardly likely to suffer any agonies as a punishment for sin. Her singing was like Mme. Flagstad's, beautiful in tonal quality, sustained and exquisitely molded phrasing, and nobility of style.

The entire performance of "Tristan und Isolde" by the cast above given was the perfection of lyricism. The drama had never before been sung as it was sung then. It has never been sung so completely since then. And Nordica's contribution was a lyric utterance of ravishing beauty and unquestionable justice.

Milka Ternina disclosed her Isolde on March 2, 1900, with Van Dyck as Tristan, Van Rooy as Kurvenal, Schumann-Heink as Brangaene and Edouard de Reszke as King Mark. This Isolde was a gracious and lovely lady, sometimes stately, always dignified, vocal with a consummate legato, an elegant aristocracy of song-speech, a loveliness of tone that was a perpetual delight, and a controlled finish that seemed almost too controlled. Mme. Ternina had not the physical force for the torrential rages of the first act nor the depth and breadth of resource demanded by the liebestod; but her second act, if not most melancholy, was certainly most musical. Hers was assuredly a "hochgeboren" Isolde, but no more likely to be desperate in passion than her Tosca. As a historical note it may be added that she was the Isolde on the one occasion when this music drama was chosen for the opening night of the subscription. The incident was of the season of 1901-02.

This brings us to two Isoldes which have been dressed in something of the glamor of legend. Mme. Gadski was heard in the rôle in seasons within the memory of young operagoers, for she sang it with the Wagnerian company at the Manhattan when Schorr and Editha Fleischer were on the roster of artists. But the truth is that her Isolde was better in the autumn of her voice than it was when she sang it on February 15, 1907, for the first time on any stage, with Carl Burrian as Tristan, Homer as Brangaene, Van Rooy as Kurvenal and Blass as Mark. The orchestra was noisy and the other singers turbulent and uncertain in pitch. Effects prepared by Mme. Gadski for subdued utterance were drowned out and in the second act she gave up the contest and joined in the general hubbub.

But in later years her Isolde became a finely drawn and genuinely dramatic impersonation. It brought the level of her achievements to an elevation which in her earlier years no music lover could have expected. She had the good sense to spend con-

siderable time with Lilli Lehmann, but that illustrious Isolde soon told her that she must work out
her interpretation to suit her own vocal gifts, and
that she did with notable success. She elaborated
the details of her singing so that the shades of significance were accorded a necessary dramatic value.

And it should be remembered that Mme. Gadski
was technically a good singer. She had a sound
legato and a very rich tone quality. Her Mozart
was always enjoyable. She had the misfortune to
come to New York at a time when great singers
were numerous and therefore she had to wait till
most of them were gone before her merits acquired
prominence. If she was never an entirely great
Isolde, she was one of high distinction.

Olive Fremstad sang her first Isolde on January
1, 1908, with Heinrich Knote as Tristan and Gustave Mahler as conductor, making his first appearance in this country. The other persons concerned
in the performance were those heard with Mme.
Gadski as listed above. Mme. Fremstad had already
been a successful Brangaene and there was doubt of
her ability to encompass the range of Isolde's music.

However, she sang all the notes, though not always with power and fullness, and in the early part of the second act two or three times with timidity and thin tone. Her interpretation was dramatically beautiful in its tenderness and yielding passion. Here was no raging Isolde, but a woman smothering a devastating love which presently was loosed from its restraint and poured itself out in longing, sighing accents. There was little of the majesty traditionally associated with the rôle, but an abundance of that feminine lure which may have been supposed to exert its fatal power over Tristan's honor.

As time passed it became clear that Mme. Fremstad had to pay the inevitable price of pushing up a voice. She suffered loss of resonance, of quality and indeed of all tone in some of the high flights of the score. But the compelling charm of her Isolde remained to the end.

Of the impersonations of Melanie Kurt and Elizabeth Ohms nothing need be said. They were commendable, but not important. Margarite Matzenauer, Frieda Leider, Anna Konetzni, Nanny Larsen-Todsen and Gertrude Kappel should be still fresh in the memories of contemporaneous operagoers. Mme. Kappel's Isolde will hold an enviable place in the gallery of portraits of the heroine. It was not planned on a large scale, but it was well drawn, tender, lovable.

Let us not forget that in the '80s and early '90s we had not yet emerged from the fog of misconceptions about the correct way to interpret the music of Wagner. We were still misled to some extent by the Bayreuth professions of faith and the elocutionary methods of the sacred Festspielhaus. Wagner was to be declaimed with heavily accented articulation, destructive of flowing legato. When Mme. Lehmann went back to Germany and sang Bruennhilde, she was charged with treating Wagner as if he were a composer of Italian opera. But to her indomitable personality we owe the opening of the gate through which "Tristan und Isolde" marched forward to the revelatory performance of 1895, when the late Henry E. Krehbiel exclaimed, "They actually sang it, sang every note of it."

And then it was discovered that this was precisely what "Tristan und Isolde" needed. It is essentially a lyric work and when it is perfectly sung it proclaims its mighty passion in its own language, that of pure music. Because Mme. Flagstad is first and last a singer, she gives us the true meaning of Isolde and proudly takes her place beside the great singers of the rôle who gave glory to the Metropolitan.

Index